Fabrizio Pregadio

Taoist Internal Alchemy

An Anthology of Neidan Texts

Golden Elixir Press

The Chinese texts translated in the present anthology are freeely available in PDF. For the download link, please visit the page on this book in the Golden Elixir Press website (www.goldenelixir.com).

Golden Elixir Press
Mountain View, CA
www.goldenelixir.com

ISBN 978-0-9855475-5-4 (paperback)

Cover: The Taoist Immortal Lü Dongbin, related to several Neidan traditions. Hanging scroll, ca. 1300.

TAOIST INTERNAL ALCHEMY

By the same author:

Great Clarity: Daoism and Alchemy in Early Medieval China (Stanford University Press, 2006)

The Encyclopedia of Taoism, editor (Routledge, 2008)

The Seal of the Unity of the Three (2 vols., Golden Elixir Press, 2011, 2012)

Cultivating the Tao: Taoism and Internal Alchemy, translator (Golden Elixir Press, 2013)

Contents

Foreword

This anthology presents complete or partial translations of sixteen important works belonging to the Taoist tradition of Neidan, or Internal Alchemy. While the selections are far from covering the whole field of Neidan—a virtually impossible task, given its width and variety—they are representative of several lineages and branches. Texts have been selected in this perspective, and they are arranged chronologically in order to provide an overview not only of Neidan, but also of the history of its discourses and practices.

The anthology opens with three foundational works, the first two of which were actually written before the rise of Neidan, but are part of its main writings: the *Seal of the Unity of the Three* (*Cantong qi*), the *Book of the Hidden Agreement* (*Yinfu jing*), and the *Mirror for Compounding the Medicine* (*Ruyao jing*). There follow several works belonging to the three main lineages created between the tenth and the twelfth centuries. The first is the *Anthology of the Transmission of the Dao from Zhongli Quan to Lü Dongbin* (*Zhong Lü chuandao ji*), associated with the Zhong-Lü lineage. Three works are related to the Southern Lineage (Nanzong), namely the *Awakening to Reality* (*Wuzhen pian*), by Zhang Boduan; the *Four Hundred Words on the Golden Elixir* (*Jindan sibai zi*), also attributed to Zhang Boduan; and the *Pointers to the Mystery* (*Zhixuan pian*), by Bai Yuchan. Next, the *Fifteen Essays by Wang Chongyang to Establish the Teaching* (*Chongyang lijiao shiwu lun*) is representative of the Northern Lineage (Beizong).

Two texts document the integration of the Southern and Northern lineages in the thirteenth and fourteenth centuries: the *Harmony of the Center: An Anthology* (*Zhonghe ji*), by Li Daochun, and the *Great Essentials of the Golden Elixir* (*Jindan dayao*), by Chen Zhixu. Later Neidan lineages, established between the sixteenth and the eighteenth centuries, are represented by Lu Xixing's *Rectifying Errors for the Seekers of the Golden Elixir* (*Jindan jiuzheng pian*); the anonymous *Principles of the Conjoined Cultivation of Nature and Existence* (*Xingming guizhi*); the *Secret of the Golden Flower* (*Jinhua zongzhi*), attributed to the Taoist immortal, Lü Dongbin; and the *Discriminations on Difficult Points in Cultivating Reality* (*Xiuzhen biannan*), by Liu Yiming.

Two other works, written in the twelfth and the thirteen centuries, are concerned with Neidan terminology: the *Model Images of the Golden Elixir* (*Jindan faxiang*), by Weng Baoguang, and the *Questions and Answers on the Golden Elixir* (*Jindan wenda*), by Xiao Tingzhi.

Four of the sixteen texts are integrally translated. Six texts and two commentaries are translated here (entirely or partially) for the first time into English. Except for the *Seal of the Unity of the Three*, the *Mirror for Compounding the Medicine*, and parts of the *Awakening to Reality*, which I had previously published in other books, all translations have been prepared for the present anthology.

The origins and main features of each text are presented in the short introductions to each chapter. Here I will only point out a few general aspects of the works translated in this book. Despite its compendious nature, this anthology attests to the variety and diversity of the Neidan tradition. While each text may be seen as a testimony to a particular aspect of Neidan, it should also be read in light of the lineage to which its author belonged, and of the time in which it was written. Only in this way can one appreciate the differences between doctrinal treatises (from the *Seal of the Unity of the Three* to Liu Yiming's *Discriminations*) and works that focus on inner alchemical practices (the commentaries to the *Mirror for Compounding the Medicine* and to the *Four Hundred Words* are two of the main examples). The different backgrounds and dates of the texts should also be taken into account in order to make sense of the evident, and often disconcerting, contrasts that exist within the literature. To give a few examples limited to this anthology, the scope of Neidan texts ranges from works that display influences of Confucianism and Neo-Confucianism (for instance, the commentary to the *Book of the Hidden Agreement* and Li Daochun's *Harmony of the Center*) to works related to sexual practices (Lu Xixing's *Rectifying Errors*); and from works that place emphasis on the Neidan views of the body (in particular, the *Transmission of the Dao*) to others that discuss points of doctrine (Bai Yuchan's *Pointers to the Mystery*, and several others), or even the adept's "life style" (the *Fifteen Essays by Wang Chongyang*).

Closely related to the above is the complex issue of the "grades" of Neidan. Not only is Neidan subdivided into different lineages and branches, but several masters emphasize that it can be understood and practiced at different levels. Even the same technical terms take on different meanings according to the "vehicles" (a term borrowed from Buddhism) that a master teaches and a disciple learns. One of Bai Yuchan's essays, as well as portions of the chapters devoted to Li Daochun and Chen Zhixu, deal with this subject and are valuable to approach this important feature of Neidan.

Two other subjects that deserve mention are the importance of poetry in Neidan, and the nature of the commentaries to earlier works. Four texts translated in this book are written in verses: the *Seal of the Unity of the Three*, the *Mirror for Compounding the Medicine*, the *Awakening to Reality*, and the *Four Hundred Words*. All of them rank among the main Neidan scriptures, and poems are found in several other works translated here. While this may be a further hurdle for a Western reader, the use of poetry, as opposed to a linear form of writing, is one of the aspects of Neidan—especially in its earlier stages—that require consideration. With regards to the three commentaries translated in this book, it is sufficient to remind that their authors did not merely explicate earlier works, but they did so according to the tradition that they followed and the time in which they lived. In other words, what we read in a commentary does not necessarily reflect the intention of the author of the original work, but in the first place the views of the commentator.

A final point that requires attention is the language of the texts. I have always tried to respect the rhetoric and the terminology of the works I have translated, with no attempt to adapt them to the taste of the modern Western reader. Two different translators of Classical Chinese texts might render the same passage in different ways, and both translations might be correct. When facing a choice between the source and the target languages, my preference as a rule has gone to the former; for this reason, independently of their accuracy, I would agree with anyone who regards my translations as being too "literal".

The book is concluded by several tables and by an index of the main terms. Coming upon an unfamiliar term, the reader may consult the index in order to refer to other pages of this book that mention or define it.

As always, I am grateful to Xiaokun, without whose help this book would have never seen the light. Any error is entirely my responsibility.

Fabrizio Pregadio
March 2019

Sources

1   *Cantong qi* 參同契 (The Seal of the Unity of the Three). Attributed to Wei Boyang 魏伯陽 (trad. second century CE). Selections translated from Chen Zhixu 陳致虛 (1290-ca. 1368), *Zhouyi cantong qi zhujie* 周易參同契注解 (Commentary and Explication of the *Cantong qi*). Jinling shufang 金陵書坊 edition, 1484.

2   *Yinfu jing* 陰符經 (Book of the Hidden Agreement). Anonymous (sixth to eighth centuries). Commentary by Yu Yan 俞琰 (1258–1314). Complete text translated from *Huangdi yinfu jing zhu* 黃帝陰符經注 (Commentary on the Yellow Emperor's *Yinfu jing*). *Daozang* 道藏 (Taoist Canon) edition, 1445.

3   *Ruyao jing* 入藥鏡 (Mirror for Compounding the Medicine). Attributed to Cui Xifan 崔希範 (ca. 880–940). Commentary by Wang Jie 王玠 (?-ca. 1380). Selections translated from *Cui gong ruyao jing zhujie* 崔公入藥鏡注解 (Commentary and Explication of the *Ruyao jing*). *Daozang* 道藏 (Taoist Canon) edition, 1445.

4   *Zhong Lü chuandao ji* 鍾呂傳道集 (Anthology of the Transmission of the Dao from Zhongli Quan to Lü Dongbin). Attributed to Shi Jianwu 施肩吾 (fl. 820–35). Selections translated from *Xiuzhen shishu* 修真十書 (Ten Books on the Cultivation of Reality), ch. 14–16. *Daozang* 道藏 (Taoist Canon) edition, 1445.

5   *Wuzhen pian* 悟真篇 (Awakening to Reality). Zhang Boduan 張伯端 (987?–1082). Selections translated from Wang Mu 王沐, ed., *Wuzhen pian qianjie* 悟真篇淺解 (A Simple Explanation of the *Wuzhen pian*). Beijing: Zhonghua shuju 中華書局, 1990.

6   *Jindan sibai zi* 金丹四百字 (Four Hundred Words on the Golden Elixir). Attributed to Zhang Boduan 張伯端 (987?–1082). Commentary by Peng Haogu 彭好古 (fl. 1586–99). Complete text translated from the *Daozang xubian* 道藏續編 (Sequel to the Taoist Canon) edition, 1952.

7   *Zazhu zhixuan pian* 雜著指玄篇 (Pointers to the Mystery: A Miscellany). Bai Yuchan 白玉蟾 (1194–1229?). Selections translated

from *Xiuzhen shishu* 修真十書 (Ten Books on the Cultivation of Reality), ch. 4. *Daozang* 道藏 (Taoist Canon) edition, 1445.

8   *Jindan faxiang* 金丹法象 (Model Images of the Golden Elixir). Weng Baoguang 翁葆光 (fl. 1173). Selections translated from *Wuzhen zhizhi xiangshuo sansheng biyao* 悟真直指詳說三乘祕要 (Straightforward Directions and Detailed Explanations on the *Wuzhen pian* and the Secret Essentials of the Three Vehicles). *Daozang* 道藏 (Taoist Canon) edition, 1445.

9   *Jindan wenda* 金丹問答 (Questions and Answers on the Golden Elixir). Xiao Tingzhi 蕭廷芝 (fl. 1260–64). Selections translated from *Xiuzhen shishu* 修真十書 (Ten Books on the Cultivation of Reality), ch. 10. *Daozang* 道藏 (Taoist Canon) edition, 1445.

10 *Chongyang lijiao shiwu lun* 重陽立教十五論 (Fifteen Essays by Wang Chongyang to Establish the Teaching). Wang Chongyang 王重陽 (1113–70). Complete text translated from the *Daozang* 道藏 (Taoist Canon) edition, 1445.

11 *Zhonghe ji* 中和集 (The Harmony of the Center: An Anthology). Li Daochun 李道純 (fl. 1288–92). Selections translated from the *Daozang* 道藏 (Taoist Canon) edition, 1445.

12 *Jindan dayao* 金丹大要 (The Great Essentials of the Golden Elixir). Chen Zhixu 陳致虛 (1290-ca. 1368). Selections translated from the *Daozang* 道藏 (Taoist Canon) edition, 1445.

13 *Jindan jiuzheng pian* 金丹就正篇 (Rectifying Errors for the Seekers of the Golden Elixir). Lu Xixing 陸西星 (1520–1606). Complete text translated from *Fanghu waishi* 方壺外史 (The External Secretary of Mount Fanghu). Ed. of 1915.

14 *Xingming guizhi* 性命圭旨 (Principles of the Conjoined Cultivation of Nature and Existence). Anonymous (ca. 1600). Selections translated from Li Jianzhang 李建章, ed., *Xingming guizhi baihua jie* 性命圭旨白话解 (The *Xingming guizhi*, with Explications in Modern Language). Beijing: Renmin tiyu chubanshe 人民体育出版社, 1993.

15   *Jinhua zongzhi* 金華宗旨 (The Secret of the Golden Flower). Attributed to Lü Dongbin 呂洞賓. Selections translated from the *Daozang xubian* 道藏續編 (Sequel to the Taoist Canon) edition, 1952.

16   *Xiuzhen biannan* 修真辨難 (Discriminations on Difficult Points in Cultivating Reality). Liu Yiming 劉一明 (1734–1821). In *Daoshu shi'er zhong* 道書十二種 (Twelve Books on the Dao). Selections translated from the Yihua tang 翼化堂 edition, 1880.

Translations

1 The Seal of the Unity of the Three

Cantong qi 參同契

Attributed to Wei Boyang 魏伯陽

The *Zhouyi cantong qi*, or *Seal of the Unity of the Three, in Accordance with the Book of Changes*, is the main text of Neidan. Traditionally attributed to Wei Boyang and dated to the mid-second century, it did not reach its present form before the mid-fifth century, and possibly one or even two centuries later. Its reputed author was an alchemist from southeastern China (present-day Zhejiang province), but clear evidence shows that the text was originally attached to the northern cosmological traditions centered on the *Yijing*, or *Book of Changes*.

Within the greatest part of the Chinese alchemical tradition, the *Cantong qi* has been read and interpreted as a work exclusively concerned with Neidan. According to a less well-known view, instead, it deals with three major subjects, which—as the title indicates—are merged and integrated into a single doctrine. The three subjects are: (1) The relation of the cosmos to the Dao, explained according to the system of the *Book of Changes*; (2) The realized state of the saintly person (*shengren*), defined according to the teachings of *Daode jing* (Book of the Way and Its Virtue) on "non-doing" (*wuwei*); (3) Alchemy as the practice that leads to the realization of the Dao and to the state of sainthood.

The selections translated in this chapter contain twelve of the eighty-eight sections of the text. They are excerpted from my complete translation, published as *The Seal of the Unity of the Three* (Golden Elixir Press, 2011). If the subdivision of the *Cantong qi* into three subjects is taken into account, sections 1 and 7 are concerned with the Dao and the cosmos; sections 18, 20, 26, 58, and 60 are concerned with the state of realization; and sections 22, 23, 39, 40, and 72 are concerned with the alchemical practice.

Section numbers correspond to those of my complete translation. Besides footnotes to several verses, I have added general notes to the translated sections.

I: QIAN AND KUN, KAN AND LI

"Qian ☰ and Kun ☷ are the door and the gate of
  change,"[1]
the father and the mother of all hexagrams.[2]
Kan ☵ and Li ☲ are the inner and the outer walls,[3]
they spin the hub and align the axle.
Female and male, these four trigrams
function as a bellows and its nozzles.

The constant conjunction of Qian and Kun, the active and the passive
principles, gives birth to all phenomena in the world of change. Therefore
Qian and Kun are "the door and the gate" through which change arises,
and "the father and the mother" of all emblems that represent change. As
they join with one another, Qian ☰ entrusts his generative potential to
Kun and, in doing this, becomes Li ☲; Kun ☷ receives the essence of Qian
to bring it to fruition and, in doing this, becomes Kan ☵. Since Kan and
Li embrace Qian and Kun, represented by the respective inner lines, they
provide "inner and outer walls" to Qian and Kun: the Yin principle (☵)
harbors True Yang (—), and the Yang principle (☲) harbors True Yin (--).

Fig. 1. "Kan ☵ and Li ☲ are the inner and the outer walls."

---

[1] This line is an almost literal quotation from the "Appended Sayings"
("Xici") of the *Book of Changes* (*Yijing*): "Qian and Kun are indeed the door
and the gate of change!" (B.5; see Wilhelm, *The I-ching or Book of Changes*,
p. 343).

[2] Compare *Book of Changes*, "Explanation of the Trigrams" ("Shuogua"): "Qian is Heaven, therefore he is called the father. Kun is Earth, therefore she is called the mother" (sec. 9; see Wilhelm, p. 274).

[3] In the trigrams Kan ☵ and Li ☲, the lower lines are the "inner wall,"
and the upper lines are the "outer wall." The central lines belong to Qian ☰
and Kun ☷, respectively.

If the two sets of walls are shaped as joined semicircles, they form a wheel (see fig. 1). The central hub is the emptiness from which existence comes forth; the axle passing through the hub is Qian and Kun, which hold the wheels in position; and the wheels with their spokes are the compass of space and the cycles of time governed by Kan and Li. The *Daode jing* (Book of the Way and Its Virtue) uses the same images to illustrate the operation (or "function," *yong*) of emptiness at the center of the cosmos: "Thirty spokes share one hub: wherein there is nothing lies the function of a carriage. . . . Therefore in what is there lies the benefit; in what is not there lies the function" (*Daode jing*, 11).

Qian, Kun, Kan, and Li are also compared to a bellows and its nozzles. The bellows (Qian and Kun) is empty, but sends forth its breath through the nozzles (Kan and Li). This image too alludes to a passage in the *Daode jing*, which refers to the empty center that brings about existence by saying: "The space between Heaven and Earth—is it not like a bellows? As empty, it is never exhausted; as it moves, it continues to pour" (*Daode jing*, 5).

7: SUN AND MOON MAKE CHANGE

WU in Kan ☵ is the essence of the Moon,
JI in Li ☲ is the radiance of the Sun.
Sun and Moon make change,
the firm and the yielding match one another.

Soil rules over the four seasons,
entwining beginning and end;
green, red, black, and white
each dwells in one direction.
All are endowed by the Central Palace
through the efficacy of WU and JI.

The Moon is Kan ☵ and the Sun is Li ☲. However, although the Yin trigram Kan is associated with the Moon, it encloses a solid Yang line that belongs to Qian ☰. This line corresponds to the celestial stem WU 戊, an emblem of the active, creative aspect of the One. Analogously, the Yang trigram Li is associated with the Sun, but encloses a broken Yin line that belongs to Kun ☷. This line corresponds to the celestial stem JI 己, representing the passive, fulfilling aspect of the One. When Qian and Kun are contained within Kan and Li, they are called the "essence" (*jing*) of the Moon and the "radiance" (*guang*) of the Sun.

The alternation of the Sun and the Moon produces change. With regard to this, the *Cantong qi* observes that when the graphs that represent the Sun and the Moon are joined to one another, with the graph for "sun" (*ri* 日) placed above the graph for "moon" (*yue* 月), they form the graph for "change" (*yi* 易). This etymology of the word "change" does not pertain to philology, but is an example of the analogical function of images and forms.

In addition to being associated with True Yang (Qian) and True Yin (Kun), the celestial stems wu 戊 and ji 己 are also emblems of the central agent Soil, which, like the One, comprises Yin and Yang halves. Soil transmits the One Breath to the four directions and the four seasons—i.e., to space and time—which correspond to the agents Wood, Fire, Water, and Metal, referred to here by the colors green, red, black, and white. In reiterating the unity of Qian and Kun, Kan and Li, and wu and ji, Soil guarantees the conjunction of the world of multiplicity to the Absolute.

18: NOURISHING INNER NATURE

Innerly nourish yourself,
serene and quiescent in Empty Non-Being.
Going back to the fundament conceal your light,
and innerly illuminate your body.[4]

"Shut the openings"[5]
and raise and strengthen the Numinous Trunk;

---

[4] In later times, *neizhao* ("to illuminate within") became the name of an inner alchemical practice, as seen, for instance, in the expression *huiguang neizhao*, "reversing the light to illuminate within" (see the selections from the *Secret of the Golden Flower* in Chapter 15 below). From the perspective of the *Cantong qi*, however, this term does not refer to a practice, or at least not to a practice in the ordinary sense: *neizhao* describes the state of the realized person, whose inner being is constantly illuminated.

[5] Compare sec. 58, which refers to the "three luminaries" as the "three treasures" (*sanbao*), saying: "Ears, eyes, and mouth are the three treasures: shut them, and let nothing pass through" (see below, p. 17).

as the three luminaries sink into the ground,[6]
warmly nourish the Pearl.

"Watching, you do not see it"[7] —
it is nearby and easy to seek.

Emptiness is the fundament from which all things arise and to which they
return; quiescence is the state required to contemplate Emptiness. The
first stanza expresses these principles with allusions to an exemplary
passage of the *Daode jing*: "Attain the ultimate of emptiness, guard the
utmost of quiescence. The ten thousand things are brought about together: accordingly, I observe their return. . . . Returning to the root
means quiescence; being quiescent means reverting to one's destiny;
reverting to one's destiny means being constant; knowing the constant
means being luminous" (*Daode jing*, 6). The subjects of the present
section of the *Cantong qi* are the same as those of this passage:
Emptiness, the return to the root, and the luminous quality of those who
achieve quiescence.

Attaining the state of Emptiness requires closing the "openings"
through which we deal with the world of multiplicity. This principle, and
its formulation, also originate in the *Daode jing*: "Shut the openings,
close the gates, and to the end of your life you will not toil. Unlock the
openings, meddle with affairs, and to the end of your life you will not
attain salvation" (*Daode jing*, 52).

For the *Cantong qi*, the openings are the "three luminaries": the eyes,
the ears, and the mouth, or the functions of sight, hearing, and speech.
When the "three luminaries" do not turn their light toward the external
world, they "sink into the ground." This expression, which derives from
the *Zhuangzi*, denotes the attitude of the saintly man who conceals his
sainthood (see the note to verse 7). Established in quiescence, he does not
turn himself toward the external objects, allowing the radiance of the
luminaries to illuminate and nourish his true nature (the "numinous

---

[6] The term *luchen* ("sinking into the ground") derives from this passage
of the *Zhuangzi*, ch. 25: "[The saint] has buried himself among the people,
hidden himself among the fields. . . . Perhaps he finds himself at odds with the
age and in his heart disdains to go along with it. This is called 'sinking into
the ground'" (see Watson, *The Complete Works of Chuang Tzu*, pp. 285–86).

[7] This verse is quoted from *Daode jing*, sec. 14, where it refers to the Dao:
"Watching, you do not see it: it is called invisible. Listening, you do not hear
it: it is called inaudible. Grasping, you do not get it: it is called imperceptible."

trunk"). Maintaining himself in the state of non-doing, he contemplates the arising of all entities and phenomena from Emptiness and their return to it, and nurtures the Pearl spontaneously generated in him by the precelestial One Breath.

This attitude and nothing else constitutes the way of superior virtue and the realized state according to the *Cantong qi*. As we are reminded with another line drawn from the *Daode jing* (see the note to verse 9), no pursuit is necessary: the Dao is invisible, inaudible, and imperceptible, but is "nearby and easy to seek."

20: SUPERIOR VIRTUE AND INFERIOR VIRTUE

"Superior virtue has no doing":[8]
it does not use examining and seeking.
"Inferior virtue does":[9]
its operation does not rest.

The *Cantong qi* upholds two ways of realization. Quoting the *Daode jing*, the present section defines the two ways as "superior virtue" (*shangde*) and "inferior virtue" (*xiade*). In superior virtue, nothing needs to be searched or investigated; the unity of the precelestial state (*xiantian*, the Absolute, Emptiness, constancy) and the postcelestial state (*houtian*, the relative, the world of change) is immediately realized. Inferior virtue, instead, seeks the precelestial One Breath (*xiantian yiqi*) within the postcelestial state. Superior virtue is the way of "non-doing" (*wuwei*), inferior virtue is the way of "doing" (*youwei*, or *wei zhi*). As a practice, alchemy—in any of its forms, "external" or "internal"—pertains to the way of inferior virtue.

[8] This line is quoted from *Daode jing*, sec. 38: "Superior virtue has no doing: there is nothing whereby it does."
[9] This line is quoted from *Daode jing*, sec. 38: "Inferior virtue does: there is something whereby it does."

22: THE PRINCIPLES OF ALCHEMY

"Know the white, keep to the black,"[10]
and the Numinous Light will come of its own.

White is the essence of Metal,
Black the foundation of Water.[11]
Water is the axis of the Dao:
its number is 1.

At the beginning of Yin and Yang,
Mystery holds the Yellow Sprout;
it is the ruler of the five metals,[12]
the River Chariot of the northern direction.[13]

That is why lead is black on the outside
but cherishes the Golden Flower within,
like the man who "wears rough-hewn clothes but

[10] This line is quoted from *Daode jing*, sec. 28: "Know the white, keep to the black, and be a mold for the world. If you are a mold for the world, the constant virtue does not depart from you, and you return to the Ultimateless."

[11] For several commentators, "white" stands for True Lead; for others, it means either mercury, or silver, or gold. These varying views reflect different configurations of the alchemical emblems, in whose contexts the same principle can be represented by different terms and symbols. "White," in all cases, alludes to the authentic principle contained within the "black." Being the True Yang within Yin, this authentic principle is the opposite of black lead, and therefore is called True Lead. For the same reason, it may be called "mercury," which in Chinese alchemy stands in a polar relation to lead. Because of its white color, it can also be called "silver," in contrast to black native lead. Finally, since True Yang is the precelestial One Breath, it may be called "gold," the metal that more than any other represents the Elixir.

[12] The five metals are gold, silver, copper, iron, and lead. Here they are meant as mere emblems of the five agents: Water is the first of the five agents, and lead, which is related to Water, is "the ruler of the five metals."

[13] In Neidan, River Chariot refers to path of the circulation of Breath (qi) through the *dumai* and *renmai* vessels, respectively running along the back and the front of the body. This circulation is analogous to the circulation of the One Breath in the cosmos along the cycles of time and the compass of space.

> cherishes a piece of jade in his bosom,"[14]
> and outwardly behaves like a fool.

Alchemy seeks the principle that gives birth to, and is hidden within, the manifest cosmos. Among the emblems of the *Book of Changes*, this principle is represented by the solid Yang line contained within Kan ☵ (Water), which originally belongs to Qian ☰. Alchemically, it is represented by the True Lead found within "black lead," or native lead.

The opening line, borrowed from the *Daode jing*, states that one should "keep to the black" in order to "know the white." Black (Yin) represents the agent Water, the outer Yin lines of Kan ☵, and native lead; it is the world in which we live. White (Yang) represents the agent Metal, the inner Yang line of Kan, and True Lead; it is the One Breath sought by the alchemist. "Keeping to the black" and "knowing the white" generates the Numinous Light (*shenming*), which in the alchemical metaphor is the Elixir.

Therefore the precelestial Breath is to be sought within Water. As a cosmological principle, Water is the first of the five agents (here called the "five metals"); it is "the beginning of Yin and Yang," and is represented by number 1 and by the northern direction. Because of its primal position within the cosmos, Water is the "axis of the Dao," and all changes and transformations derive in the first place from it. For the same reason, Water is also the element that supports the River Chariot (*heche*), the vehicle that transports the One Breath (Metal, True Lead, True Yang) back and forth in its cycles of ascent and descent within the cosmos.

Water is the "mystery" (*xuan*): it stands for obscurity, the north, and black lead, but it holds light and, being the "axis of the Dao," is intimately connected to the center. In alchemical language, this hidden principle is referred to as the Yellow Sprout (*huangya*), a term that connotes both the essence of Metal (True Yang) found within Water (Yin), and the first intimation of the birth of the Elixir (denoted as "yellow" for its association with Soil, the agent that represents the center). Analogously, lead is black outside, but harbors the white and luminous Golden Flower (*jinhua*) within. Quoting another passage from the *Daode jing*, the *Cantong qi* likens the authentic principle hidden in the darkness of the world to the treasure concealed by the saintly man, who disguises himself as a common mortal.

---

[14] This line is quoted from *Daode jing*, sec. 70: "It is only because they have no understanding that they do not understand me; but since those who understand me are few, I am honored. Thus the saint wears rough-hewn clothes, but cherishes a piece of jade in his bosom."

23: METAL AND WATER, MOTHER AND CHILD

Metal is the mother of Water —
the mother is hidden in the embryo of her son.
Water is the child of Metal —
the child is stored in the womb of its mother.

This short section describes two movements. The first is the movement of "ascent" from the postcelestial (*houtian*, the relative) to the precelestial (*xiantian*, the absolute); the second is the movement of "descent" from the precelestial to the postcelestial. The precelestial domain is symbolized by Metal; the postcelestial domain, by Water. In a strict sense, alchemy deals only with the first movement, which is the way of "inferior virtue," but its path is fulfilled when the second movement, the way of "superior virtue," is also performed.

The return from the postcelestial to the precelestial is described as the inversion of the generative sequence of the five agents. In this sequence, Metal (the "mother") generates Water (the "son"), but in the alchemical process it is Water ("black lead") that generates Metal (True Lead). Thus the son generates the mother, and "the mother is hidden in the embryo of her son." The extension of the precelestial into the postcelestial, which occurs after the first movement has been completed, is represented as the common course of the generative sequence of the five agents. In this movement, Metal (the "mother") once again generates Water (the "son"). Thus "the child is stored in the womb of its mother."

After the first, "ascensional" part of the alchemical work is completed, the movement of "descent" does not lead to a new shift from the precelestial to the postcelestial. It realizes, instead, the unity the precelestial and the postcelestial.

26: INCORRECT PRACTICES

This is not the method of passing through the viscera, of
     inner contemplation and having a point of concentration;
of treading the Dipper and pacing the asterisms, using the six
     JIA as markers of time;[15]

_____

[15] The six JIA (*liujia*) are the six days of the sexagesimal cycle marked by

of sating yourself with the nine-and-one in the Way of Yin,
   meddling and tampering with the original womb;
of ingesting breath till it chirps in your stomach, exhaling the
   pure and inhaling the evil without.[16]

Day and night you go without slumber,
month after month, you never take rest.
From exhaustion your body daily grows weak:
you may be "vague and indistinct," but look like a fool.

Your hundred vessels stir and seethe like a cauldron,
unable to settle and clear.
Amassing soil you set up space for an altar,
and at daybreak and sunset you worship in awe.

Demonic creatures reveal their shapes,
at whose sight in your dreams you sigh with
   emotion.
Rejoiced in your heart, pleased in your thoughts,
you tell yourself, surely, your life will grow long.

But death, unexpected, comes ahead of its time,
and you forsake your body to rot.
Your deeds have rebounded,
for you were defiant and let slip the hinge.

The arts are so many[17] —
for each thousand, there are ten thousand more.
Their tortuous routes run against the Yellow
   Emperor and the Old Master,

the celestial stem JIA (see table 7, p. 263). Being especially important in hemerology, these days are associated with deities and with talismans that grant communication with those deities.

[16] This is one of the few passages in prose of the *Cantong qi*.

[17] *Shu*, here translated as "art," refers to various cosmological sciences and techniques—for instance, divination, physiological techniques, and alchemy—including both their doctrinal foundations and their specific methods.

their winding courses oppose the Nine Capitals.[18]
Those who are bright comprehend the meaning of
    this:
in all its breadth they know where it comes from.

The *Cantong qi* repeatedly warns against the performance of practices deemed to be incorrect or unproductive for true realization. This section rejects meditation methods, breathing practices, sexual techniques, and the worship of minor deities and spirits. "Passing through the viscera" (*lizang*) is an early term that refers to visualizing in succession the gods residing within the five viscera. "Inner contemplation" (or "inner observation," *neishi*, the reading found in other redactions of the *Cantong qi*) also refers to meditation on the inner deities. "Treading the Dipper and pacing the asterisms" denotes the meditation methods of "pacing the celestial net" (*bugang*). "Six JIA" alludes to protective calendrical deities, and in particular to those associated with the talismans of the "six decades," each of which begins on a day marked by the celestial stem JIA 甲. "Way of Yin" indicates the sexual techniques, and the expression "nine-and-one" hints to the phrase *jiuqian yishen* ("nine shallow and one deep" penetrations in intercourse). "Ingesting breath" designates the breathing practices.

Not only does the *Cantong qi* reject these methods; it also refers to them with irony. "Exhaling the old and inhaling the new [breath]" (*tugu naxin*), a common designation of the breathing practices, becomes "exhaling the pure and inhaling the evil without" (from the perspective of the *Cantong qi*, the "pure" is to be found in the first place within). Breath is ingested "till it chirps in your stomach." The adept who devotes himself to these practices is "vague and indistinct," an image that in the *Daode jing* denotes the Dao itself, but here quite literally refers to the practitioner who "looks like a fool." Apart from this, the rejected practices,

---

[18] *Quzhe* ("winding courses," "crouchings and bendings") connotes pointless and unproductive pursuits. See this passage of the *Zhuangzi*, ch. 8: "The crouchings and bendings of rites and music, the smiles and beaming looks of humanity and righteousness, which are intended to comfort the hearts of the world, in fact destroy their constant naturalness" (see Watson, 100). — The precise connotation of the term *jiudu* ("nine capitals") is unclear in this context; it may refer to the Nine Palaces (*jiufu*) of the administration of Fengdu, the subterranean realm of the dead. The implication, nevertheless, is clear: the death of the adept of incorrect practices is a punishment delivered by Heaven.

says the *Cantong qi*, are ineffective because they focus on the body and on the hope of extending one's lifetime. For this reason, they go against the true Taoist teaching, which the *Cantong qi* associates with the Yellow Emperor and with Laozi, the Old Master.

39: COMPOUNDING THE ELIXIR (*FIRST PART*)

Make dikes and embankments with Metal,
so that Water may enter and effortlessly drift.
Fifteen is the measure of Metal,
the same is the number of Water.

Tend to the furnace to determine the scruples and
    ounces:
five parts of Water are more than enough.
In this way the two become True,
and Metal will weigh as at first.
The other three are thus not used,
but Fire, which is 2, is fastened to them.

The three things join one another:
in their transformations their shapes are divine.[19]
The Breath of Great Yang lies underneath,
within an instant it steams and subdues.
First it liquefies, then coagulates;
it is given the name Yellow Carriage.[20]

When its time is about to come to an end,
it wrecks its own nature and disrupts its life span.

---

[19] This verse might also be translated as "in their transformations their shapes are like [those of] a spirit."

[20] Yellow is the color associated with the central Soil in the system of the five agents. Yu primarily means "carriage," but this word also includes "earth" among its meanings. The term "Yellow Carriage," therefore, alludes to the Center as the unity of Yin and Yang, respectively represented in alchemy by Mercury and Lead.

Its form looks like ashes or soil,[21]
its shape is like dust on a luminous window.

This and the next section contain the main description of the method for compounding the Elixir found in the *Cantong qi*. The description is divided into two parts: the first one ends with the compounding of the Yellow Carriage, and the second one, with the compounding of the Reverted Elixir proper. Although most later commentators have explained these verses from the perspective of the tradition to which they belonged, namely Neidan, terminology and images in both sections are explicitly Waidan. Nevertheless, the emblematic functions of the ingredients and the process described here can apply to both Waidan and Neidan.

The Elixir is made of two ingredients, here called Metal and Water. Metal is True Lead, and Water is True Mercury. The two ingredients are placed in the vessel, so that mercury circulates but does not volatilize when it is heated. Each ingredient is assigned a symbolic weight of fifteen ounces. Together, their weights correspond to the number of days in the lunar month.

In addition, the weights have another and more important symbolic connotation: 5 and 10 respectively are the "generation number" and the "accomplishment number" of the central agent Soil (see table 2, p. 258). This correspondence ties both Lead and Mercury to Soil, an association that is already implicit in the emblematic functions of the two ingredients: the Yang line within Kan ☵ (True Lead) is equivalent to the celestial stem wu 戊, which is the active, Yang aspect of Soil, while the Yin line within Li ☲ (True Mercury) is equivalent to the celestial stem ji 己, which is its passive, Yin aspect (see sec. 7, translated above). Being comprised within both ingredients, Soil can play a mediating function between them, enabling the Yin and Yang principles to conjoin.

Five parts of Water (Mercury) are suitable—"more than enough"— for compounding the Elixir, together with the same amount of Metal (Lead); at the end, Metal will weigh as it did at the beginning. The agent Fire, whose "generation number" is 2, is used for heating the compound. Through the action of fire, which is placed underneath the open vessel, the "three things"—Metal, Water, and Soil—undergo transmutation, taking at first a liquid form and then a solid form, similar to ashes or dust. The compound obtained at the end of the first part of the method is called Yellow Carriage (*huangyu*). It serves as the basis for making the

[21] Note again the mention of Soil, the agent that represents the conjunction of Lead and Mercury.

Elixir in the second part of the method, which is described in the next section.

40: COMPOUNDING THE ELIXIR (*SECOND PART*)

Pound it and mix it,
and let it enter the Red-colored Gates.
Seal the joints firmly,
striving to make them as tight as you can.

A blazing fire grows below:
by day and by night its sound is unchanging and
    steady.
At first make it gentle so that it may be adjusted,
at the end make it fierce and let it spread out.

Watch over it with heed and caution:
inspect it attentively and regulate the amount of its
    warmth.
It will rotate through twelve nodes,
and when the nodes are complete, it will again need
    your care.

Now its Breath is worn out, and its life is about to
    be severed;
it pauses and dies, losing its *Po* and its *Hun*.
Then its color changes to purple:
the Reverted Elixir, radiant and glowing, is attained.

Minutely powder it and make it into a pellet —
even one knife-point is supremely divine.

The description of the refining of True Lead and True Mercury that had began in the previous section continues here. The compound obtained in the first part of the method is placed in a tripod and is heated in a furnace. The vessel, this time, should be hermetically closed, as even the slightest leakage of Breath (*qi*) would prevent the Elixir from being compounded. The intensity of heat is regulated according to the system of the Fire phases (*huohou*), which subdivides each heating cycle into twelve stages ("twelve nodes") modeled on the growth and decline of the Sun during the year. Fire is mild at the beginning, then grows stronger until it reaches the highest intensity, then decreases until it is finally extinguished. After several cycles of heating, Lead and Mercury go through a symbolic death. When Yin and Yang cease to exist as separate entities, the *Hun*-soul returns to Heaven, the *Po*-soul returns to the Earth, and the luminous Reverted Elixir (*huandan*) is achieved.

58: THE THREE TREASURES

Ears, eyes, and mouth are the three treasures:
shut them, and let nothing pass through.[22]
The True Man withdraws in the depths of the abyss;
drifting and roaming, he keeps to the compass.

Watch and listen while wheeling around,[23]
and opening and closing will always accord.[24]
Take this as your lynchpin,
and movement and quiescence will never be
       exhausted.

The Breath of Li ☲ strengthens and guards you within,
and Kan ☵ is not employed for listening.

[22] Compare the expression "Shut the openings" in sec. 18 above, and the passage of the *Daode jing*, sec. 52, quoted in the note to that section.

[23] For the expressions "wheeling around" in this verse and "keeping to the compass" in the previous verse, compare this passage of the *Liezi* that describes the art of charioteering as a metaphor of the state of the True Man or Realized Man: "What you sense within in your innermost heart will accord outside with the horse's temper. In this way you will be able to drive back and forth as straight as a stretched cord, and wheel around as exactly as a compass" (ch. 5; see Graham, *The Book of Lieh-tzu*, p. 114).

[24] According to the explications given by Liu Yiming (1734–1821), this verse means that the two phases of activity and inactivity are fulfilled in a non-dual state. In his commentary, Liu Yiming defines this state as follows: "'One's mind (*xin*) is dead and one's spirit lives; one severs evil and preserves sincerity; one neither forgets nor assists."

Dui ☱ is closed and not used for talking:
you follow the boundless with inaudible words.

The "three treasures" spoken of here are the "three luminaries" of sec. 18 above: the ears, the eyes, and the mouth, respectively corresponding to the functions of hearing, seeing, and speaking. These treasures should be guarded and cherished, and their light should be turned within.

The mention of Breath (*qi*) in conjunction with Li ☲, the trigram that represents the eyes, shows that this passage refers to certain fundamental correspondences that pertain to the Taoist view of the human being:

(1) The ears are represented by Kan ☵ (Water, Yin), which is placed below (in correspondence with the lower Cinnabar Field) and holds the Original Essence (*yuanjing*).

(2) The eyes are represented by Li ☲ (Fire, Yang), which is placed above (in correspondence with the upper Cinnabar Field) and holds the Original Breath (*yuanqi*).

(3) The mouth is represented by Dui ☱ (Metal), which is placed in the center (in correspondence with the middle Cinnabar Field) and holds the Original Spirit (*yuanshen*).

When the "three treasures" are secured, Essence does not flow downward, as water does, but instead ascends; Breath does not rise upward, as fire does, but instead descends; and one's individual traits (*qing*, i.e., attitudes, temperament, personality, and other features related to one's individual existence) do not spring forth as emotions or passions, but emerge as qualities that enable spirit, or one's own true nature (*xing*), to operate.

The true nature is referred to in this passage as the True Man, or Realized Man. Withdrawn "in the depths of the abyss" (compare the expression "sinking into the ground" in sec. 18 above), the True Man leads his carriage (see sec. 43 above) and meets no obstructions. Quiescence and activity are equivalent for him, and he enters and exits the world without distinction. Seeing, hearing, and speaking are turned inward: he watches and listens to the boundless, and communicates with it in words that no one can hear.

60: THE BREATHING OF THE TRUE MAN

Cultivate this unceasingly,
and your plentiful breath will course like rain from
    the clouds,
overflowing like a marsh in the spring,
pouring forth like ice that has melted.

It will stream from the head to the toes;
on reaching the end, it will rise once again.
In its coming and going, it will spread limitless,
pervading throughout and extending all around.

Return is the attestation of the Dao,
weakness is "the handle of virtue."
When the long gathered filth is removed,
the fine and tenuous are attuned and laid forth.
The turbid is the path of the clear:
after a long dusk, the gleaming light.

This section describes the way of breathing of the True Man, or Realized
Man. His breath is joined with the One Breath, and circulates within his
entire person. This is not a description of a practice: it happens spontaneously to the realized beings who take the operation of the Dao as a
model for their operation in the world.

72: THE THREE THINGS ARE ONE FAMILY

When the Wooden essence of cinnabar
finds Metal, they pair with each other:
Metal and Water dwell in conjunction,
Wood and Fire are companions.

These four, in indistinction,
arrange themselves as Dragon and Tiger:
the Dragon is Yang, its number is odd,
the Tiger is Yin, its number is even.

The liver is green and is the father,
the lungs are white and are the mother,
the kidneys are black and are the son,
the heart is red and is the daughter.

The spleen is yellow and is the forefather,
and the son is at the origin of the five agents.
The three things are one family:
all of them return to WU and JI.

The Elixir is made of two ingredients, which in terms of the five agents respectively correspond to Metal and Wood, and in alchemical terms respectively correspond to True Lead and True Mercury. In the generative sequence of the agents, Metal generates Water, and Wood generates Fire. Through the inversion of this sequence that occurs in the alchemical process, Water (Yin) generates Metal (True Yang), and Fire (Yang) generates Wood (True Yin). In the language of alchemy, "black lead" (Water, Yin) generates True Lead (Metal, True Yang), and cinnabar (Fire, Yang) generates True Mercury (Wood, True Yin).

This inversion causes the postcelestial (*houtian*) aspects of Yin and Yang to be reintegrated within their precelestial (*xiantian*) aspects, which are of the opposite signs: the postcelestial Yin (Water) returns to precelestial True Yang (Metal), and the postcelestial Yang (Fire) returns to True Yin (Wood). The precosmic and cosmic aspects of Yin and Yang are now joined again to one another: "Metal and Water dwell in conjunction, Wood and Fire are companions."

Since the four initial elements are merged "in indistinction," they are reduced to two, symbolized by the Yang Dragon (whose numerical emblem is 3) and the Yin Tiger (whose numerical emblem is 4). With the addition of the central Soil, which enables True Yin and True Yang to conjoin, there are three sets, each of which has a numerical value of 5. The first set is made of Water and Metal (1+4); the second, of Fire and Wood (2+3); and the third, only of Soil (5). The main symbolic associations of each element are shown below:

(1)	WATER	1	north	dark warrior	black lead	kidneys	son
	METAL	4	west	white tiger	true lead	lungs	mother
(2)	FIRE	2	south	vermilion sparrow	cinnabar	heart	daughter
	WOOD	3	east	green dragon	true mercury	liver	father
(3)	SOIL	5	center	yellow dragon		spleen	forefather

The next verses mention the standard associations of the five viscera (liver, heart, spleen, lungs, and kidneys) with the five agents, here represented by their colors (green, red, yellow, white, and black) and by the family relations that occur among them (father, daughter, "forefather," mother, and son).[25] The verse translated as "the son is at the origin of the five agents" can be understood in two ways, and the double meaning is certainly intended. In the first sense, *zi* 子 means "son"; the son is Water, which is generated by the One and is the first element in the "cosmogonic sequence" of the five agents (see the notes to sec. 22 above). In the second sense, *zi* 子 is the name of the first earthly branch (see table 6, p. 262), and the verse should be translated as "ZI is the origin of the five agents." In both interpretations, the sense is the same: ZI is the branch emblematic of the North, and the North corresponds to the agent Water.

The final two verses reiterate the reversion process: from 5 to 3 (Metal and Water; Wood and Fire; Soil), and from 3 to 1, when True Yin and True Yang are joined to one another in the Elixir. The One is indicated by WU 戊 and JI 己, the two celestial stems that represent Soil with its Yin and Yang halves.

[25] The associations of the five viscera with the five agents will play an important role in Neidan, where the Elixir is often said to be formed by joining the "fire of the heart," which holds True Yin, with the "water of the kidneys," which holds True Yang.

2   The Hidden Agreement

Yinfu jing 陰符經

Anonymous (sixth to eighth centuries)

Commentary by Yu Yan 俞琰 (1258–1314)

Despite its brevity, the *Yinfu jing*, or *Book of the Hidden Agreement*, is one of the most obscure and difficult Taoist texts. Traditionally attributed to the Yellow Emperor (Huangdi, one of mythical founders of Chinese civilization, and the foremost in the eyes of the Taoists), it dates from between the late sixth and the eighth century. It exists in two main versions, containing slightly more than 300 and slightly more than 400 characters, respectively.

Later Neidan texts have often placed the *Yinfu jing* with the *Daode jing* (Book of the Way and Its Virtue) and the *Cantong qi* (The Seal of the Unity of the Three) at the origins of their teachings (for one example, see below, p. 84). Within Neidan, the text is especially well-known for its idea of "stealing the mechanism" (*daoji*), which Neidan adepts understand as meaning the inversion of the process that leads from the precelestial to the postcelestial domains.

Several dozen commentaries to the *Yinfu jing* are found both within and outside the Taoist Canon. The commentary translated here is by Yu Yan (born in Suzhou, 1258–1314), a learned and prolific author who wrote both independent works and commentaries to earlier texts. Part of his works examine the *Book of Changes* (*Yijing*) and Chinese cosmology, while others are concerned with Neidan (including a major commentary to the *Cantong qi*). While Yu Yan is one of the authors who incorporate key concepts of Neo-Confucianism in their Neidan, his writings display a remarkable knowledge of both Nanzong (Southern Lineage) and Beizong (Northern Lineage) literature.

This chapter contains a complete translation of the *Yinfu jing* with Yu Yan's commentary. As he explains at the end of his work, Yu Yan uses the shorter version of the *Yinfu jing*. Divisions into sections follow the original Chinese text; I have added section numbers.

1

Contemplate the Way of Heaven, hold to the operation of Heaven: this is completeness.

COMMENTARY

Being of itself as it is is the Way of Heaven; revolving to the left and turning to the right, without interruption day and night, is the operation of Heaven.

The *Zhongyong* (The Middle Course) says: "Sincerity is the Way of Heaven."[1] It also says: "Utmost sincerity has no pause."[2] Sincerity means to "be true and devoid of artificiality," and to "match the principle of Heaven" of being so of itself.[3] As this sincerity has no pause, it nourishes with continuity, moment after moment, without interruption for even one instant. If one can contemplate the Way of Heaven and preserve one's sincerity, and if one can hold to the operation of Heaven by being "strong and untiring," then one is a "companion of Heaven."[4]

"This is completeness" means that although the words "contemplate the Way of Heaven, hold to the operation of Heaven" are concise, their meaning is complete. There is nothing to add.

2

Heaven has five bandits; the one who sees them flourishes. The five bandits are in the Heart; they perform their operation in Heaven.

---

[1] *Zhongyong*, sec. 20. The *Zhongyong*, one of the main early Confucian works, is often quoted by authors of Neidan texts.

[2] *Zhongyong*, sec. 26.

[3] These sentences are drawn from Zhu Xi's (1130–1200) works; see *Zhuzi yulei*, ch. 16 and 61, respectively.

[4] The expression "strong and untiring" derives from the *Book of Changes* (*Yijing*), "Image" ("Xiang") on the hexagram Qian ䷀ (no. 1; see Wilhelm, *The I-ching or Book of Changes*, p. 6). "Companion of Heaven" derives from the *Zhuangzi*, ch. 4 (see Watson, *The Complete Works of Chuang Tzu*, p. 56).

COMMENTARY

The five bandits are the five agents. Zhu Ziyang (Zhu Xi) said:

> What is good in the world is born from those five, and what is
> bad is also due to those five. Therefore [the *Yinfu jing*] uses
> words to the contrary and calls them the five bandits.[5]

The five agents of Heaven are Water, Fire, Wood, Metal, and Soil; and
the five agents of Man are sight, hearing, speech, behavior, and
thinking. The five agents of Heaven are in Heaven and can be seen.
The five agents of Man are in the Heart; how can they be seen? If one
can see not only what is easy to see, but also what is difficult to see,
then there is nothing that one cannot see. Therefore it says, "The one
who sees them flourishes."

Why does it say that they are "in the Heart"? This means that "sight
is concerned with seeing clearly; hearing is concerned with hearing
sharply; speech is concerned with being loyal; and behavior is concerned with being respectful"; but concern is the function of the Heart.[6]

Why does it say that "they perform their operation in Heaven"?
This refers to wind, rain, sunshine, cold, and warmth.

3

The cosmos is in one's own hands, the ten thousand transformations
are born from oneself.

COMMENTARY

If one is able to set that mechanism in motion and to seize the mechanism of Heaven and Earth, then the creation and transformation of

---

[5] Yu Yan quotes this passage from Zhu Xi's commentary to the *Yinfu
jing*. About "using words to the contrary," compare the statement in the
Daode jing (Book of the Way and Its Virtue), sec. 78: "The right words seem
to go contrary to fact."

[6] These are four of the "nine concerns" (*jiusi*) of the noble man mentioned in the *Lunyu* (Sayings of Confucius), 16:10 (see Legge, *The Chinese
Classics*, vol. 1, p. 314).

Heaven and Earth are in oneself. Therefore it says, "The cosmos is in one's own hands, the ten thousand transformations are born from oneself."

Shao Kangjie (Shao Yong) says in his "Guanyi yin" (Chant on Contemplating Change):

> Each thing since its beginning has a body,
> and each body has a Qian ☰ and a Kun ☷ of its own.
> For one who knows that the ten thousand things are complete
>   in oneself,
> how could the Three Powers have a separate root?[7]
>
> Heaven from the One Center makes creation and
>   transformation;
> Man from his Heart weaves the warp and the weft.
> Could Heaven and Man have two different minds?
> But keeping away from following vain courses lies only with
>   Man.[8]

This is what [the *Yinfu jing*] means.

4

The Nature of Heaven is Man; the Heart of Man is the mechanism.

COMMENTARY

Quiescence in the life of Man is the Nature of Heaven. Therefore it says, "the Nature of Heaven is Man." The mechanism moving in the Center is the Heart of Man. Therefore it says, "the Heart of Man is the mechanism."

---

[7] The Three Powers (*sancai*) are Heaven, Earth, and Man.
[8] This poem is found in Shao Yong's (1012–77) *Yichuan jirang ji* (Beating on the Ground at Yichuan: An Anthology), ch. 15.

5

Establish the Way of Heaven, and thereby stabilize Man.

COMMENTARY

When Man is able to establish his sincerity and is not moved by human desires, then Heaven is stabilized and Man is also stabilized. Therefore it says, "establish the Way of Heaven, and thereby stabilize Man."

6

Heaven releases the mechanism of taking life, and dragons and snakes arise from the ground. The Earth releases the mechanism of taking life, and stars and constellations fall and disappear.[9] Man releases the mechanism of taking life, and Heaven and Earth are overturned.

COMMENTARY

When Heaven above releases the mechanism of taking life, dragons and snakes respond to it, and they arise from the ground. When the Earth below releases the mechanism of taking life, stars and constellations respond to it, and they fall and disappear. When Man in the middle releases the mechanism of taking life, what is above and what is below respond to it, and Heaven and Earth are overturned.

Those who are skilled in strategy (*quanmou*) and tactics (*zhishu*) know this principle, and therefore they make the example of the snake of Mount Heng: if you hit it in the head, its tail responds; if you hit it in the tail, its head responds; and if you hit it in the middle, both its head and tail respond.[10]

Those who cultivate themselves know this principle, and therefore take the head as Heaven, the belly as the Earth, and the Heart as Man.

[9] Falling stars, meteors, and similar unpredictable astronomical phenomena were considered ill omens in premodern China.

[10] These sentences are found in the *Sunzi bingfa* (The Art of War by Master Sun), ch. 11.

Their method consists in concealing the spirit within. They guide the coming and going of inhalation and exhalation, so that it reaches the Muddy Pellet (*niwan*) above and the Gate of Life (*mingmen*) below;[11] and they cause the five agents to operate within oneself by inverting their course. In the descending phase, "Metal and Water dwell in conjunction" and descend with Soil; in the ascending phase, "Wood and Fire are companions" and ascend with Soil.[12] Their rise and fall and their coming and going are inexhaustible and endless. This is "Heaven and Earth being overturned" within oneself.

The discourses of these two groups have their own motives, but their principles are obscurely joined.[13] In fact, those who have humanity (*ren*) see this and call it "humanity," and those who have knowledge see this and call it "knowledge"; however, the principles are the same. Otherwise, why would this book be called *The Hidden Agreement*?

I have seen that the book of Laozi says:

> The Spirit of the Valley does not die:
> it is called the Mysterious-Female.
> The gate of the Mysterious-Female
> is called the root of Heaven and Earth.
> Unceasing and continuous,
> its operation never wears out.[14]

These words refer to the cultivation of oneself. It also says:

---

[11] The Muddy Pellet is the upper Cinnabar Field. The name Gate of Life can refer to several points in the region of the abdomen; here Yu Yan clearly means the lower Cinnabar Field.

[12] The two sentences are quoted from the *Cantong qi* (The Seal of the Unity of the Three), 72:3–4 (translated above, p. 19). They refer to the inversion of the ordinary sequence of the five agents that occurs in the alchemical process, so that Water is not generated by Metal, but returns to Metal, and Fire is not generated by Wood, but returns to Wood. Soil, the central agent, makes their conjunction possible.

[13] The "two groups" are "those who are skilled in strategy and tactics" and "those who cultivate themselves," described in the previous two paragraphs.

[14] *Daode jing*, sec. 6.

Governing a great kingdom is like cooking a small fish.[15]

And it also says:

Good weapons are inauspicious tools.[16]

Indeed, instead of speaking only from the perspective of self-cultivation, [the book of Laozi] also speaks of the Way of government. The *Zihua zi*, the *Guanyin zi*, the *Wenzi*, the *Liezi*, and the *Zhuangzi* all do the same. Some people hold to just one of the two perspectives and only talk of that perspective. This is deceitful. When Zhan Gu wrote a commentary on this Book (the *Yinfu jing*), he took "Strengthening the army to win the battle" to refer to the filthy arts of "riding women" and the "battle of collecting." This is the utmost of deceit.[17]

<h1 style="text-align:center">7</h1>

When Heaven and Man release it together, the ten thousand transformations have a stable foundation.

COMMENTARY

The mechanism of Heaven and the mechanism of the Heart of Man respond to one another: in their movements, this and that are in agreement (*fu*) with each other. This is the meaning of "Heaven and Man release it together."

Without knowing the Dao, who can know the mechanism released together by Heaven and Man? When one knows that mechanism and does not recklessly set it in motion, the root of the ten thousand transformations is stable. Therefore it says, "when Heaven and Man release it together, the ten thousand transformations have a stable foundation."

[15] *Daode jing*, sec. 60.
[16] *Daode jing*, sec. 31.
[17] In several editions of the *Yinfu jing*, the phrase "Strengthening the army to win the battle" is the title of the third and last section of the text (in his text, Yu Yan does not use these subdivisions). "Riding women" (*yunü*) is a common name of the sexual practices. The "battle of collecting" (*caizhan*) refers to absorbing the female "essence" (*jing*) in those practices.

Those who cultivate themselves know the mechanism released together by Heaven and Man. Hence at night, sitting in quiescence, they coagulate their Spirit and coalesce their Breath. In the blink of an eye, the Spirit enters the Breath, and they join one another. Then, "silent and unmoving,"[18] they continue until the end of the HAI hour and the beginning of the ZI hour; when the Breath of Heaven and Earth arrives, they "quickly collect" it.[19] If it does not arrive, they maintain themselves empty and wait for it: they do not dare to go ahead of it.

8

In [human] nature there are skillfulness and clumsiness; they can be hidden and stored.

COMMENTARY

Among people, there are those who have knowledge and those who are foolish. Therefore their nature differs in skillfulness or clumsiness. With regard to [the statements] "great knowledge seems to be foolish" and "great skill seems to be clumsy,"[20] [they mean that] one's nature is hidden and stored within and is not perceived by other people. Therefore it says, "in [human] nature there are skillfulness and clumsiness; they can be hidden and stored."

9

The wickedness of the nine openings depends on the three essential ones; they can be in movement or in quiescence.

---

[18] This expression is used in a large number of Neidan and other Taoist texts. It is originally found in the *Book of Changes*, "Appended Sayings" ("Xici"), sec. A.9 (see Wilhelm, p. 315).

[19] "Quickly collect" (*jicai*) is a recurrent Neidan phrase, first found in the *Wuzhen pian* (Awakening to Reality), "Lüshi," poem 7 (translated below, p. 72).

[20] *Daode jing*, sec. 45.

COMMENTARY

The "wickedness" is the human desires: when human desires burn, the principle of Heaven is extinguished. Therefore the noble man wards off and protects himself against that wickedness.

There are nine openings, but three of them are the essential ones: the ears, the eyes, and the mouth. In his movement, the noble man "does not watch what is not proper, does not listen to what is not proper, and does not speak of what is not proper";[21] this is being sincere in movement. In his quiescence, he does not watch and does not listen, and cautiously keeps his mouth closed; this is being sincere in quiescence.

Thus the noble man is sincere in his movement as well as in his quiescence. Since he is sincere in both movement and quiescence, wherever he goes there is no place where he could not [be sincere]. Therefore it says, "The wickedness of the nine openings depends on the three essential ones; they can be in movement or in quiescence."

IO

Fire is born in wood: as calamity occurs, there is surely conquest. Treachery is born in the kingdom: as time moves, there is surely disruption. The one who knows this and cultivates himself is called a sage.

COMMENTARY

When fire is born within the wood, the wood is burnt by that fire. Therefore it says, "fire is born in wood: as calamity occurs, there is surely conquest." When treachery is born within the kingdom, the kingdom is impaired by that treachery. Therefore it says, "treachery is born in the kingdom: as time moves, there is surely disruption."

In the method of cultivating oneself, one "stores the Heart in the abyss and polishes the Numinous Root."[22] When there is [a state of]

---

[21] *Lunyu*, 12:2 (see Legge, *The Chinese Classics*, vol. 1, p. 250).

[22] This sentence is quoted form the *Taixuan jing* (Book of the Great

rest (*an*), fire does not cause damage by blazing upward; this is the same as wood that stores fire within itself, but is not conquered by that fire. "Warding off evil and maintaining sincerity"[23] is the same as a kingdom that stores treachery within itself, but is not destroyed by that treachery. Therefore it says, "the one who knows this and cultivates himself is called a sage."

11

Heaven gives life and Heaven gives death: this is the principle of the Dao.

COMMENTARY

As there is the rain of spring that gives forth life, so there is the frost of autumn that causes life to wither. This is the Way of Heaven being as it is, and the Principle being so of itself.

12

Heaven and Earth are the thieves of the ten thousand things. The ten thousand things are the thieves of Man. Man is the thief of the ten thousand things. When the three thieves find what is proper, the Three Powers are at rest.

Mystery), tetragram "Yang" ("Nourishment"). The *Taixuan jing* is a Han-dynasty work written by Yang Xiong (53 BCE–18 CE). It is based on "tetragrams" or emblems made of four lines, instead of the hexagrams of the *Book of Changes* that are made of six lines.

[23] This expression, which defines one of the cardinal principles of Neidan, derives from the *Book of Changes*, "Explanation of the Sentences" ("Wenyan") on the hexagram Qian ☰ (no. 1): "Even in ordinary speech he is trustworthy, and in ordinary actions he is careful. He wards off evil and maintains his sincerity" (see Wilhelm, p. 380). "Sincerity" is equivalent to the True Intention (*zhenyi*), which is the operation of Spirit.

COMMENTARY

Heaven and Earth nourish the ten thousand things, but they also harm the ten thousand things; therefore it says, "Heaven and Earth are the thieves of the ten thousand things." Man nourishes the ten thousand things, but he also harms the ten thousand things; therefore it says, "the ten thousand things are the thieves of Man." The ten thousand things nourish Man, but they also harm Man; therefore it says, "Man is the thief of the ten thousand things." In fact, the reason why [the *Yinfu jing*] does not speak of nourishment and only speaks of harm is that it uses words to the contrary.

If each of those three finds what is proper for itself, then Heaven and Earth acquire their positions and the ten thousand things are nourished. Therefore it says, "when the three thieves find what is proper, the Three Powers are at rest."

13

Therefore it is said: Eat at the right time, and the hundred bones are regulated.[24] Set that mechanism in motion, and the ten thousand transformations are at rest.

COMMENTARY

"Time" means the time of Heaven and Earth. If I can "eat at the right time" and be joined with Heaven and Earth, then "the hundred bones are regulated."

"Mechanism" means the mechanism of the Heart of Man. If I can "set that mechanism in motion" and be joined with Heaven and Earth, then "the ten thousand transformations are at rest" in me.

---

[24] "Eating at the right time" refers to taking one's nourishment from the precelestial Original Breath (*yuanqi*) as it manifests itself in the time cycles of the postcelestial domain.

I4

Man knows the Spirit that is spirit, but does not know why what is
not spirit is Spirit.[25]

COMMENTARY

Spirit is "that in which Yin and Yang are unfathomable."[26] "It is the
name given to what makes the ten thousand things wondrous."[27] It
does not mean the numina and ghosts of the common people of the
world.

The foolish people do not know how to investigate the principles:
they are confused by odd and weird discourses about numina and
ghosts, and say that those are "spirit." As for the cyclical movements
of the Sun and the Moon, the shifting of the four seasons, and the
transformations of the ten thousand things, they are accustomed to
them and take them as ordinary, and say that all this "is not spirit."
Who among them could know "what makes Spirit what is not Spirit"?

In the past, I heard a recluse saying:[28]

> Heaven is empty and its shape is similar to a chicken egg. The
> Earth has a precise location in the middle of Heaven; therefore
> it is like the yolk in an egg. Above and below and all around the

---

[25] In other versions of the *Yinfu jing*, this sentence reads: "Man knows the
Spirit that is spirit, but does know why the Spirit that is not spirit is Spirit."
For another explanation of this passage, see below, p. 252. (For the sake of
clarity, I use uppercase and lowercase letters to distinguish the two senses of
shen, "spirit.")

[26] This sentence is found in the *Book of Changes*, "Appended Sayings,"
sec. A.5 (see Wilhelm, p. 301). It defines spirit as the state of unity in which
Yin and Yang are not distinguished from one another.

[27] *Book of Changes*, "Explanation of the Trigrams" ("Shuogua"), sec. 5
(see Wilhelm, p. 272).

[28] In the remaining part of his commentary on this section, Yu Yan provides examples, drawn from the astronomical and biological knowledge of his
time, to document the principle that even phenomena often deemed to be
obvious are owed to the operation of spirit. He also criticizes, by means of a
sentence found in the *Suishu* (History of the Sui Dynasty), an example of the
erroneous understanding of that operation.

Earth it is all empty: that emptiness is Heaven. The Earth is suspended in emptiness but has never fallen from the antiquity to the present day because Heaven moves outside and turns around day and night, without interruption. Heaven is higher in the north and lower in the south and turns in an oblique way; therefore the North Pole is 36 degrees inside the Earth's axis, and the South Pole is 36 degrees outside the Earth's axis. The ecliptic surrounds the Heaven's belly; the Sun and the Moon move within the emptiness [of Heaven] but never leave the ecliptic.

The *Suishu* (History of the Sui Dynasty) says that the Sun enters the water.[29] This is senseless, because "water flows within the Earth"[30] and never leaves it. [Moreover,] all around the four directions of the Earth there is only Heaven; how could there be water? Saying that water floats in Heaven and supports the Earth is thoroughly senseless.

On the winter solstice, the Sun in the morning is close to the South Pole and moves in the southern part of Heaven. The Yang Breath is distant from the human beings. Thus the cold at night is hidden in the emptiness under the ground, and the Yang Breath stays under the people's feet. This is why the water in the wells is warm. On the summer solstice, the Sun in the morning is close to the North Pole and moves above the people's heads. The Yang Breath directly irradiates what is below. Thus the heat at night is hidden outside the Earth, in the emptiness of the north, and the Yang Breath does not stay under the ground. This is why the water in the wells is cool.

The ten thousand things are born in the spring and grow in the summer, because the Breath of Great Yang steams upwards from the ground. They withdraw in the autumn and are stored in the winter, because the Breath of Great Yang leaves the ground and gradually goes away. This principle is clear, but those who are blind to it just do not understand it.

[29] This seems to refer to a discussion in the *Suishu*, ch. 19, that contains the following statement: "Heaven is something Yang, and moreover, it enters and exits water; it is similar to a dragon, and therefore it is represented by a dragon."

[30] *Mengzi*, 3:2 (see Legge, *The Chinese Classics*, vol. 2, p. 280).

As for the birds, the mammals, the worms, and the fishes; the different creatures born from wombs, from eggs, from moist, or by transformation;[31] and the flowering and the fruiting of plants, [in all these cases] the white [gives birth] to the white; the red, to the red; the large, to the large; and the small, to the small. Everyone knows that it is so, but no one knows what makes it so.

Therefore [the *Yinfu jing*] says, "Man knows the Spirit that is spirit, but does not know why what is not spirit is Spirit."

15

The Sun and the Moon have rules, the large and the small have laws. The efficacy of the sage comes forth from this, the Numinous Light comes forth from this.

COMMENTARY

The Sun and the Moon are Spirit! "Sun and Moon follow their courses and it is now cold, now hot,"[32] and "when cold goes, heat comes, when heat comes, cold goes."[33] This is Spirit. If not the sage, who could understand this? Indeed, in understanding Spirit,[34] the efficacy lies in the sage.

The Sun in one day moves by 1 degree. In one full term,[35] it moves by 365$\frac{1}{4}$ degrees and makes a whole celestial revolution. The Moon in one day moves by a little more than 13 degrees. When it makes a celestial revolution in twenty-eight days, it moves for two more days, then meets the Sun and they align with one another. When it makes a celestial revolution in twenty-seven days, it moves for three more days, then meets the Sun and they align with one another. Therefore it says, "the Sun and the Moon have rules, the large and the small have laws."

[31] These are the "four kinds of birth" (*sisheng*) in Buddhism.
[32] *Book of Changes*, "Appended Sayings," sec. A.1 (see Wilhelm, p. 284).
[33] *Book of Changes*, "Appended Sayings," sec. B.3 (see Wilhelm, p. 338).
[34] *Book of Changes*, "Appended Sayings," sec. A.12 (see Wilhelm, p. 324; Yu Yan's use of this sentence requires a translation different from the one given by Wilhelm).
[35] *Yiqi*, i.e., one year.

The sage is concerned that people do not know that the Sun and the Moon have rules, and thus could miss the times of sowing in the spring and harvesting in the autumn. Hence he sets the calendar and defines the seasons for their benefit. He establishes the seasons to complete a whole year by means of the intercalary months. There is one intercalary month in the third year, and two in the fifth year [after the third one]; in nineteen years there are [altogether] seven intercalary months, and this is called a "division" (zhang). In this way, the first day of the month always falls on the same day.[36] The rules are indeed fixed and cannot change.

The sage supports the fostering of Heaven and Earth: this is his efficacy. He causes everyone to know that the Sun and the Moon are Spirit: this is the principle that he enables to shine. Therefore it says, "the efficacy of the sage comes forth from this, the Numinous Light comes forth from this."

16

No one in the world is able to see the stealing of the mechanism, and no one is able to know it. When the noble man obtains it, he strengthens himself.[37] When the small man obtains it, he makes light of his destiny.

COMMENTARY

When the mechanism is not released, and it is hidden and not exposed, who is able to see it? Who is able to know it? This is why it calls this "the stealing of the mechanism."[38]

---

[36] I.e., on the day in which the Sun and the Moon are aligned with one another with respect to the Earth, and the Moon seen from the Earth is black.

[37] Several editions of the Yinfu jing read guqiong 固窮 instead of gugong 固躬: "When the noble man obtains it, he endures want." The expression guqiong is found in a passage of the Lunyu, 15:1, that is close in import to the present passage of the Yinfu jing: "The noble man endures want; the small man, when he is in want, gives way to unbridled license" (see Legge, The Chinese Classics, vol. 1, p. 294).

[38] The "mechanism," as Yu Yan explains in his commentary to sec. 6, is the ordinary course that leads from life to death. "Stealing the mechanism"

If the noble man obtains this mechanism, he uses it to strengthen himself: he knows his destiny and does not set it in motion carelessly. If the small man obtains it, he uses it to make light of his destiny: he does not know his destiny and sets it in motion carelessly.

17

The blind is skilled in hearing, the deaf is skilled in seeing. By cutting off one source of profit, the function increases by ten times compared to the common people. By returning three times day and night, the function increases by ten thousand times compared to the common people.[39]

COMMENTARY

The eyes of a blind man do not see, but his ears are skilled in hearing. The ears of a deaf man do not hear, but his eyes are skilled in seeing. This is because they focus only on one thing.

If those who study the Dao are able to eliminate the selfishness of greed and to maintain their will undivided, then their function is ten times superior to that of a common person. People's afflictions are caused by not examining themselves. If they are able to carefully guard the three essentials, namely the ears, the eyes, and the mouth, and to maintain their sincerity day and night, then their function is ten thousand times superior compared to that of a common person.[40]

allows one to "invert the course." This process is secret and hidden; therefore it should be "stolen."

[39] The word *shi* also means "soldier," and this sentence has often been understood as meaning "Cutting off one source of profit is ten times better than using soldiers." This understanding may suit the use of the *Yinfu jing* in the context of the military arts. *Shi*, however, also means "common person" or "common people." In the present case, the "common people" are those whose senses of hearing and seeing function in the ordinary ways. Compared to them, the blind and the deaf lack one function ("one source of profit"), but the other one increases in efficacy.

[40] This section of the *Yinfu jing* contains the word *fan* ("to return") in the sentence *sanfan zhouye*, literally translated above as "returning three times

18

The Heart lives in things and dies in things. The mechanism is in the eyes.

COMMENTARY

The Heart moves because of things; thus it "lives in things." It follows them and forgets to come back; thus it "dies in things."

The Heart is the residence of spirit, and the eyes are the windows of spirit. Wherever the eyes go, the Heart also goes; thus its mechanism indeed lies in the eyes.[41]

19

Heaven has no mercy, and great mercy is born. Shift of thunders, blasts of wind, and all things wiggle.

COMMENTARY

The relation of Heaven to things is that it lets them be as they are. Therefore it is comprehensible that [the *Yinfu jing*] calls this "no

day and night." Yu Yan intends *fan* as meaning *zifan*, a term that in Confucian texts means "to examine oneself" (e.g., *Mengzi*, 2:1; see Legge, *The Chinese Classics*, vol. 2, p. 187). For Yu Yan, however, self-examination does not only consist in questioning oneself from ethical or moral points of view; it consists, especially, in guarding the "three essentials," each of which is "inverted" (another sense of *fan*) so that it operates inwardly instead of outwardly. For instance, the eyes are not used to look outside, but to look within. This is done "three times," once for each of the "three essentials," and is done "night and day," i.e., continuously. The analogy with the blind and the deaf is clear: by eliminating each "source" (*yuan*) of dispersion (such as the eyes looking outwardly), the opposite function (looking inwardly) increases in efficacy.

[41] The view that the eyes direct the course of the Heart (or the mind) seems to be first stated in the *Huangdi neijing suwen* (Inner Book of the Yellow Emperor: The Plain Questions), sec. 18, which says: "The eyes are the envoys of the Heart. The Heart is the residence of spirit." This view has had a large number of applications in both medicine and Taoism.

mercy." However, when it comes to "arousing them by thunder and lightning, and fertilizing them by wind and rain,"[42] everything under Heaven, from the wriggling worms to the sentient creatures, is affected by its beneficence. Does this not mean that within "no mercy" there is "great mercy"?

20

In utmost happiness, one's nature is overflowing; in utmost quiescence, it is pure.

COMMENTARY

When one who has knowledge is happy, in his happiness he knows his destiny and is not distraught. Therefore his nature is overflowing: it is plentiful and unrestricted. When one who has humanity is quiescent, in his quiescence he is stable and has no desires. Therefore his nature is uncorrupt: it is pure and devoid of greed.

21

What is most partial in Heaven is most universal in its operation.

COMMENTARY

The Way of Heaven is most universal and devoid of partiality. People only see the birth of a single thing or the growth of a single thing, and think that this is Heaven being most partial.[43] They do not reflect on "what is illuminated by the Sun and the Moon, and what is reached by rain and dew."[44]

---

[42] *Book of Changes*, "Appended Sayings," sec. A.1 (see Wilhelm, p. 284).

[43] In other words, they think that Heaven has accorded some favor to that particular thing.

[44] These expressions are drawn from the *Baopu zi waipian* (Outer Chapters of the Master Who Embraces Spontaneous Nature), ch. 2.

Among all the species of birds, fishes, animals, and plants, there is not even one that does not "receive its correct nature and destiny, and does not embrace and join with the Great Harmony."[45] This is Heaven being "most universal." How could Heaven be partial to a single thing?

22

The command of birds lies in Breath (qi).[46]

COMMENTARY

When the oriole sings in the spring, what makes it sing? When the swan goose returns in the autumn, what makes it return? The reason is that "the command of birds lies in Breath."

23

Life is the root of death; death is the root of life. Mercy is born in harm, harm is born in mercy.

COMMENTARY

Life means the movement of the ten thousand things. "When movement culminates, it returns to quiescence"; therefore "life is the root of death." Death means the quiescence of the ten thousand things. "When quiescence culminates, it returns to movement"; therefore "death is the root of life."[47]

[45] Book of Changes, "Commentary on the Judgment" ("Tuanzhuan") on the hexagram Qian ䷀ (no 1; see Wilhelm, p. 371).

[46] According to one of several ways in which this sentence has been understood, birds are able to fly because they can control (zhi, i.e., "be in command of") the qi ("breath") of the clouds. Yu Yan's commentary follows this understanding, but he also emphasizes that birds spontaneously know how to follow the transformations of qi, such as those that occur with the coming of spring and autumn.

[47] The two sentences, "When movement culminates, it returns to quies-

"Mercy" means that Heaven gives life; "harm" means that Heaven takes life. There are withdrawal and storing in autumn and winter, and thus there are birth and growth in spring and summer. There are spreading out and flourishing in spring and summer, and thus there are withering and ending in autumn and winter. Therefore it says, "life is the root of death; death is the root of life."

24

The foolish ones take the signs and the patterns of Heaven and Earth as sagehood. I take the signs and the patterns of time and things as wisdom.[48]

COMMENTARY

"The foolish ones take the signs and the patterns of Heaven and Earth as sagehood" because sagehood is unfathomable. As they deem it to be unfathomable, people refrain from inquiring into its principles. They consider it sagehood but do not know what makes it sagehood.

"I take the signs and the patterns of time and things as wisdom" because wisdom can be known. Those who have knowledge inquire into its principles in order to "extend that knowledge to the utmost."[49] Thus I am able to fathom the sagehood of Heaven and Earth; and how much more can I do this with time and things?

cence" and "When quiescence culminates, it returns to movement," are found at the beginning of Zhou Dunyi's (1017–73) *Taiji tu shuo* (Explication of the Chart of the Great Ultimate).

[48] "Signs of Heaven" (*tianwen*) refers to Sun, Moon, planets, stars, wind, rain, and other similar objects and phenomena that are found or occur in Heaven. "Patterns of the Earth" (*dili*) refers to mountains, seas, rocks, plants, animals and other similar objects that are found on the Earth. — In the second sentence, "time and things" refers to time as defined and measured by the movements of the astral bodies in Heaven, and to the things and creatures that exist and live on the Earth.

[49] This famous sentence derives from another major early Confucian text, the *Daxue* (The Great Learning), sec. 4 (see Legge, *The Chinese Classics*, vol. 1, p. 358)

The signs and the patterns of time and things are the same as those of Heaven and Earth. If one does not know the signs of Heaven, one just contemplates the proper times of Heaven. If one does not know the patterns of the Earth, one just observes the circumstances of the things of the Earth. What need is there of searching on high and afar?

At the end of this text (the *Book of the Hidden Agreement*) there are slightly more than one hundred other characters. Some think that they belong to a commentary, others think that they belong to the main text. For example, it says: "The Way of Heaven and Earth impregnates [all things]; therefore Yin and Yang prevail." This means that between Heaven and Earth, when the Yang flourishes it prevails over the Yin, and when the Yin flourishes it prevails over the Yang. Like water does when it impregnates something, [the Way of Heaven and Earth] operates in a gradual way.

Although Zhu Ziyang (Zhu Xi) thought that [this part of the text] belongs to a commentary and did not write his own explications on it, he did answer the questions of his disciples about it, showing that he deeply understood its meaning. I follow his example.

3   Mirror for Compounding the Medicine

Ruyao jing 入藥鏡

Attributed to Cui Xifan 崔希範 (ca. 880–940)

Commentary by Wang Jie 王玠 (?-ca. 1380)

The *Ruyao jing*, or *Mirror for Compounding the Medicine*, is attributed to Cui Xifan (ca. 880–940). With the *Cantong qi* (The Seal of the Unity of the Three; above, Chapter 1), the *Yinfu jing* (Book of the Hidden Agreement; above, Chapter 2), and the *Wuzhen pian* (Awakening to Reality; below, Chapter 5), it is one of the texts most frequently quoted in works belonging to the Neidan tradition.

The text has been transmitted in different forms, among which the version at the basis of this translation is the only one to have entirely survived. This version summarizes the main Neidan principles and practices in twenty-one short poems, each of which is made of four verses of three characters (except for the last poem, which contains only two verses). The term *ruyao* in the title, literally meaning "to enter the ingredients," is used in Waidan (External Alchemy) and in pharmacology to mean that the ingredients are placed in a vessel to compound an elixir or a medicine. The word "mirror" (*jing* or *jian*) appears in the titles of several Chinese texts to indicate that they provide models for the application of fundamental principles or ideas.

The commentary translated here is by Wang Jie (?-ca. 1380). Also known as Wang Daoyuan and Hunran zi (Master of the Inchoate), he was a second-generation disciple of Li Daochun (late thirteenth century; see below, Chapter 11) and is the author of several Neidan works, including both original writings and commentaries to earlier texts.

These selections contain ten of the original twenty-one poems. They are drawn from my complete translation of both text and commentary, published in Wang Jie, *Commentary on the Mirror for Compounding the Medicine* (Golden Elixir Press, 2013).

I

Precelestial Breath,
postcelestial Breath.
Those who obtain them
always seem to be drunk.

COMMENTARY

The precelestial Breath is the original and initial Ancestral Breath.
This Ancestral Breath is in the true center of Heaven and Earth within
the human body. [Placed between] the Secret Door and the Gate of
Life, hanging in the middle, it is the Heart of Heaven.[1] The self-
cultivation of the divine immortals only consists in collecting the
precelestial One Breath and using it as the Mother of the Elixir.

The postcelestial Breath is the Breath that circulates internally: one
exhalation, one inhalation, once coming, once going. "Exhaling
touches onto the root of Heaven, inhaling touches onto the root of
Earth. On exhaling, 'the dragon howls and the clouds rise'; on inhaling, 'the tiger roars and the wind blows.'"[2]

When [the postcelestial Breath] is "unceasing and continuous,"[3] it
returns to the Ancestral Breath. The internal and the external in-

---

[1] This sentence alludes to the description of the center of the human
body in the *Huangting jing* (Book of the Yellow Court): "Above is the *Hun*
Numen, below is the Origin of the Barrier; on the left is the Minor Yang, on
the right is the Great Yin; behind is the Secret Door, in front is the Gate of
Life" ("Inner" version, poem 2). The Secret Door (*mihu*) is the kidneys, or a
point in their region. The Gate of Life (*shengmen*) is the lower Cinnabar
Field, or a point in its region. — The *Huangting jing*, originally dating from
the second or the third century, is one of the main texts on early Taoist
meditation. It exists in two versions, called "Outer" and "Inner." The "Inner"
version" is later and longer compared to the "Outer" version.

[2] This passage is quoted, without attribution, in the *Jindan wenda* (Questions and Answers on the Golden Elixir). It is also found in Li Daochun's
Zhonghe ji (The Harmony of the Center: An Anthology), ch. 4, translated
below, p. 174.

[3] This expression derives from the passage of the *Daode jing* (Book of the
Way and Its Virtue) quoted at the end of the commentary to the present
section.

choately merge, and coalesce to form the Reverted Elixir (*huandan*).
Then you become aware of a burning fire in the Cinnabar Field that
spreads to the four limbs. You look like a fool or like drunk, but "its
beauty lies within."[4] This is why it says, "those who obtain them
always seem to be drunk."

This is what the *Daode jing* (Book of the Way and Its Virtue)
means when it says:

> The Spirit of the Valley does not die:
> it is called the Mysterious-Female.
> The gate of the Mysterious-Female
> is called the root of Heaven and Earth.
> Unceasing and continuous,
> its operation never wears out.[5]

And this is what the *Book of Changes* means when it says about the
Kun ䷁ hexagram:

> From the Yellow Center it spreads to the veining, as it places
> itself in the correct position. Its beauty lies within, and extends
> to the four limbs.[6]

3

> Ascend to the Magpie Bridge,
> descend from the Magpie Bridge.
> In Heaven it responds to the stars,
> on Earth it responds to the tides.[7]

[4] This expression derives from the passage of the *Book of Changes*
(*Yijing*) quoted at the end of the commentary to the present section.

[5] *Daode jing*, sec. 6.

[6] *Book of Changes*, "Explanation of the Sentences" ("Wenyan") on the
hexagram Kun ䷁ (see Wilhelm, *The I-ching or Book of Changes*, p. 395). The
first sentence is also found in the *Cantong qi* (The Seal of the Unity of the
Three), 19:1 (see Pregadio, *The Seal of the Unity of the Three*, p. 77).

[7] On the translation of the first two verses, see the next footnote.

COMMENTARY

In the human body, the spinal column corresponds the Milky Way in Heaven. The Milky Way separates [Heaven into two parts], but a divine magpie builds a bridge; this is why we speak of the Magpie Bridge. In the human being, the tongue is called Magpie Bridge.[8]

When you compound the Elixir, you always use the Yellow Dame to lead the Infant to ascend to the Muddy Pellet and conjoin with the Lovely Maid.[9] This is called "ascending to the Magpie Bridge." [Then] the Yellow Dame again goes back and forth; smiling, she leads the Infant and the Lovely Maid to return together to the Cavern Chamber.[10] [To do so], they must come down from the Muddy Pellet; therefore it says, "descend from the Magpie Bridge."

It is not that there are truly a Yellow Dame, an Infant, and a Lovely Maid: this is a speech made through metaphors (*piyu*), and concerns nothing outside the body, the mind, and the Intention (*yi*). Through the efficacy of silent operation, internally you rely on the movement of the Celestial Net, and externally you use the motion of

---

[8] According to a Chinese legend, the Magpie Bridge connects the Altair and Vega stars across the Milky Way. As a consequence, the Herdboy and the Weaving Girl, who live in those stars and love one another, can meet once a year. In Neidan, the Magpie Bridge connects the Control and Function vessels (*dumai* and *renmai*), respectively running along the back and the front of the body. According to different texts, this Bridge is either the tongue or the nose. In another view, there are an upper Bridge, which is the tongue, and a lower Bridge, which is found at the bottom of the spine. In accordance with the second view, the first two verses of this stanza should be translated as "The upper Magpie Bridge, / the lower Magpie Bridge." In his commentary, Wang Jie mentions only the tongue, and understands *shang* and *xia* ("upper" and "lower") as verbs meaning "to ascend" and "to descend," respectively to and from the Magpie Bridge. I have translated this stanza in accordance with Wang Jie's reading.

[9] Muddy Pellet (*niwan*) is the most common name for the upper Cinnabar Field, located in the region of the head.

[10] Cavern Chamber (*dongfang*) is usually a name of one of the "chambers" of the Niwan Palace, the upper Cinnabar Field. Here, however, it clearly connotes the lower Cinnabar Field. Note that in both premodern and present-day Chinese, this term is also used to mean "nuptial chamber."

the Dipper's Handle.[11] When you kindle the Fire, you become aware of the Breath ascending without interruption. Similar to the initial rise of a tide, it goes upwards by inverting its flow; therefore it says, "in Heaven it responds to the stars, on Earth it responds to the tides."

This is what a book on the Elixir means when it says:

The practice is easy, the Medicine is not far away.[12]

And this is what we mean when we say: "The wheel of Heaven revolves, and the Earth responds with the tides."

6

The Lead-Dragon ascends,
the Mercury-Tiger descends.
Force the Two Things,
do not be indulgent.

COMMENTARY

Lead is the one particle of True Yang within Kan ☵; we call it the Dragon. Mercury is the one particle of True Yin within Li ☲; we call it the Tiger.

When you compound the Elixir, you always move the wu-Soil upwards to extract the Lead within Kan.[13] Wood generates Fire, which blazes and ascends to the Muddy Pellet. Since the Dragon comes forth from the Fire, it says "the Lead-Dragon ascends." You [also] use the ji-Soil to draw the Mercury within Li. Metal generates Water, which flows and descends to the [lower] Cinnabar Field. Since the Tiger is born in the Water, it says "the Mercury-Tiger descends."

[11] Celestial Net (tiangang) is the name of the first four stars of the Northern Dipper, and Dipper's Handle (doubing) is the name of its last three stars.

[12] Wuzhen pian (Awakening to Reality), "Xijiang yue," poem 2 (see Cleary, Understanding Reality, p. 132).

[13] The wu-Soil and the ji-Soil (mentioned below in this paragraph) are the Yang and the Yin aspects of Soil, respectively. Soil is the agent that represents the unity of Yin and Yang.

In the practice of seizing [the ingredients], if you do not apply the strength of the fierce Fire, the Lead-Dragon would not ascend; and if you do not use the strength of the gentle Fire, the Mercury-Tiger would not descend. The wonder of the cyclical flow [that occurs] during each breath lies in the amount of force [that you apply]. Use your strength to seize the Dragon and the Tiger, and place them in the Tripod. Heat and refine them, and they will transmute themselves into a royal jelly (*wangjiang*). Therefore it says, "force the Two Things, do not be indulgent."

This is what Zhang Ziyang (Zhang Boduan) meant when he said:

> The White Tiger in the Western Mountain by nature goes wild,
> the Green Dragon in the Eastern Sea cannot be defied.
> Grab each of them in your hands and let them battle to death;
> refine them, and they will turn into a chunk of purple golden
>   frost.[14]

8

Steal Heaven and Earth,
seize creation and transformation.
Gather the five agents,
bring the eight trigrams together.

COMMENTARY

Clenching Heaven and Earth, grasping Yin and Yang, gathering the five agents, and bringing the eight trigrams together: this is the learning of the divine immortals.

Heaven and Earth are Qian and Kun. Creation and transformation are Yin and Yang. The five agents are Metal, Wood, Water, Fire, and Soil. The eight trigrams are Qian ☰, Kun ☷, Kan ☵, Li ☲, Zhen ☳, Xun ☴, Gen ☶, and Dui ☱.

However, the greatness of Heaven and Earth, and the depth of creation and transformation, lies in the fact that the five agents part and

---

[14] *Wuzhen pian*, "Jueju," poem 20.

distribute themselves, and that the eight trigrams arrange themselves in a ring. By which art can you steal them and seize them, cause them to gather and bring them together?

"To steal" means to rob; "to seize" means to take; "to gather" means to converge; "to bring together" means to join. This concerns the methods of the Masters of the Elixir, whose wonder lies in the oral transmission. The true instructions on compounding the Elixir always pertain to this and nothing else. Wait until the time comes and the Breath transmutes itself: when the Medicine is produced, the Spirit knows it. Then you must shut the Barrier of Wind, close the Door of Gen ☶, turn the Celestial Net, and revolve the Dipper's Handle.[15] As each breath allows the Matching Fires [of Yin and Yang] to circulate, it causes 3,600 correct Breaths (zhengqi) to converge, and inverts the series of the 72 periods.[16]

When you have reversed the five agents and have brought the eight trigrams together, and all of them have returned to the Earthenware Crucible, close it and firmly seal it.[17] Immediately harmonize the Fire that you send forth, and refine by means of an intense, fierce heat. [The Medicine] will coalesce and form the Embryo of Sainthood.

In this way, the work of one notch seizes the nodal phases of one whole year.[18] A book on the Elixir says:

If the human Heart joins with the Heart of Heaven,
reversing Yin and Yang takes only one instant.[19]

---

[15] The Barrier of Wind (fengguan) is one of the two openings under the palate that allow the passage of air during inhalation and exhalation. For "door of Gen ☶," the text in the Daozang jiyao has "door of Dui ☱." Dui usually represents the mouth.

[16] The 3,600 correct Breaths are those of the "double hours" contained in the ten months of gestation of the embryo. The 72 periods are the 5-day phases that form one year.

[17] Earthenware Crucible (tufu), a name derived from Waidan (External Alchemy), denotes in Neidan the lower Cinnabar Field.

[18] For the "notch" (ke), see the entry "The Fire Phases" in the Jindan wenda (Questions and Answers on the Golden Elixir), p. 139 below.

[19] These verses are quoted from Xiao Tingzhi's Jindan da chengji (A Great Anthology on the Golden Elixir), in Xiuzhen shishu, ch. 9.

This means that with one exhalation and one inhalation you can "seize creation and transformation." In one day, a human being makes 13,500 exhalations and 13,500 inhalations. One exhalation and one inhalation correspond to one breath; thus in the space of one breath, you covertly seize the number of a celestial revolution of 13,500 years. In one year, you make 4,860,000 breaths, and you covertly seize the number of a celestial revolution of 4,860,000 years. At that point, you entirely change your impure Yin body and transform it into a body of Pure Yang.

The transformations of Spirit are unlimited: coagulation results in form, dispersion results in wind.[20] You exit Being and enter Non-Being, and whether you conceal yourself or let yourself to be seen, you cannot be fathomed. Is this not extraordinary?

9

Water is True Water,
Fire is True Fire.
Water and Fire conjoin:
you will never grow old.

COMMENTARY

Water dwells in the North. Among the trigrams it is Kan ☵, and in the body it is the kidneys. Fire dwells in the South. Among the trigrams it is Li ☲, and in the body it is the heart. Water stores Fire within itself, and Fire stores Water within itself. In the human being, the one particle of True Liquor within the heart is the True Water, and the one particle of True Yang within the kidneys is the True Fire.

Water and Fire are divided between above and below. How can they be conjoined? You must avail yourself of the True Soil of WU and JI in order to seize and control the True Fire and the True Water, and to apply pressure on them. Thus you can cause them to ascend and descend, and to return together to the Earthenware Crucible.

---

[20] These sentences are found in many Taoist texts. The last word is usually "breath" (*qi*) instead of "wind" (*feng*), but the two terms are equivalent in this context.

After Water and Fire have been balanced, they coalesce and form the Golden Elixir. In the Pure Yang of the One Breath, you will live as long as Heaven. Therefore it says, "Water and Fire conjoin: you will never grow old."

II

It is Nature and Existence,
it is not Spirit and Breath.
Lead in the village of Water,
the one ingredient.

COMMENTARY

One's Nature (*xing*) is Spirit, one's Existence (*ming*) is Breath. The inchoate merging of Nature and Existence is the precelestial foundation; the cyclical transformations of Spirit and Breath are the postcelestial operation. Therefore it says, "it is Nature and Existence, it is not Spirit and Breath."

If those who devote themselves to self-cultivation want to make their Nature numinous and their Existence firm, from the moment they set to practice they must collect the Lead in the village of Water. "Lead in the village of Water" means that Kun ☷ loses her virginity because of Qian ☰ and becomes Kan ☵. [Therefore] within the Kan-Water there is the Qian-Metal:

Metal is the mother of Water —
the mother is hidden in the embryo of her son.[21]

One particle of True Yang dwells in it. As soon as you meet the movement of the Yang principle in the ZI hour within yourself, you should immediately collect it. Ziyang (Zhang Boduan) said:

When Lead meets the birth of GUI, quickly you should collect it.[22]

---

[21] *Cantong qi*, 23:1–2 (translated above, p. 11).
[22] *Wuzhen pian*, "Lüshi," poem 7 (translated below, p. 72).

He meant that at the time of the collection you must use the Intention, which goes back and forth, and lead the Fire so that it forces the Metal [to ascend]. This is exactly what is meant by the words:

> Fire forces Metal into movement, following an inverted course, and the Great Elixir coagulates of its own within the Tripod.[23]

This one ingredient is the root of the Great Dao.

Yunfang (Zhongli Quan) said:

> The Gate that gives me life is the Door that gives me death:
> how many people are aware of this, how many are awakened to it?
> When the night comes, even the toughest of all men ponders meticulously:
> living a long life without dying depends on each of us.[24]

He pointed to this one ingredient just because he wished the people of this world to seek it in this way, as it is the foundation for refining the Elixir. This is what the books on the Elixir mean when they say:

> Hold True Lead firmly and seek with intention[25]

and when they say:

> Just take the one ingredient, the Metal within Water.[26]

---

[23] I have not identified the source of these verses, but similar sentences are found in many Neidan texts.

[24] These verses are attributed to Zhongli Quan in the *Jinlian zhengzong ji* (Records of the Correct Lineage of the Golden Lotus), ch. 1. This work, dating from the mid-thirteenth century, contains biographies of Quanzhen patriarchs and early masters.

[25] *Wuzhen pian*, "Lüshi," poem 10 (see Pregadio, *Awakening to Reality*, p. 52).

[26] In the form translated above, this verse derives from Chen Nan's *Cuixu pian* (The Emerald Emptiness). Wang Jie's text reads, "The one ingredient in the Flowery Pond (*huachi*) is Metal within Water."

14

Count on the Yellow Dame
as match-maker for the Lovely Maid.
Lightly,
silently, it rises.

COMMENTARY

Yellow Dame and Lovely Maid are names used by necessity.[27] The
Yellow Dame is the Kun ☷ Soil, that is, the Soil of WU and JI; it is also
called the Intention. The Lovely Maid is the Dui ☱ Metal; Dui is the
youngest daughter, and Metal hides itself within Water. When you
compound the Elixir, you must always count on the Yellow Dame as
the match-maker, as she thoroughly understands the feelings of the
Lovely Maid.

The WU-Soil stores Fire, and Fire forces Metal into movement.
When you begin to kindle the Fire, the Breath (qi) received [by the
Lovely Maid] is still weak. You should turn the gear of the barrier in
the sinciput, and let [the Fire] rise "lightly, silently" from the Caudal
Cavity. Suddenly the force of Fire becomes intense, and the River
Chariot cannot be halted.[28] After [the Lovely Maid] enters the South-
ern Palace, she returns to the original position.[29] [Then] she "marries

---

[27] Lit., "forced names" (qiangming). This expression alludes to the passage in the Daode jing, sec. 25, that says: "I do not know its name, but call it
Dao; if I am forced to give it a name, I say 'great.'"

[28] The term River Chariot (heche) has different meanings in Neidan. Here
it denotes the route formed by the Control and Function vessels (dumai and
renmai, in the back and the front of the body, respectively), through which a
"chariot" transports the ingredients of the Elixir. Along the back of this
route—where one proceeds by ascending and "inverting the course" (ni)—are
found the "three barriers" (sanguan), i.e., the Caudal Funnel (weilü), the
Spinal Handle (jiaji), and the Jade Pillow (yuzhen). Along its front—where
one proceeds by descending and "following the course" (shun)—are found the
three Cinnabar Fields. See Wang Mu, Foundations of Internal Alchemy, pp.
71–74.

[29] The Southern Palace (nangong) here is upper Cinnabar Field. (In traditional Chinese cartography, the south is placed "above" and the north is

the Lord of Metals making him an old gentleman."[30]

Master Cui earnestly warns us and urges us. Thinking that the people of this world would not realize the teachings on the Reverted Elixir, he uses the metaphor of "counting on the Yellow Dame as a match-maker for the Lovely Maid," only because he wishes that everyone comprehends this principle.

This is what the *Wuzhen pian* means when it says:

> The roaming of the Lovely Maid follows set directions:
> her journey in the front takes a shorter time, and the one in the back, a longer time.
> Coming back, she enters the Yellow Dame's dwelling,
> and marries the Lord of Metals making him an old gentleman.[31]

15

Within one day,
during the twelve hours,
wherever the Intention goes,
all can be done.

COMMENTARY

The Intention is the operation of one's Nature (*xing*); it is the True Soil. Within the twelve [double] hours of one day there are the time phases of a whole year. The six [hours] from ZI to CHEN and SI pertain

placed "below.")

[30] These words derive from the *Wuzhen pian* poem quoted at the end of the commentary to the present section.

[31] *Wuzhen pian*, "Jueju," poem 26. The journey "in the back" is longer, because the Lovely Maid ascends from the Caudal Funnel to the upper Cinnabar Field by "inverting the course." The journey "in the front" is shorter, because she descends from the upper to the lower Cinnabar Fields by "following the course."

to Yang; the six [hours] from WU to XU and HAI pertain to Yin.[32] When the initial Yang returns with Fu ䷗, it is the time of ZI within the body; when the initial Yin is born with Gou ䷫, it is the time of WU within the body.[33]

However, Water and Fire are divided between North and South, and Wood and Metal are separated between East and West. How can these four images be joined? You must avail yourself of the Intention in order to move through the ebb and the flow.[34] By doing so, in a short while you can seize the creation and transformation of Heaven and Earth.

In the twelve [double] hours of one day there is no daytime or nighttime; concentrate on this, examine it, and always be watchful.[35] When your thoughts are in motion, the Fire circulates; when you pause them, the Fire nourishes warmly. This is why it says, "wherever the Intention goes, all can be done."

19

The Fire phases are sufficient:
do not harm the Elixir.
Heaven and Earth are numinous,
creation and transformation are mean.

[32] In other words, the first six earthly branches (dizhi), i.e., ZI, CHOU, YIN, MAO, CHEN, and SI, represent the Yang part of the day, while the last six, i.e., WU, WEI, SHEN, YOU, XU, and HAI, represent its Yin part. In premodern China, the day was divided into twelve "hours" (shi), corresponding to two hours in modern reckoning.

[33] Fu ䷗ and Gou ䷫ are the hexagrams that represent the beginning of the growth of the Yang the Yin principles, respectively, during the day and the year. Among the earthly branches, Fu corresponds to ZI, and Gou corresponds to WU. See table 6, p. 262.

[34] "Ebb and flow" (xiaoxi) refers to the two main parts of a time cycle of any length. The first half is marked by the growth of the Yang principle, and the second half by the decrease of the Yang principle and the parallel growth of the Yin principle. In Neidan, the ebb and flow of the time cycles is reproduced by the Fire phases.

[35] In other words, the Fire phases of Neidan are not related to ordinary time.

COMMENTARY

Through the refining, the Yellow Sprout fills the Tripod, the White Snow pervades Heaven, and the Infant achieves an image. Therefore "the Fire phases are sufficient."[36]

When the Fire phases are sufficient, you only have to "bathe" and "nourish warmly." If you do not know how to stop when it is sufficient, and with errant intention you [continue to] circulate the Fire, this would harm the Elixir.[37] After the Elixir has been formed, Heaven and Earth will be inchoately merged, and Breath and Spirit will be numinous of their own. This is what the immortal Masters meant when they said, "in the empty chamber, brightness is born,"[38] and "the Numinous Light will come of its own."[39] Therefore it says, "Heaven and Earth are numinous."

At that time, you must provide protection and love. In harmonizing breathing, the main point lies in making it subtle and fine. In quiescence and concentration, what is inside does not exit, and what is outside does not enter. Forms are forgotten, things are forgotten. The Heart is equal to the Great Emptiness, in the Pure Yang of the One Breath. Therefore "creation and transformation are mean."[40]

---

[36] The Yellow Sprout (*huangya*) and the White Snow (*baixue*) represent the True Yang and the True Yin principles, respectively.

[37] The Neidan concept of "knowing when to stop" (*zhizhi*) or "knowing what is sufficient" (*zhizu*) has antecedents in both Taoism and Confucianism. See *Daode jing*, sec. 44: "Know what is sufficient and you will not be disgraced; know when to stop and you will not be in danger"; *Daode jing*, sec. 46: "There is no calamity greater than not knowing what is sufficient"; and *Daxue* (The Great Learning), sec. 2: "Only if you know when to stop there is stability; and only if there is stability there is quiescence" (see Legge, *The Chinese Classics*, vol. 1, p. 356).

[38] *Zhuangzi*, ch. 4: "Look into that closed room, the empty chamber where brightness is born!" (Watson, *The Complete Works of Chuang Tzu*, p. 58).

[39] *Cantong qi*, 22:2 (translated above, p. 9).

[40] "Creation and transformation" are "mean" (or "miserly, impoverished," *qian*) because multiplicity is brought back to the state of Emptiness and Unity.

21

Practice this word by word,
and it will respond sentence by sentence.[41]

COMMENTARY

These two lines summarize all the previous eighty lines [of the *Mirror for Compounding the Medicine*]. They mean that in the Great Way of the Golden Elixir, "advancing the Fire and withdrawing in response" are the wondrous instructions on seizing creation and transformation.[42] When they are practiced, the whole person becomes like an empty valley that responds to a sound, or like the *yangsui* mirror that collects Water and the *fangzhu* mirror that collects Fire. Spirit pervades and Breath responds: could anything happen faster than this? Therefore it says, "practice this word by word, and it will respond sentence by sentence."

A book on the Elixir says:

> Watching, you do not see it, listening, you do not hear it —
> but if you call it, it responds.

---

[41] *Mimi* can mean either "closely" or "secretly." I translate "word by word" to maintain the parallelism with the next verse.

[42] In this sentence, I read *jindan dadao* 金丹大道 for *dadao jindan* 大道金丹, which would mean, "the Golden Elixir of the Great Way."

4 The Transmission of the Dao from Zhongli Quan to Lü Dongbin

Zhong Lü chuandao ji 鍾呂傳道集

Attributed to Shi Jianwu 施肩吾 (fl. 820–35)

The *Zhong Lü chuandao ji*, or *Anthology of the Transmission of the Dao from Zhongli Quan to Lü Dongbin*, is the main text of the Zhong-Lü school, the first clearly identifiable lineage in the history of Neidan. Both Zhongli Quan and Lü Dongbin are among the most renowned Taoist immortals. In addition to being placed at the origins of the Zhong-Lü lineage, which takes its name from their surnames, they are also among the patriarchs of both the Southern and the Northern lineages (Nanzong and Beizong) of Neidan.

After the foundational works at the basis of the previous three chapters of this anthology, the *Zhong Lü chuandao ji*—which, despite its traditional attribution, probably dates from the tenth century—is the first major doctrinal treatise of Neidan. It is divided into eighteen chapters, concerned with different aspects of Internal Alchemy, such as "Heaven and Earth," "Sun and Moon," "The Five Agents," "Water and Fire" "Lead and Mercury," and "Having Audience at the Origin." In each chapter, Lü Dongbin asks a question, Zhongli Quan replies, then Lü Dongbin summarizes the main points of the reply and asks a new question. Another Zhong-Lü text, the *Lingbao bifa* (Complete Methods of the Numinous Treasure), is said to outline the practices related to the principles described in the *Zhong Lü chuandao ji*.

The chapter translated below is concerned with two of the main emblems of Neidan. It is representative of the perspectives of the Zhong-Lü lineage, which is characterized by extremely detailed correlations between cosmos, human body, and Neidan practice.

8: DRAGON AND TIGER

Lü Dongbin said: The Dragon is in the first place the image of the liver, and the Tiger is the form of the lungs. [However,] the Liquor generated within the Fire of the heart is the True Water; this Water, "dim and obscure," hides the True Dragon. Thus the Dragon is not the liver but comes forth from the Palace of Li ☲.[1] What is the reason?

[Similarly,] the Breath generated within the Water of the kidneys is the True Fire; this Fire, "vague and indistinct," stores the True Tiger. Thus the Tiger is not the lungs but comes forth from the position of Kan ☵.[2] What is the reason?

Zhongli Quan said: The Dragon is something Yang. It flies in Heaven, and when it howls, the clouds rise. When it finds a marsh, it gives benefit to the ten thousand things. Among the images, it is the Green Dragon; among the directions, it is JIA and YI; among the substances, it is Wood; among the seasons, it is spring; among the ways, it is benevolence; among the trigrams, it is Zhen ☳; and among the five viscera of the human body, it is the liver.

The Tiger is something Yin. It runs on the Earth, and when it roars, the wind blows. When it finds a mountain, it subdues the hundred animals. Among the images, it is the White Tiger; among the directions, it is GENG and XIN; among the substances, it is Metal; among the seasons, it is autumn; among the ways, it is righteousness; among the trigrams, it is Dui ☱; and among the five viscera of the human body, it is the lungs.

The liver is Yang but is found in the position of Yin. Therefore the Breath of the kidneys is conveyed to the Breath of the liver.[3] As the Breath follows the mother-child relationship, Water generates Wood. When the Breath of the kidneys is plentiful, it generates the Breath of the liver. After this, the excess of Yin in the kidneys is extinguished, and what ascends is the Pure Yang Breath.[4]

---

[1] Li ☲ is the trigram that represents Fire and the heart.

[2] Kan ☵ is the trigram that represents Water and the kidneys.

[3] The kidneys, like the liver, are also found in the "position of Yin."

[4] The "Lun wuxing" (On the Five Agents) chapter of the *Zhong Lü chuandao ji* says: "What generates is called the mother, and what is generated

The lungs are Yin but are found in the position of Yang. Therefore the Liquor of the heart is conveyed to the Liquor of the lungs.[5] As the Liquor follows the husband-wife relationship, Fire conquers Metal. When the Liquor of the heart reaches [the lungs], it generates the Liquor of the lungs. After this, the excess of Yang in the heart is extinguished, and what descends is the Pure Yin Liquor.[6]

As the liver pertains to Yang, it extinguishes the excess of Yin in the kidneys. Therefore we know that when the Breath [of the kidneys] goes through the liver, it becomes Pure Yang. This Pure Yang Breath stores the Water of True Unity; "vague and indistinct," it is formless. It is called Yang Dragon.

As the lungs pertain to Yin, they extinguish the excess of Yang in the heart. Therefore we know that when the Liquor [of the heart] reaches the lungs, it becomes Pure Yin. This Pure Yin Liquor carries the Breath of Correct Yang; "dim and obscure," it is invisible. It is called Yin Tiger.

The Breath ascends and Liquor descends, but normally they cannot conjoin. Yet, when the Water of True Unity within the Breath [of the kidneys] sees the Liquor [of the heart], they join with one another; and when the Breath of Correct Yang within the Liquor [of the heart] sees the Breath [of the kidneys], they gather together. If while they are being conveyed [to the liver and the lungs, respectively] you control them by means of your practice, you cause the Breath of the kidneys not to be lost, so that you gather the Water of True Unity; and you cause the Liquor of the heart not to be wasted, so that you collect the Breath of Correct Yang. Mother and child come across each other and long for one another.

As the Medicine, day after day, becomes as large as a grain of millet, in one hundred days, providing that you do not make errors, its

---

is called the son." In the "generation" sequence of the five agents, Water (associated with the kidneys) generates Wood (associated with the liver); therefore the Breath of the kidneys generates the Breath of the lungs.

[5] The heart, like the lungs, is also found in the "position of Yang."

[6] The "Wuxing" chapter says: "What conquers is called the husband, and what is conquered is called the wife." In the "conquest" sequence of the five agents, Fire (associated with the heart) conquers Metal (associated with the lungs); therefore the Liquor of the heart generates the Liquor of the lungs.

strength becomes whole; in two hundred days, the Womb of Saint-hood is solid; and in three hundred days, the Embryo-Immortal is complete. "In shape, it is similar to a pellet, in color, it is the same as a red orange."[7] This is called the Elixir (*danyao*). Constantly guard it in your lower Cinnabar Field. You will preserve your [bodily] form and dwell in the world, and you will enjoy a life as long as a great kalpa. This is what we call being a divine immortal on earth.

Lü Dongbin said: The Water of the kidneys generates the [Pure Yang] Breath, and within this Breath there is the Water of True Unity. This is called Yin Tiger; when the Tiger sees the Liquor, they unite with one another. The Fire of the heart generates the [Pure Yin] Liquor, and within this Liquor there is the Breath of Correct Yang. This is called Yang Dragon; when the Dragon sees the Breath, they join with one another. "Directions come together according to their kinds, things are divided according to their classes."[8] The principle is entirely natural.

While the [Pure Yang] Breath is generated, the Liquor [of the heart] descends. Does the Water of True Unity within this Breath continue to follow that Liquor, so that it is conveyed below among the five viscera? While the [True Yin] Liquor is generated, the Breath [of the kidneys] ascends. Does the Breath of Correct Yang within this Liquor continue to follow that Breath, so that is comes forth above through the trachea?[9]

If the True Water follows the Liquor and circulates below, the Tiger cannot conjoin with the Dragon. If the True Yang follows the Breath and ascends above, the Dragon cannot conjoin with the Tiger. If Dragon

[7] This sentence derives from the *Baopu zi neipian* (Inner Chapters of the Master Who Embraces Spontaneous Nature), ch. 6.

[8] *Book of Changes* (*Yijing*), "Appended Sayings" ("Xici"), sec. A.I; see Wilhelm, *The I-ching or Book of Changes*, p. 280. The word *fang* 方 in this sentence has been translated in different ways (Wilhelm has "events"), but in the present context is seems to be understood in the sense of "directions." As said above, liver (east) and kidneys (north) belong together, and so do lungs (west) and heart (south).

[9] With these questions, Lü Dongbin asks whether the True Yin and the True Yang continue to follow the ordinary cycles and courses within the body after they are generated.

and Tiger do not conjoin, how can one obtain the Yellow Sprout? And without the Yellow Sprout, how can one obtain the Great Medicine?

Zhongli Quan said: After the Breath of the kidneys has been generated, it is like the Sun emerging from the ocean. Even the fog cannot conceal its radiance. The Liquor that descends is like a thin bamboo window shade: how could it overcome the Breath? When the Breath is strong, the Water of True Unity is plentiful of its own.

After the Liquor of the heart has been generated, it is like the cold days taking a creature's life. Even the warmth of breath cannot moderate that coldness. The Breath that ascends is like an emerald curtain: how could it overcome the Liquor? When the Liquor is plentiful, the Breath of Correct Yang may be strong or weak: this cannot be determined in advance.

Lü Dongbin said: The birth of the Breath and the birth of the Liquor have their own times. At the time of the birth of the Breath, if the Breath is plentiful then the Water of True Unity is also plentiful. At the time of the birth of the Liquor, if the Liquor is plentiful then the Breath of Correct Yang is also plentiful. I still do not know what is the meaning of "plentiful" and "insufficient."

Zhongli Quan said: The Breath of the kidneys is easy to dissipate: what is difficult to obtain is the True Tiger. The Liquor of the heart is difficult to gather: what is easy to lose is the True Dragon. The ten thousand scrolls of books on the Elixir do not discuss anything but Yin and Yang; and concerning these two subjects, the essential is always the Dragon and the Tiger.

Among ten thousand persons who revere the Dao, those who understand them are no more than one or two. Some may hear many things and read plenty of books; they may know the principles of the Dragon and the Tiger, but they do not understand the time of their conjunction or do not know the method of the collection. Therefore the knowledgeable people of ancient and modern times practice until old age, but do not go beyond the degree of the "small achievement." From generation to generation, they do not hear about transcending worldliness.[10] Indeed, they cannot conjoin the Dragon and the Tiger, collect the Yellow Sprout, and achieve the Elixir.

---

[10] "Transcending Worldliness and Separating from the Form" (*chaotuo fenxing*) is the final and highest stage of the Neidan practice in the *Lingbao bifa* (Complete Methods of the Numinous Treasure), the main text based on the principles of the *Zhong Lü chuandao ji*. See Baldrian-Hussein, *Procédés Secrets du Joyau Magique*, 185–93 and 284–87.

5   Awakening to Reality

Wuzhen pian 悟真篇

Zhang Boduan 張伯端 (987?–1082)

The *Wuzhen pian*, or *Awakening to Reality*, describes in a poetical form, and in a typically cryptic and allusive language, several facets of Neidan. Its author, Zhang Boduan, was placed in the early thirteenth century at the origins of the Southern Lineage (Nanzong) of Neidan. Since that time, it has been the main textual source of that lineage. The *Wuzhen pian*, however, has played a vast and visible influence on the whole history of Internal Alchemy.

The text is divided into three main parts, all of which consist of poems written in different meters. The first part contains sixteen poems in "regulated verses" (eight-line heptasyllabic poems, known as *lüshi*). The second part contains sixty-four poems in "cut-off lines" (four-line heptasyllabic poems, *jueju*). The third part contains eighteen poems, written in different meters and divided into three sets: one pentasyllabic poem, twelve "lyrics" (*ci*) of irregular length, and five more poems in "cut-off lines." Certain editions also include a final series of poems that use Buddhist terminology, probably added after the completion of the main text. Many Nanzong adepts have read in the *Wuzhen pian* allusions to the different stages of the Neidan practice.

The selections translated in this chapter consist of eight poems in "regulated verses" and eighteen poems in "cut-off lines." The translations of the poems in "regulated verses" are based on those in my *Awakening to Reality* (Golden Elixir Press, 2009), which contains a general introduction to the *Wuzhen pian*, line-by-line annotated translations, and selections from the commentary by Liu Yiming (1734–1821). The poems in "cut-off lines" have been translated for the present anthology.

Poems are numbered as in the original Chinese text. Several other poems or verses of the *Wuzhen pian* are translated in different chapters of the present book. Another work attributed to Zhang Boduan (the *Jindan sibai zi*, or *Four Hundred Words on the Golden Elixir*) is translated in Chapter 6.

POEMS IN "REGULATED VERSES"

3

If you study immortality, you should study celestial
  immortality:
only the Golden Elixir is the highest principle.
When the two things meet, emotions and nature
  join one another;
where the five agents are whole, Dragon and Tiger
  coil.

Rely in the first place on WU and JI that act as go-
  betweens,
then let husband and wife join together and rejoice.
Just wait until your work is achieved to have
  audience at the Northern Portal,
and in the radiance of a ninefold mist you will ride
  on a soaring phoenix.

This poem uses traditional images to describe the main features and
benefits of the Golden Elixir. There are several grades of transcendence,
but for the very fact of being graded, they pertain to the realm of relativ-
ity in which we live. Only "celestial immortality," says Zhang Boduan,
grants complete transcendence, the removal of distinctions between the
precelestial and postcelestial domains.

Inner nature (*xing*) is essentially pure and unaffected by phenomena
or events of any kind. Emotions (*qing*, a word also meaning feelings,
sentiments, passions) tend to disjoin from one's inner nature and become
uncontrolled. Only when True Yin and True Yang (the "two things")
merge can one's inner nature and emotions be in agreement with one
another.

"The five agents are whole" refers to the inversion from multiplicity to
Unity, or from the postcelestial (*houtian*) to the precelestial (*xiantian*).
This reversal is performed first by reducing the five agents to three, and
then to one (see Poem 14 below).

The conjunction of Yin and Yang occurs by means of WU and JI.
These are the two celestial stems related to the agent Soil (see table 5, p.
261). Soil, which is placed at the center, is an emblem of Unity giving

birth to multiplicity. To generate the "ten thousand things," the One first divides itself into the Two, or Yin and Yang. The stems WU and JI respectively represent the Yang and the Yin halves of Soil, or the One. In the human being, Soil is associated with the Intention (*yi*), the faculty of focusing the mind on a goal or an object. In Neidan, the True Intention (*zhenyi*) brings about the union of Yin and Yang. This is possible because intention, just like Soil, embraces both Yin and Yang, or WU and JI. For this reason, WU and JI are often said in Neidan texts to be the "go-betweens" (*meiping*) that enable the conjunction of Yin and Yang.

Fulfilling the Way of the Golden Elixir is analogous to ascending to Heaven as an immortal and having audience with the highest deities.

4

> This is the method of wondrous Reality within Reality,
>   where I depend on myself, alone and different from
>   all others.[1]
> I know for myself how to invert, starting from Li ☲
>   and Kan ☵:
> who else can comprehend the floating and the
>   sinking, and determine the host and the guest?
>
> If in the Golden Tripod you want to detain the
>   Mercury in the Vermilion,
> first from the Jade Pond send down the Silver in the
>   Water.
> The cycling of fire in the spiritual work before the
>   light of dawn
> will cause the whole wheel of the Moon to appear in
>   the Deep Pool.

The subject of this poem is the "inversion" that produces the Golden Elixir. While True Yin and True Yang are separate from one another in the postcelestial world, the alchemical process allows them to conjoin.

Kan ☵ (Water) is postcelestial Yin containing True Yang, and Li ☲

---

[1] This line derives in part from the *Daode jing* (Book of the Way and Its Virtue), sec. 20: "I am alone and different from all others, and value being fed by the mother." The "mother" is the Dao as the origin of the world.

(Fire) is postcelestial Yang containing True Yin. In the postcelestial, conditioned state, Kan is placed below and Li is placed above (see table 3, p. 259). Li and Kan harbor the True Yin and True Yang essences of the precelestial state. Just like fire and water do in nature, Li and Kan respectively move upward and downward, and in doing so, they also carry the true principles that they hold. True Yin and True Yang, therefore, are constantly separated from one another. Only if the positions of Kan and Li are inverted (i.e., when Kan becomes the "host" and Li the "guest") can True Yin and True Yang meet and conjoin.

The next lines have been explained in different ways by commentators and later authors. I will refer here only to the explication given by Liu Yiming (1734–1821) in his commentary to these verses. The Golden Tripod is the human mind and its conscious knowledge. It is the Yang (Vermilion) containing True Yin (Mercury); this True Yin is the "innate capacity" (*liangneng*) of the human being in the precelestial state, represented by "the Mercury within the Vermilion". Just like mercury "flies away" when it is submitted to the action of fire, so does the human mind lose its "innate capacity" and produce illusions when it comes in touch with the postcelestial cognitive spirit. The Jade Pond, vice versa, is the "mind of the Dao" and its true knowledge. It is the Yin (Water) containing True Yang (Silver); this True Yang is the "innate knowledge" (*liangzhi*) in the precelestial state, represented by "the Silver within the Water". Because of the shift to the postcelestial state, "the real is covered by the artificial," and True Yang is hidden within Yin. The "innate knowledge" of the "mind of the Dao" is lost and, as Liu Yiming says, "one sinks into the ocean of desires".

Although the conscious knowledge of the human mind "moves easily," it can be controlled by the true knowledge of the mind of the Dao. In order to "detain" it, one should first invert the respective positions of the human mind and the "mind of the Dao," and "send down the true knowledge of the mind of the Dao" in order to reach the conscious knowledge of the human mind. In this way, "the conscious knowledge of the human mind spontaneously coalesces and does not disperse itself." Liu Yiming concludes: "By employing the mind of the Dao to control the human mind, one complies with the mind of the Dao by means of the human mind; one commands conscious knowledge by true knowledge; and one nourishes true knowledge by conscious knowledge."

In the final two verses, the "cycling of fire" refers to the Fire phases (*huohou*). One complete cycle of heating symbolically lasts one day and one night, as it includes a Yang phase followed by a Yin phase. When the heating is completed, the Elixir takes form in the lower Cinnabar Field, here called Deep Pool (*shentan*). Zhang Boduan compares the Elixir to the "whole wheel of the Moon." This is an allusion to the fact that the Elixir is equivalent to Pure Yang (*chunyang*), a common name in Taoism for the state prior to the division of the One into Yin and Yang. It might at first seem odd that this state is described with the image of the full Moon. When the Moon is full, however, it is thoroughly exposed to the rays of the Sun. The full Moon, therefore, is an image of the elimination of the impurities of the conditioned state, associated with the Yin principle, and of the return to Pure Yang.

6

> All people on their own have the Medicine of long
>   life;
> it is only for insanity and delusion that they cast it
>   away to no avail.
> When the Sweet Dew descends, Heaven and Earth
>   join one another;
> where the Yellow Sprout grows, Kan ☵ and Li ☲
>   conjoin.
>
> A frog in a well would say that there are no dragon
>   lairs,
> and how could a quail on a fence know that
>   phoenix nests exist?
> When the Elixir ripens, spontaneously Gold fills the
>   room:
> what is the point of seeking herbs and learning how
>   to roast the reeds?

The Golden Elixir is fundamentally possessed by every human being; it is an image of one's innermost true nature. In this poem, the Elixir is described as the conjunction of the Sweet Dew and the Yellow Sprout.

The term Sweet Dew (*ganlu*) derives from a passage of the *Daode jing* (Book of the Way and Its Virtue), sec. 32: when the world followed the Dao, "Heaven and Earth were joined to one another, causing sweet dew to descend." Just like dew comes down from the Yang heaven and partakes of the Yin nature of water, so does the Sweet Dew refers to the True Yin component of the Elixir, or True Mercury.

Yellow Sprout (*huangya*) is a common alchemical term that connotes True Lead (True Yang). The yellow color refers to the association of the Elixir with Soil, the agent that resides at the center and is made of Yin and Yang, or Kan ☵ and Li ☲, joined together. A sprout emerges from the Yin earth and partakes of the nature of the Yang wood: the term Yellow Sprout refers to the True Yang aspect of the Elixir, or True Lead.

·

7

> You should know that the source of the stream, the
>   place where the Medicine is born,
> is just at the southwest—that is its native village.
> When Lead meets the birth of GUI, quickly you
>   should collect it:
> if Metal goes past the full moon, it is not fit to be
>   savored.
>
> Send it back to the earthenware crucible, seal it
>   tightly,
> then add the Flowing Pearl, so that they are match
>   for one another.
> For the Medicine to weigh one pound the Two
>   Eights are needed;
> regulate the Fire phases relying on Yin and Yang.

This poem concerns an essential aspect of Neidan: the collection of True Yang, which is the initial ingredient of the Elixir. As soon as one comes upon True Yang, one should store it safely and let it join with one's True Yin, the fundamentally pure consciousness underlying the cognitive mind.

The symbolism of the first half of this poem is complex. The Medicine is True Yang. In the postcelestial domain (the world in which we live), True Yang is contained within Yin and is represented by the unbroken line within Kan ☵, the trigram that replaces Kun ☷ (Pure Yin) in the postcelestial state. Since Kun, in the postcelestial domain, is positioned at the southwest (see table 3, p. 259) Zhang Boduan says that "the place where the Medicine is born is just at the southwest," and calls this the "native village" of True Yang.

Kan ☵ is Water, but contains Metal—the True Yang—as its inner solid line. Water is represented by two celestial stems, REN and GUI. REN stands for the precelestial aspect of Water, and GUI stands for its postcelestial aspect. Therefore the True Yang should be collected from Water during its REN stage, before it "meets the birth of GUI."

This True Yang should be sent to the "earthenware crucible" (*tufu*), the lower Cinnabar Field (*dantian*), where it joins with the Flowing Pearl (*liuzhu*), or True Mercury. Their conjunction generates the Elixir. In the traditional Chinese weight system, one pound (*jin*) corresponds to sixteen ounces (*liang*). The symbolic "pound" of Elixir, therefore, is made of eight ounces of Lead and eight ounces of Mercury.

9

The Yin essence within Yang is not a firm substance:
if you cultivate only this thing you will become ever
more weak.
Toiling your body by pressing and pulling is
certainly not the Way,
ingesting breath and swallowing mist is entirely
foolish.

The whole world recklessly tries to subdue Lead and
Mercury —
when will they be able to see Dragon and Tiger
submitted?
I exhort you to probe and grasp the place where one
comes to life:
return to the fundament, revert to the origin, and
you are a Medicine King.

This poem refers to several practices that Zhang Boduan deems to be erroneous: cultivating "the Yin essence within Yang" (instead of the Yang essence within Yin), performing *daoyin* and massage, and carrying out breathing exercises.

The first line refers to the different forms of the Yin essence in the human body, which include saliva, semen, and blood. In the third line, "pressing and pulling" (*anyin*) is an abbreviation for "pressing and rubbing" and "guiding and pulling" (*anmo daoyin*). "Pressing and rubbing" means performing massage. *Daoyin* is a practice based on postures that favor the circulation of breaths and essences found within the body. It performs in Taoism the same function that *hatha yoga* performs in Hinduism. In the fourth line, "ingesting breath" and "swallowing mist" refer to breathing practices.

In the view of the *Wuzhen pian*, these practices do not make it possible for True Yin and True Yang to join one another. Only this, according to Zhang Boduan, makes it possible to return to the "fundament" and the "origin," the ultimate source of existence.

12

> In plants and trees, Yin and Yang are equal to one
>   another;
> let either be lacking, and they do not bloom.
> First the green leaves open, for Yang is the first to sing,
> then a red flower blossoms, as Yin follows later.
>
> This is the constant Dao that everyone uses daily;
> but returning to the True Origin—does anyone
>   know about this?
> I announce to all of you who study the Dao:
> if you do not comprehend Yin and Yang, do not
>   fiddle around.

In nature, the Yang principle precedes the Yin principle, but both of them are necessary: Yang gives the initial impulse to life, Yin brings it to achievement. The green color is an emblem of the initial stage of the True Yang principle. The red color is the symbolic color of the Elixir, which "blossoms" when the True Yin principle joins the True Yang principle.

The same priority of Yang over Yin is seen in the treatment of the ingredients of the Golden Elixir, when True Lead is first refined from "black lead" and is then joined to True Yin refined from cinnabar; and in the Fire phases (*huohou*), where the Yang phase of increasing heat is followed by the Yin phase of decreasing heat. At the same time, however, the alchemical process is based on the "inversion" of the natural processes, which makes it possible to revert to the original state, here called the True Origin. Both movements—the forward and the backward ones—are needed in order to fulfill the alchemical path.

14

Three, Five, One—all is in these three words;
but truly rare are those who understand them in
    past and present times.
East is 3, South is 2, together they make 5;
North is 1, West is 4, they are the same.

Wu and ji dwell on their own, their birth number is 5;
when the three families see one another, the Infant
    coalesces.
The Infant is the One holding True Breath;
in ten months the embryo is complete—this is the
    foundation for entering sainthood.

The verses of this poem are often quoted in later Neidan texts. The poem describes the compounding of the Internal Elixir in terms of the five agents; it provides an example of the inversion that was the subject of the previous poem. The inversion process here consists in joining Wood and Fire, on the one hand, and Metal and Water, on the other hand. When this is done, there are two ingredients, namely True Yin and True Yang. Through the mediation of Soil, the central agent that partakes of the nature of both, Yin and Yang merge and generate the Elixir.

The first half of the poem is based on the "generation numbers" (*shengshu*, lit. "birth numbers," or precelestial numbers) associated with the five agents (see tables 1 and 2, pp. 257 and 258). The four external agents are reduced to two by reintegrating those that represent the postcelestial state into those that represent the precelestial state: Wood (East, 3) is reintegrated into Fire (South, 2); Metal (West, 4) is reintegrated into Water (North, 1). Each dyad has a numeric value of 5.

> Wood + Fire   3+2 = 5   Inner Nature + Original Spirit
>
> Metal + Water   4+1 = 5   Emotions + Original Essence

In this way, inner nature returns to partake of Original Spirit, and emotions are turned into qualities manifested in the world of form.

In the second half of the poem, wu and ji are the two celestial stems associated with Soil, the central agent (see table 5, p. 261, and Poem 3 above). Soil represents the Intention (*yi*), the driving force of the alchemical process, and 5 is its "birth number" (i.e., its "generative number," or precelestial emblematic number).

There are therefore three entities, which Zhang Boduan and many Neidan masters after him call "the three families" (*sanjia*): True Yin, True Yang, and the Intention. Each has a numeric value of 5 (the "three fives") and is in a balanced relation to the others. Through the mediation the Intention (Soil), True Yin and True Yang conjoin. The state of Unity is represented by the Infant, an image of the Elixir and of the One Breath (*yiqi*) of the Dao, who is born after ten symbolic months of gestation (in China, gestation is traditionally deemed to last ten months).

15

> If you do not comprehend that True Lead is the
>   proper ancestor,
> the ten thousand practices will all be vain
>   exercises:
> leaving your wife and staying in idle solitude will
>   separate Yin and Yang,
> and cutting off the grains will only cause your
>   stomach to be empty.
>
> Herbs and trees and gold and silver are all dregs,
> clouds and mist and Sun and Moon partake of
>   haziness;
> and as for exhaling and inhaling, or visualizing and
>   meditating,
> these pursuits are not the same as the Golden Elixir.

As he does in other poems, Zhang Boduan here criticizes several approaches to self-cultivation, such as celibacy, abstention from cereals, ingestion of herbal and alchemical drugs, breathing techniques, and visualization of the inner deities.

The third verse refers to maintaining celibacy. In the fourth verse, "cutting off the grains" (*jueli*) is equivalent to "abstaining from cereals" (*bigu*), the common name of one of the practices for Nourishing Life (*yangsheng*). Cereals were deemed to leave dregs in the intestines that feed the "three corpses" (*sanshi*) and the "nine worms" (*jiuchong*), the agents of death residing within the human body. Some practitioners, therefore, replaced cereals with other substances, including herbs, minerals, and most importantly breath (*qi*).

The fifth verse alludes to ingesting herbal medicines or alchemical elixirs. The sixth verse criticizes the methods for absorbing external breath (*qi*) and those for ingesting the essences (*jing*) of the Sun and the Moon.

In the seventh verse, "exhaling and inhaling" refers to breathing practices, and "visualizing and meditating" (*cunxiang*) refers to methods based on the visualization of the inner gods.

All these methods pertain to what Neidan texts often call the "side gates" (*pangmen*), i.e., inadequate techniques of realization. In the perspective of the *Wuzhen pian*, only the knowledge of True Lead, which gives birth to the Elixir and is ultimately equivalent to it, is effective to achieve true realization.

POEMS IN "CUT-OFF LINES"

I

First take Qian ☰ and Kun ☷ as the tripod and the
furnace,
then catch the crow and the hare and boil the
Medicine.
Once you have chased the two things and they have
returned to the Yellow Path,
how could the Golden Elixir not be born?

The crow and the hare represent True Yin and True Yang, respectively, as the two ingredients of the Elixir. The term Yellow Path (*huangdao*) usually denotes the apparent circuit of the Sun around the Earth. In Neidan, it refers instead to the circular path along which the Essence (*jing*) is circulated within the practitioner's body in a sense contrary to its ordinary flow, in order to generate the first seed of the Elixir.

5

Swallowing saliva and ingesting breath are human
actions;
only when you have the Medicine can you form and
transform.

If in the tripod there is no True Seed,
this is like using water and fire to boil an empty pot.

This is one of several poems in the *Wuzhen pian* that criticize practices different from Neidan. "Swallowing saliva" (*yanjin*) and "ingesting breath" (*naqi*) allude to early Taoist meditation and visualization practices. "Form and transform" translates *huasheng*, lit., "generate by transformation."

10

Empty the heart, fill the belly: the meanings are
both profound.
It is just in order to empty the heart that you should
know the heart.
Nothing is better than first filling the belly by
refining Lead;
then, by guarding and collecting, you load the hall
with Gold.

The Southern Lineage model of Neidan practice initially gives priority to the cultivation of Existence (*ming*), but assigns the final and highest part of its three-stage process to the cultivation of Nature (*xing*).[2] The present poem addresses this subject by drawing two expressions from sec. 3 of the *Daode jing*: "Thus the saint in his government empties the people's minds and fills their bellies." According to commentators and later Neidan authors, "emptying the heart" (or "the mind," *xuxin*) and "filling the belly" (*shifu*) refer to cultivating Nature and Existence, respectively: the heart and the abdomen are the symbolic locations of Nature and Existence in the human being. The poem as a whole maintains that both Nature and Existence should be cultivated, but the third line shows that, according to the Southern Lineage, one should begin by cultivating Existence.

---

[2] See Wang Mu, *Foundations of Internal Alchemy*, 4–5 and 109–17.

12

The Dao from Empty Non-Being generates the One
    Breath,
then from the One Breath gives birth to Yin and
    Yang;
Yin and Yang join again and form the three bodies,
the three bodies repeatedly generate, and the ten
    thousand things flourish.

This poem summarizes the main principles of the unfolding of the Dao
into the cosmos. It is clearly based on the account found in sec. 42 of the
Daode jing: "The Dao generates the One, the One generates the Two, the
Two generate the Three, the Three generate the ten thousand things. The
ten thousand things sustain the Yin and embrace the Yang, blending their
breaths to make them harmonious." The "three bodies" are, in the
macrocosm, Heaven, Earth, and Man; and in the microcosm, Essence
(*jing*), Breath (*qi*), and Spirit (*shen*).

14

If Li ☲ and Kan ☵ do not return to WU and JI,
    they may hold the four images but will not make the
    Elixir.
It is only because that and this harbor the True Soil
    that they cause the reversion of the Golden Elixir.

Li ☲ is Fire and contains Wood (True Yin), Kan ☵ is Water and contains
Metal (True Yang). These two trigrams, therefore, represent all four
"external" agents: Wood, Fire, Metal, and Water. Their conjunction in
the Elixir, however, can occur because both trigrams hold the Yin and
Yang aspects (JI and WU, respectively) of the central agent, Soil. "That"
and "this" are technical terms in Neidan. "This" (*ci*) is one's own True
Yin (the inner line of Li ☲). "That" (or "the other," *bi*) is the True Yang
(the inner line of Kan ☵), which in the postcelestial state is not found in
oneself. The purpose of Neidan is often defined as recovering the True
Yang that is lost in the transition from the precelestial to the postcelestial
state (*xiantian* to *houtian*).

16

Gather the solid [line] from the center in the
     position of Kan ☵,
and transmute by projection the innermost Yin in
     the palace of Li ☲.
Thus it alters itself and forms the strong body of
     Qian ☰:
withdrawing and concealing or leaping into flight
     depends entirely on the mind.

This poem summarizes the main points of the representation of the Neidan process by the trigrams of the *Book of Changes*. In that representation, the Neidan process initially consists in recovering the True Yang found within the Yin (i.e., the inner solid line of Kan ☵, found within two broken lines). The recovered True Yang is then used to transmute the Yin of the postcelestial world (the inner broken line of Li ☲, found within two solid lines). In this way, Li ☲ turns into Qian ☰, an image of original, precelestial Unity.

17

The Mercury of the Dragon-Zhen ☳ comes forth
     from the village of Li ☲,
the Lead of the Tiger-Dui ☱ is born from the land
     of Kan ☵.
The two things entirely depend on the child giving
     birth to its mother;
the five agents should all enter the center.

In the postcelestial state, the trigram Zhen is placed in the East, the direction of the Green Dragon, and the trigram Dui is placed in the West, the direction of the White Tiger (see table 3, p. 259). Li is the trigram associated with the South, or Fire, and Kan is the trigram associated with the North, or Water. In the ordinary sequence of the five agents, Wood generates Fire, and Metal generates Water. In the inverted sequence at the basis of Neidan, Fire (Yang, Li ☲) produces Wood (True Yin, Mercury), and Water (Yin, Kan ☵) produces Metal

(True Yang, Lead). Therefore "the child (Fire, Water) gives birth to its mother (Wood, Metal)." When the pairs Fire-Wood and Metal-Water are conjoined in the alchemical process, the five agents return to their original state of Unity in the center. — For the phrase "the child gives birth to its mother" see sec. 23 of the *Cantong qi*, translated above, p. 11.

27

> Even if you discern the Vermilion Sand and the
>   Black Lead,
> it will be useless if you do not know the Fire phases.
> On the whole, it all depends on the force of practice:
> with an error as fine as a hair, you will not make the
>   Elixir.

Vermilion Sand (*zhusha*) is the literal translation of one of the common names of cinnabar, deemed to be a Yang substance in both Chinese pharmacology and in Waidan (External Alchemy). In Neidan, this term is often understood as meaning Sand in the Vermilion; in other words, it refers to the Yang ("vermilion") containing True Yin ("sand"). Analogously, Black Lead (*heiqian*) is one of the names of native lead, which in both Waidan and Neidan is the material or emblematic Yin substance that contains True Yang. This poems reminds that although one may know these basic principles, their true understanding requires the practice of the Fire phases, which belongs to the first stage of the Neidan process and is therefore one of its most crucial aspects.

28

> The *Seal* and the treatises, the scriptures and the
>   songs expound the utmost Reality
> but do not commit the Fire phases to writing.
> If you want to know the oral instructions and
>   comprehend their mysterious points,
> you must discuss them in detail with a divine
>   immortal.

As the Fire phases are the most secret aspect of the alchemical practice, they are not revealed in writing. "The *Seal*" is the *Cantong qi*, or *Seal of the Unity of the Three*.

37

The images of the hexagrams are established on the
    basis of their meanings:
understand the images and forget the words—the
    idea is clear of itself.
The whole world delusively clings to the images:
people practice the "breaths of the hexagrams" and
    hope to rise in flight.

The term "breaths of the hexagrams" (*guaqi*) has several meanings in Chinese cosmology. Here it refers to the properties of the twelve hexagrams that represent the twelve-stage cycle of the Fire phases (see table 4, p. 260). Those hexagrams provide therefore a model for the Neidan practice. This poem points out that one should not follow that model literally, in particular with regard to the associations of the hexagrams with ordinary time, i.e., the twelve months of the year and the twelve "double hours" of the day.

39

If you want to obtain the Spirit of the Valley and
    live forever,
you must rely on the Mysterious-Female to establish
    the foundation.
Once the True Essence has returned to the Golden
    Chamber,
the Luminous Pearl will never depart.

The terms Spirit of the Valley (*gushen*) and Mysterious-Female (*xuanpin*) derive from the *Daode jing*, sec. 6 (see below, Chapter 7). "Golden Chamber" (*jinshi*) here is an image of the Center. Several editions of the *Wuzhen pian* have "the pearl of Luminous Radiance" for "the Luminous Pearl."

40

Few in the world know the Gate of the Mysterious-
    Female:
stop fiddling around with your mouth and your nose.
You may inhale and exhale for one thousand years,
but how can you find the golden crow and seize the
    baby hare?

This poem criticizes the view that the Gate of the Mysterious-Female (*xuanpin zhi men*) corresponds to the mouth and the nose. Those who hold that view devote themselves to breathing practices, but by doing so they will not be able to obtain the "crow" and the "hare," two metaphors for the ingredients of the Elixir (see "Poems in Cut-Off Lines," no, 1 above).

42

It begins with action, and hardly can one see a
    thing,
when it comes to non-doing, all begin to understand.
But if you only see non-doing as the essential
    marvel,
how can you understand that action is the
    foundation?

The Neidan practice of the Southern Lineage ends with "non-doing" (*wuwei*), needed to cultivate one's Nature (*xing*). It begins, however, with "action" (*youzuo*), which is the foundation for cultivating one's Existence (*ming*).

51

The ten thousand things, abounding and
    overflowing, revert to the root;
reverting to the root and returning to the mandate,
    they are constantly preserved.

Knowing the constant and returning to the
foundation are difficult to understand,
foolishly bringing about misfortune is something
heard of again and again.

This poem is based on *Daode jing*, sec. 16: "Things are abounding and
overflowing, but each of them reverts to its root. Reverting to the root is
called quiescence, and this means returning to the mandate (*ming*);
returning to the mandate is called constancy; knowing constancy is called
brightness. By not knowing constancy, one foolishly brings about misfortune." The "mandate" (*ming*) is the fundamental "destiny" or function
for which a person or an object is generated, and which they are supposed
to fulfill in their existence.

57

The Three Powers are the thieves of one another
and "eat at the right time":
this is the mechanism of the Dao and its Virtue for
divine immortality.
When "the ten thousand transformations are at
rest" and all thoughts come to an end,
"the hundred bones are regulated" and each of them
manifests non-doing.

This poem draws several phrases and expressions from the *Yinfu jing* (Book
of the Hidden Agreement), and in particular from sections 12 (translated
above, p. 32) and 13 (p. 33). There are several variants for the second verse,
e.g., "The divine immortals of the Dao and its Virtue conceal this mechanism." In the last verse, "hundred bones" denotes the whole person.

58

The precious words of *The Hidden Agreement* are
just over three hundred,
and the sacred text of *The Way and Its Virtue* is
complete with five thousand.

Countless immortals of superior rank in the present
  and the past
have understood the true principles trough them.

The Hidden Agreement is the *Yinfu jing* (translated in Chapter 2 of the present book). *The Way and Its Virtue* is the *Daode jing*.

59

Virtuous gentlemen, sharp and discerning more
  than a Yan Hui and a Min Qian,
if you do not encounter a true master, do not
  struggle to make conjectures.
If you only follow the books on the Elixir without
  oral instructions,
where could you coagulate the Numinous Embryo?

The sense of this poem is clear. Significantly, it is placed immediately after other poems (nos. 57 and 58) that pay tribute to the *Daode jing* and the *Yinfu jing*, two of the main texts whose doctrines have provided the foundations of Neidan. Yan Hui and Min Qian were two of Confucius' disciples.

61

If you have not yet refined the Reverted Elixir, then
  quickly refine it;
having refined it, you should know to stop when it is
  enough.
If you still hold it and fill your mind with it, instead
  of halting it,
you will not avoid danger, and before long you will
  suffer humiliation.

The third verse alludes to *Daode jing*, sec. 9: "You hold something to fill it up, but this is not as good as halting."

6 Four Hundred Words on the Golden Elixir

Jindan sibai zi 金丹四百字

Attributed to Zhang Boduan 張伯端 (987?–1082)

Commentary by Peng Haogu 彭好古 (fl. 1586–99)

The *Jindan sibai zi*, or *Four Hundred Words on the Golden Elixir*, is attributed to Zhang Boduan (the author of the *Wuzhen pian*, partly translated in Chapter 5 above). Although this attribution does not seem to be trustworthy, the association with the first master of the Southern lineage (Nanzong) is one of the reasons of the popularity enjoyed by this work within the Neidan tradition.

The text, here entirely translated with a commentary, is made of twenty poems, each containing four verses of five characters. Several verses or parts of them are repeatedly quoted in later Neidan works, often with no need of a precise reference to their source given its renown. To give two examples, these include the verse "This Opening is not a common opening" (in poem 7) and the whole poem 13, concerned with the difference between ordinary time and the inner time of Neidan.

The commentary translated here is by Peng Haogu (fl. 1586–99, from Hubei). Few details about him and his life are available. He is also known for a commentary to the *Cantong qi* (The Seal of the Unity of the Three) and for several other works on Neidan, which he published in 1599 in a collection entitled *Daoyan neiwai bijue quanshu* (Complete Writings of Secret Instruction on Internal and External Taoist Teachings). Peng Haogu's work is one of many examples showing that commentaries to Neidan texts not only offer explications of the original texts, but are Neidan works to all effects and reflect the perspectives of their authors.

I

True Soil seizes True Lead,
True Lead controls True Mercury.
Lead and Mercury return to the True Soil,
body and mind are silent and unmoving.

COMMENTARY

When a human being is born, Heaven, whose number is 1, generates
the Kan ☵ Water, which is the kidneys. The Water of the kidneys,
which sinks downwards, is an image of Lead. The kidneys generate
the Breath (qi). The one particle of Essence of True Unity within the
Breath is True Lead.

The Earth, whose number is 2, generates the Li ☲ Fire, which is
the heart. The Fire of the heart, which flies upwards, is an image of
Mercury. The heart generates the Liquor (ye). The one particle of
Breath of Correct Yang within the Liquor is True Mercury.[1]

Within Kan there is the WU-Soil, and within Li there is the JI-Soil.[2]
Water in the first place is Yin, but within the Yin there is True Yang;
Fire in the first place is Yang, but within the Yang there is True Yin.
These two are the True Soil. The conjunction of Yin with Yang and of
Yang with Yin entirely depends on the True Soil.

True Lead is the Breath within the body; True Mercury is the
Spirit within the mind; True Soil is the Intention within the body and
the mind.[3] Sincerity (*cheng*) can set in motion one's own True Intention: it causes Mercury constantly to greet Lead, and Lead constantly
to control Mercury. When "Lead and Mercury return to the True

---

[1] The terminology used in these two initial paragraphs is complex, but
the main points can be rephrased as follows: The first paragraph says that the
kidneys are Yin and pertain to Kan ☵ and Water. The Yin Breath (qi) of the
kidneys contains the True Yang, which is True Lead and is also called Essence
of True Unity. The second paragraph says that the heart is Yang and pertains
to Li ☲ and Fire. The Yang Liquor (ye) of the heart contains the True Yin,
which is True Mercury and is also called Breath of Correct Yang.

[2] The WU-Soil and the JI-Soil are the Yang and the Yin aspects of Soil,
respectively. Soil is the agent that represents the unity of Yin and Yang, and
therefore makes their conjunction possible.

[3] In Chinese, the word for "heart" and "mind" is the same, *xin*.

Soil," Spirit and Breath inchoately merge, nature (*xing*) and emotions (*qing*) join as one, and body and mind are "silent and unmoving."[4]

Although it says "unmoving," within pure Suchness (*ruru*) there is complete realization (*liaoliao*), and within darkness there is brightness. The errant mind is removed, but the bright mind is not obscured; the body of flesh appears to be dead, but the dharma-body (*fashen*) is constantly alive.[5] This is not falling into "idle emptiness" or coveting to be "withered and rotten."[6]

2

Emptiness and Non-Being generate the White Snow,
silence and quiescence send forth the Yellow Sprout.
In the Jade Furnace the fire is warm,
a purple mist flies above the Tripod.

COMMENTARY

Emptiness and Non-Being, silence and quiescence concern the work done when one practices in order to collect the Medicine. The White Snow and the Yellow Sprout are images of the birth of the Medicine within oneself. There is a difference, however, between the White Snow, which pertains to Emptiness and Non-Being, and the Yellow Sprout, which pertains to silence and quiescence: while the White Snow is born from Emptiness, the Yellow Sprout needs nourishment by Fire to be born, because it is from Fire that one can generate Soil.[7]

[4] In the conditioned state, emotions are separated from one's inner nature. The Neidan practice allows them to reconjoin to one another. When that happens, the emotions become qualities that express one's nature.

[5] On the dharma-body see p. 246, note 16 below.

[6] With these words, Peng Haogu criticizes erroneous practices performed by Buddhist and Taoist adepts. The first expression is often used to disapprove of Buddhist meditation on Emptiness. The second expression derives from the *Daode jing* (Book of the Way and Its Virtue), sec. 76: "When the ten thousand things and trees and plants are born, they are yielding and supple; when they die, they are withered and rotten."

[7] In other words, according to Peng Haogu the appearance of the White

At the time of the Gou ䷫ hexagram, Heaven conjoins with the Earth; in Emptiness and Non-Being, the White Snow is spontaneously generated. At the time of the Fu ䷗ hexagram, the Earth conjoins with Heaven; in silence and quiescence, the Yellow Sprout is spontaneously sent forth.[8] It is just like in our world:[9] after the Yang culminates there is the Yin, and the white snow falls from the sky; after the Yin culminates there is the Yang, and the yellow sprouts grow from the earth.

The Jade Furnace is the Yellow Court (*huangting*), and the "fire" is Spirit. When Spirit guides Breath, Fire is within the Jade Furnace. "Warm" means that one is practicing the Fire phases (*huohou*).

The Tripod is the position of Qian ☰, and it is Spirit's own palace. As the black turns red and becomes purple, Fire flies upwards and becomes mist. This mist and this Fire are not two different things.

"In the Jade Furnace the fire is warm" means that the brightness of Spirit from the Palace of Qian ☰ enters the Palace of Kun ☷. When "a purple mist flies above the Tripod," Kun receives the Fire of Qian. As it manifests itself outside the Palace of Kun, there is the image of "flying."

3

In the Flowery Pond the lotus flowers bloom,
in the Spirit Water the golden waves are quiescent.
Deep at night the Moon is fully bright,
Heaven and Earth are one round mirror.

Snow (True Yin) pertains to "non-doing" (*wuwei*) and occurs of its own in the higher stage of the Neidan practice, while the appearance of the Yellow Sprout (True Yang) pertains to "doing" (*youwei*) and is the result of the initial stage or stages. — In the "generation sequence" of the five agents, Fire generates Soil.

[8] These two hexagrams represent the rebirth of the Yin principle and of the Yang principle, respectively, and thus symbolize the appearance of the White Snow and the Yellow Sprout.

[9] Lit., "between Heaven and Earth."

COMMENTARY

Ziyang (Zhang Boduan) says in his Preface: "When Lead calls on Mercury, this is called Flowery Pond (*huachi*). When Mercury enters Lead, this is called Spirit Water (*shenshui*)."[10] This shows that the Flowery Pond is the Stem of Existence (*mingdi*) and the Spirit Water is the Root of Nature (*xinggen*).[11] If you wish to merge Nature (*xing*) and Existence (*ming*) inchoately, first use Mercury to seize Lead, then use Lead to control Mercury. The Essence of True Unity in the Palace of Kan ☵ ascends carrying the Breath of Correct Yang; Breath is similar to the blooming of the lotus flowers. The Breath of Correct Yang in the Palace of Li ☲ descends following the Essence of True Unity; its quietude and purity are similar to the purity of golden waves.[12]

When the time of the zi hour comes,[13] Water is pure and Metal is white: these are Nature and Existence, Spirit and Breath inchoately joined with one another. Therefore it says: "Heaven and Earth are one round mirror."

All of this lies only in joining Nature with Existence, and in coagulating Spirit so that it enters the Cavity of Breath (*qixue*).[14] An ancient man said:

> To refine the Elixir there is no other method: just lead the Spirit Water to enter the Flowery Pond, and the ten thousand pursuits are completed.[15]

[10] These words are found in the preface to the *Jindan sibai zi*.

[11] The Stem of Existence is located in the lower Cinnabar Field, and the Root of Nature is located in the upper Cinnabar Field. In this section, Peng Haogu refers to the two Fields as Palace of Kan and Palace of Li, respectively.

[12] The main subject of this paragraph is the inversion of the ordinary courses of "essence" and "breath" of Yin and Yang. Instead of descending and being wasted, Lead (the Essence of True Unity, True Yang) ascends; and instead of ascending and being lost, Mercury (the Breath of Correct Yang, True Yin) descends. As Lead and Mercury are conjoined, they "carry" and "follow" one another.

[13] Formally corresponding to 11pm–1am, but actually signifying the rebirth of the Yang principle.

[14] The Cavity of Breath is the middle Cinnabar Field (also called Cavity of Spirit and Breath, *shenqi xue*).

[15] These words are found in the *Jinhua bijue* (Secret Instructions on the Golden Flower), one of many Neidan texts associated with Lü Dongbin.

This is exactly what he meant.

4

The Vermilion Sand refines into Yang Breath,
the Water Silver boils into Essence of Metal.
Essence of Metal with Yang Breath:
Vermilion Sand and Water Silver.

COMMENTARY

The Vermilion Sand is the Breath of Correct Yang within the Liquor.
The Water Silver is the Essence of True Unity within the Breath.[16] To
replenish the Yin within the Palace of Li ☲, collect the Breath of
Correct Yang within the Liquor. To take the Yang within the Palace of
Kan ☵, collect the Essence of True Unity within the Breath.

"Essence of Metal with Yang Breath" means that you refine one by
means of the Yang Fire (*yanghuo*), and it becomes like the Vermilion
Sand; and you nourish the other by means of the Yin Response
(*yinfu*), and it becomes like the Water Silver. They are not two different things.[17]

5

The Sun's *Hun*-soul, the lard of the Jade Hare;
the Moon's *Po*-soul, the marrow of the Golden Crow.
Once collected, they return to the Tripod,
and transmute themselves into a clear pool of water.

---

[16] The Vermilion Sand (to be understood as Sand in the Vermilion) is Yin
within Yang (the Yin Breath within the Yang Liquor, or Li ☲). The Water
Silver (i.e., Silver in the Water) is Yang within Yin (the Yang Essence within
the Yin Breath, or Kan ☵). The Yang Breath is True Yang, and the Essence of
Metal is True Yin.

[17] Fire makes it possible to extract the Yang from the Yin and to replenish
the Yin within the Yang (in the first and the second halves of the cycle of the
Fire phases, respectively). Thus the two become the same.

COMMENTARY

The Wood and Fire of Great Yang are the *Hun*-soul of the Sun. The *Hun*-soul stores the Spirit, but within the Yang there is the Yin: that Yin is the *Po*-soul of the Moon. Without the Moon, the Sun could not generate its radiance. Therefore it says "the lard of the Jade Hare," because the lard pertains to Essence.

The Metal and Water of Great Yin are the *Po*-soul of the Moon. The *Po* stores the Essence, but within the Yin there is the Yang: that Yang is the *Hun*-soul of the Sun. Without the Sun, the Moon could not complete its body.[18] Therefore it says "the marrow of the Golden Crow," because the marrow pertains to Spirit.[19]

It is like the Vermilion Sand, which is the Essence of the Sun; as it is touched by the glow of the Moon, it generates the True Breath. [It is also like] the Water Silver, which is the glow of the Moon; as it is touched by the Essence of the Sun, it generates the True Lead.

Among those who practice the great cultivation, the superior persons transmute Breath by means of Spirit, and Essence by means of Breath; the average persons preserve Breath by means of the Essence, and Spirit by means of Breath. When Essence and Spirit inchoately join and harmonize with one another within the precious Tripod, the Sweet Dew spontaneously descends and becomes "a clear pool of water."

[18] The Moon "completes its body" in the middle of the lunar month, when it appears to be full. At that time, which is the peak of the Yang principle, the Yin principle is at the lowest stage of its course: the Moon appears to be full because it is entirely enlightened by the Sun.

[19] The complex imagery of this and the previous paragraphs can be summarized as follows. Although the Sun is Yang, it holds the Yin soul of the Moon as its "essence" (*jing*). This essence is symbolized by the hare, the animal that, according to a Chinese myth, lives on the Moon. Conversely, the Moon is Yin but holds the Yang soul of the Sun as its "spirit" (*shen*). This spirit is symbolized by the crow, the animal said to live on the Sun.

6

The Medicine is born in the Mysterious Opening,
the Fire phases come forth from the Yang Furnace.
When Dragon and Tiger conjoin,
the Golden Tripod gives birth to the Mysterious Pearl.

COMMENTARY

The Mysterious Opening is the Mysterious-Female. The Mysterious is Yang, the Female is Yin. Together they are called "Mysterious Opening."

In the human body, the lower [Cinnabar] Field is the Furnace, the place where Spirit lodges. Fire is sent forth from here; therefore it is called "the Yang Furnace." Above the Furnace there is the Tripod. When quiescence culminates and there is movement, the Medicine is spontaneously born. You should collect it at that time. After you have obtained it, if it is not heated and refined by means of the Fire phases, it would disperse again. If that happens, how could the Mysterious Pearl be generated? This is why you must "turn the gear of the barrier in the sinciput" and "steal the Pearl under the chin of the Black Dragon."[20]

The Medicine is Fire, and Fire is the Medicine. When Medicine and Fire join as one, Dragon and Tiger conjoin, and the precious Tripod of the Suspended Womb spontaneously gives birth to the Mysterious Pearl, sized as a grain of millet.[21] Therefore you can send forth the Fire from the Yang Furnace only after the Mysterious Opening has generated the Medicine. If the right moment has not yet come,

[20] The first sentence is found in several texts, including Wang Jie's commentary to the *Ruyao jing* (Mirror for Compounding the Medicine), sec. 14 (translated above, p. 55). The second sentence is a line in a poem found in the *Lifeng laoren ji* (The Old Man of the Solitary Peak: An Anthology), ch. 1.

[21] This simile is drawn from the *Cantong qi* (The Seal of the Unity of the Three), 79:20, which says of the Elixir: "Ingest it in pills sized as a grain of millet." — The Tripod of the Suspended Womb (*xuantai ding*) is, according to Weng Baoguang's *Jindan faxiang* (Model Images of the Golden Elixir), an image of the Center; see below, p. 135.

and you cause it to grow it ahead of time, the external Fire (*waihuo*) would circulate, but the internal Response (*neifu*) would not be in accord with it. You would just set your body on fire.

Substantially, when Spirit and Breath harmonize and merge with one another, the Mysterious Opening spontaneously appears. After the Mysterious Opening has appeared, the Fire phases (*huohou*) are spontaneously known. After the Fire phases are known, Dragon and Tiger spontaneously pair with one another. After Dragon and Tiger have paired with one another, the Mysterious Pearl is spontaneously formed. The wonder of this lies between "movement" and "quiescence": you cannot make an error as fine as a hair.

7

This Opening is not a common opening:
it is formed by the joining of Qian ☰ and Kun ☷.
It is called Cavity of Spirit and Breath,
and within there are the essences of Kan ☵ and Li ☲.

COMMENTARY

"This Opening" means the Mysterious Opening mentioned above.[22] It does not pertain to Being or Non-Being, and it does not fall into any category or rule; it lies outside and beyond the body and mind, and it emerges from the "vague and indistinct."[23] Therefore it says, "is not a common Opening."

In the human body, Qian ☰ is above and Kun ☷ is below. The central line within Qian seeks Kun and forms Kan ☵. Kan dwells in the position of Kun, and Breath dwells there. The central line within Kan seeks Qian and forms Li ☲. Li places itself in the position of Qian, and Spirit dwells there.[24]

---

[22] See the previous poem.

[23] *Daode jing*, sec. 21: "Vague and indistinct! Within there is something. Dim and obscure! Within there is an essence."

[24] The different positions of the trigrams represent the shift from the precelestial to the postcelestial domains. See table 3, p. 259.

Spirit is the Mercury within the mind, Breath is the Lead within the body. The mind is the chamber of Spirit, the body is the seat of Breath.[25] Therefore it says, "it is called Cavity of Spirit and Breath."

Within the body there is a particle of Breath of True Yang; that Breath pertains to Li ☲. Within the mind there is a particle of Essence of True Yin; that Essence pertains to Kan ☵. Therefore it says, "within there are the essences of Kan ☵ and Li ☲."

8

> Wooden Mercury, one particle of red,
> Metallic Lead, four pounds of black.[26]
> Lead and Mercury coalesce and form the Pearl:
> shining, it takes on the color of purple gold.

COMMENTARY

The one particle of Essence of True Yin within the heart is called "Wooden Mercury." Wood pertains to number 3 and holds the Breath of True Yang, whose number is 1; therefore it says "one particle." Since Wood is able to generate Fire and the color of Fire is red, it says "one particle of red."

The one particle of Breath of True Yang within the body is called "Metallic Lead." Metals pertains to number 4; therefore it says "four pounds of Lead, black in color."[27] Since Metal and Water share the same Palace, it says "four pounds of black."

First you cause the red to enter the black, then you refine the black so that it enters the red. When the red and the black seize one another, they coalesce within the precious Tripod into the Mysterious Pearl sized as a grain of millet, which shines with a color similar to purple.

[25] Here again it is necessary to remember that the "mind" is also the "heart."

[26] Other versions of the *Jindan sibai zi* have "three pounds," explained either as the symbolic weight of Lead in the Lead-Mercury compound, or (just like "one particle" in the previous line) as a number with no precise material correspondence.

[27] This is not a precise quotation of the line in the poem above.

Since purple is midway between red and black, it says "it takes on the color of purple gold."

However, Lead and Mercury are not fixed objects, red and black are not fixed colors, and "one particle" and "four pounds" are not fixed numbers. Those who are accomplished know this by themselves.

9

In the house garden the sight is beautiful:
wind and rain are like those of deep spring.
Without spending your strength for plowing and digging,
the whole great Earth is yellow gold.

COMMENTARY

The "house garden" is the True Soil within the body. The "sight" is the images of the ingredients within the body.

At the moment of the return of the initial Yang, you should only activate the wind of Xun ☴ so that it blows upon Kan ☵.[28] This means leading the Spirit Water to moisten the Flowery Pond. At the time of the conjunction in Tai ䷊ (Peace), with its three Yang lines,[29] you should carefully refrain from spending your strength in order to collect [the Medicine]. Just "neither forget nor assist," and the Yellow Sprout of the Great Earth will burst forth of its own from the soil.[30] It is called "gold" because it will coalesce and form the Golden Elixir.

[28] Among natural phenomena, the trigram Xun ☴ is represented by the wind. The expression "wind of Xun" therefore means the breath. Kan ☵ represents the lower Cinnabar Field.

[29] Tai (Peace) is the hexagram (containing three Yang lines below and three Yin lines above) that represents the perfect state of conjunction and balance between Yin and Yang. Compare the "Image" ("Xiang") on this hexagram in the Book of Changes (Yijing): "Heaven and Earth are conjoined: Peace" (see Wilhelm, The I-ching or Book of Changes, p. 49).

[30] The expression "neither forget nor assist" originates in Mengzi, 3:2: "Let not the mind forget it, but let there be no assisting it" (see Legge, The Chinese Classics, vol. 2, p. 190).

10

True Lead is born in Kan ☵,
but its operation is in the Palace of Li ☲.
From black it turns red:
in the whole tripod the cloud's breath is dense.

COMMENTARY

The kidneys generate Breath (*qi*); the Water of True Unity within
Breath is True Lead. This Water of True Unity [is collected] when the
Breath of Correct Yang in the Palace of Li ☲ sees the Liquor, and they
conjoin. What you should collect is the Water of True Unity within
the Breath, and not the Breath of Correct Yang within the Liquor.[31]

Just like a mother and a child meeting and not wishing to leave
one another, so does Metal hide itself within Water, and there is no
way to cause it to ascend. Indeed, that Spirit should guide the Breath
is the most important instruction transmitted from Heart to Heart
throughout all times. Therefore it says "its operation is in the Palace
of Li ☲," because the foundation (*ti*) is in Kan and the operation
(*yong*) is in Li.[32]

After Lead has emerged by means of Fire, Water "from black turns
red." The Medicine is Fire. It will go through the route of the Three
Barriers until it reaches the top of the ninefold Heaven.[33] It rises
vividly, it ascends as if it drifts in the air, it steams harmoniously, and

---

[31] For the terminology and imagery used in this paragraph see page 88, n.
1 above. Here, however, Peng Haogu refers to the True Yang as Water of True
Unity instead of Essence of True Unity. Essentially, this paragraph states that
True Yang (the Water of True Unity) must be collected by means of True Yin
(the Breath of Correct Yang, represented by the Yin line within the Yang
trigram Li ☲). At that time, one should collect the Yang (the Water of True
Unity) within the Yin (Breath), and not the Yin (the Breath of Correct Yang)
within the Yang (the Liquor in the heart).

[32] That is, True Lead is found within Kan ☵, but it operates by means of
the True Mercury found within Li ☲.

[33] In ancient China, Heaven was described as made of nine horizontal
layers. Here the term "ninefold" also alludes to the nine "palaces" or "rooms"
of the upper Cinnabar Field (see the note to the section "The Muddy Pellet"
in the *Jindan wenda*, p. 143 below.)

it coagulates like mist. Its Breath is as dense as the clouds, and it
ascends until it enters the Tripod.

11

True Mercury is born in Li ☲,
its operation instead is in Kan ☵.
The Lovely Maid goes past the southern garden
holding a jade olive in her hands.

COMMENTARY

Mercury is born in the Palace of Li ☲, but until it finds the Correct
Breath of the North that controls and subdues it, it "desires ever to
leave you"[34] and cannot coagulate. Therefore it says, "its operation
instead is in Kan ☵."[35]

The Lovely Maid is Mercury, and the "southern garden" is Li. As
soon as the Mercury within Li sees the Lead within Kan, Lead and
Mercury seize one another. Mercury leaves the Palace of Li ☲, then
they descend together to the position of Kan ☵.[36] Therefore it says,
"goes past the southern garden."

As soon as it has gone past the "southern garden," Mercury forms
the White Snow. Jade represents the whiteness of its color, and the
olive represents the fact that it is neither square nor round.[37]

12

Zhen ☳ and Dui ☱ are not East and West,
Kan ☵ and Li ☲ are not South and North.

---

[34] *Cantong qi*, 62:1–2: "The Flowing Pearl of Great Yang (*i.e., Mercury*)
desires ever to leave you" (Pregadio, *The Seal of the Unity of the Three*, p. 101).

[35] Just like Li ☲ contains True Mercury, so does Kan ☵ contain True
Lead, which controls True Mercury and prevents its dispersion.

[36] The Palace of Li is the upper Cinnabar Field, the "position of Kan" is
the lower Cinnabar Field.

[37] "Jade olive" (*yugan*) is a synonym of Mysterious Pearl (*xuanzhu*).

As the Dipper's handle revolves along the Celestial Circuit,
   all the people should gather together.

COMMENTARY

Zhen ☳ in the East, Dui ☱ in the West, Li ☲ in the South, and Kan ☵ in the North are the positions of the eight trigrams. The Way of Heaven follows its course without pause, and the Dipper's Handle turns around, pointing each month to a different direction. Yin and Yang, cold and heat never make errors in their time spans.

The human body is a whole Heaven and Earth. Rising from the Mysterious Valley to the Muddy Pellet, and then descending again through the Storied Pavilion to return to the Northern Ocean, is called the Celestial Circuit (*zhoutian*).[38] The mechanism of this rotation also depends on the Dipper's Handle.

In one year there are 12 months, in one month there are 30 days, and altogether there are 360 days. In one day there are 100 notches, and one year amounts to 36,000 notches.[39] The practice of one day can seize the Breath of 36,000 notches. Those who cultivate the Elixir revolve the Fire phases of an entire Celestial Circuit in one day. By replacing the year with the day, and the 12 months with the 12 [double] hours, they gather one year in one day and converge one month into one [double] hour.

To establish the circular movement, it is sufficient to follow the Dipper's Handle; then there is no more need to mention East, West, North, and South. However, if there is a single error in the Dipper's Handle, the time segments would be mistaken. Be careful! Be careful!

---

[38] The Mysterious Valley (*xuangu*) is the kidneys. The Muddy Pellet (*niwan*) is the upper Cinnabar Field. The Storied Pavilion (*chonglou*) is the trachea. The Northern Ocean (*beihai*) is the lower Cinnabar Field (note that the North is traditionally placed "below" in premodern China).

[39] For the "notches" (*ke*), see the entry "The Fire Phases" in the *Jindan wenda* (Questions and Answers on the Golden Elixir), p. 139 below.

13

The Fire phases do not use the hours,
and the winter solstice is not at ZI.
As for the method of bathing,
the times of MAO and YOU are empty similitudes.

COMMENTARY

Fire is something that causes burning if is too strong, and chilling if it is too weak. The essential lies in harmonization and in finding the balance. This is why, with regard to Fire, it is necessary to speak of its phases.

In one [double] hour there are six phases (*hou*); these are the nodal phases (*jiehou*) found within oneself. No matter what the hour may be, when quiescence culminates and there is movement within oneself, this corresponds to the winter solstice with regard to the months, and to the ZI hour with regard to the day. Greet that opportunity and move in agreement with it. The Fire phases consist in this.

On the whole, the initial Yang ascends from ZI, and the initial Yin descends from WU; the Yang ascending and the Yin descending are MAO, and the Yin ascending and the Yang descending are YOU. When we say, "distinguish ZI and WU within the time that has no notches,"[40] we mean that one should not take the winter solstice as ZI, the summer solstice as WU, and the months of the hare and the rooster as MAO and YOU.[41] For example, with regard to the External Elixir, advancing the Fire is ZI, reducing the Fire is WU, and neither increasing nor decreasing the Fire is "bathing." Do not rigidly adhere either to ZI and WU, or to MAO and YOU.[42]

[40] In a slightly different form, this saying is attributed to Ma Ziran; see p. 150 below.

[41] The months of the hare and the rooster are the second and the eighth lunar months, corresponding to the earthly branches MAO and YOU, respectively.

[42] In Neidan, the term External Elixir (*waidan*) usually does not refer to External Alchemy. It denotes, instead, the initial stage of the compounding of the Internal Elixir, achieved by the practice of the Fire times. This seems to be the sense in which Peng Haogu uses the term in this passage of his commentary.

14

The Crow's liver and the Hare's marrow
are seized and share the same place.
Grain after grain,
from tenuous it becomes manifest.

COMMENTARY

The human being is endowed with the True Original Breath of Heaven and Earth. There are 384 scruples (*zhu*) of this Breath, which altogether amount to one pound. Eight ounces are the Essence of the Sun; therefore it says "the Crow's liver," which is the Liquor of Wood. Eight ounces are the Essence of the Moon; therefore it says "the Hare's marrow," which is the Essence of Metal.[43]

Since Metal and Wood are separated from one another, you should avail yourself of WU and JI as go-betweens, and use Fire to refine them. Each day one grain is generated, sized as a grain of millet and weighing 1 scruple and 8 parts. "From tenuous it becomes manifest," and by accumulation it forms the [required] ounces: after 30 days it weighs 38 scruples and 4 parts, and after 300 days it weighs 384 scruples.[44] "Square and round, one inch is its diameter," and it weighs one pound.[45]

[43] This paragraph uses images drawn from the ancient Chinese weight system. One pound (*jin*) contains 16 ounces (*liang*), and one ounce contains 24 scruples (*zhu*). Therefore one pound is made of 384 scruples. The symbolic "pound" of Elixir requires 8 ounces of True Yin (here called "Crow's liver") and 8 ounces of True Yang (here called "Hare's marrow").

[44] Three hundred days correspond to ten months, the duration of gestation in the Chinese reckoning.

[45] The phrase "Square and round, one inch is its diameter" derives from the *Huangting jing* (Book of the Yellow Court), "Inner" version, poem 7. In the *Huangting jing*, it refers to the upper Cinnabar Field. Neidan texts often borrow this verse and use it as a metaphor to the Elixir: "square and round" refer to Heaven and Earth, and "one inch" refers to the unity of Yin and Yang.

15

The Inchoate embraces Emptiness,
Emptiness holds the Three Worlds in its hands.
Seek its origin and root:
one grain sized as millet.[46]

COMMENTARY

As there is the world, there are the Three Powers; as there are the Three
Powers, there is Emptiness; as there is Emptiness, there is the Inchoate.
The Inchoate is prior to Heaven and Earth. "The Inchoate embraces
Emptiness, Emptiness holds the Three Worlds in its hands."[47]

When you seek the instant in which you first received Breath
within yourself, it was nothing more than "one grain sized as millet."
This is the "origin and root" of human life: those who cultivate the
Elixir should know this. Therefore it is said:

If anyone wants to look for the instructions on long life,
Just go seek the root of creation and transformation.[48]

16

Heaven and Earth exchange their true liquors,
Sun and Moon hold their true essences.
If you comprehend the foundation of Kan ☵ and Li ☲,
the Three Worlds return to the one body.

COMMENTARY

The Liquor of the heart descends, and the Breath of the kidneys
ascends. [In the present poem] this Liquor and this Breath are both

[46] See above, note 21.
[47] The "three powers" (*sancai*) here are True Yin, True Yang, and Soil.
They are equivalent to the "three worlds," on which see p. 104, note 49 below.
[48] These verses are quoted from Bai Yuchan's "Xuanguan xianbi
lun" (Manifesting the Secret of the Mysterious Barrier), in *Haiqiong wendao
ji* (Questions on the Dao by the Master of Haiqiong: An Anthology), ch. 2.

called "liquors." This is the meaning of "Heaven and Earth exchange their true liquors."

The *Hun*-soul is the Essence of the Crow, and the *Po*-soul is the Marrow of the Hare. [In this poem] they are both called "essences." This is the meaning of "Sun and Moon hold their true essences."

Kan ☵ pertains to the Yin. Kan stores WU within, which is the Yang Soil. This Yang is the "foundation of Kan." Li ☲ pertains to the Yang. Li stores JI within, which is the Yin Soil. This Yin is the "foundation of Li."

If you comprehend that the WU-Soil within Kan has its foundation and origin in the Yang, and that the JI-Soil within Li has its foundation and origin in the Yin, then the Heaven and the Earth within the body, and the Sun and the Moon within the body, will operate by relying on True Soil. Then "the Three Worlds return to the one body."[49]

17

The Dragon comes from the Eastern Sea,
the Tiger rises from the Western Mountains.
The two beasts fight in the same place
and transmute themselves into the marrow of Heaven and Earth.

COMMENTARY

The Breath of Correct Yang within the heart is the Dragon. Wood can generate Fire. Since Zhen ☳ pertains to Wood, "the Dragon comes from the Eastern Sea."[50]

The Essence of True Unity within the kidneys is the Tiger. Metal can generate Water. Since Dui ☱ pertains to Metal, "the Tiger rises from the Western Mountains."[51]

---

[49] The "three worlds" (*sanjie*) here are True Yin (found within Li ☲), True Yang (found within Kan ☵), and Soil (which contains both True Yin and True Yang). When they are joined to one another through the intermediation of Soil, they become "one body."

[50] In the system of the five agents, Wood is associated with the East (the position of the trigram Zhen ☳). Wood generates Fire, which is "the Breath of Correct Yang within the heart."

[51] In the system of the five agents, Metal is associated with the West (the

If, when "the Dragon howls and the clouds rise," you are able to cause it to descend, and, when "the Tiger roars and the wind blows," you are able to cause it to ascend, then the "two beasts" will meet and fight against one another in front of the Yellow Room.[52] Then the Dragon ingests the Tiger's marrow, and the Tiger swallows the Dragon's essence. Wind and clouds will have the "blissful meeting." As they inchoately merge to become one, they transmute into "the marrow of Heaven and Earth."

18

The Golden Flower opens petals of Mercury,
the Jade Stem grows branches of Lead.
Kan ☵ and Li ☲ have never been separate,
Qian ☰ and Kun ☷ stand through the whole of time.

COMMENTARY

The Golden Flower is in the first place the embryo achieved when True Lead avails itself of Mercury. The Jade Stem is in the first place the form achieved when True Mercury avails itself of Lead. In the human body, Mercury is Spirit, and Lead is the Essence. "The Golden Flower opens petals of Mercury" means that in the "vague and indistinct," Spirit is born within Water. "The Jade Stem grows branches of Lead" means that in the "dim and obscure," Essence is born within Fire.[53] Those who receive the instructions should wait until the Golden Flower manifests its dew and the Jade Stem sends forth its buds. These are the "petals" and the "branches," or JI and WU, of Lead and Mercury.[54]

position of the trigram Dui ☱). Metal generates Water, which is "the Essence of True Unity within the kidneys."

[52] For the phrases "the Dragon howls and the clouds rise" and "the Tiger roars and the wind blows," see page 170 note 24. In Neidan, the term Yellow Room (huangwu) denotes both the middle and the lower Cinnabar Fields. This passage seems to refer to the middle Field.

[53] For "vague and indistinct," "dim and obscure," see above, page 95 note 23.

[54] The "petals of Mercury" are the Yin born from the Yang, and the

At that time, you should advance the Fire to collect the Medicine, causing Kan and Li to revolve between the East and the West, and Qian and Kun to rotate between the top and the bottom. One comes, the other goes, one ascends, the other descends, like a ring that has no end or beginning and cannot be paused for even one instant.[55]

Indeed, before you obtain the Medicine you must recognize the opening of the petals of Mercury and the growth of the branches of Lead. After you obtain the Medicine, you should also know the wonder of "coming and going" and the principle of "ascending and descending." Only then will beginning and end be both completed, and will the Embryo of Sainthood be attained.

If Qian ☰, Kun ☷, Kan ☵, and Li ☲ do not move in a ring for ten months, the Medicine within the tripod would be entirely lost. How could you protect the Golden Flower so that it does not languish? How could you protect the Jade Stem so that it does not wither?

19

When you bathe, avoid all dangers,
when you extract and augment, be careful and continuous.
Altogether there are thirty thousand notches:
make an error as fine as a hair, and you lose it.

COMMENTARY

In one year there are twelve months, which altogether amount to 36,000 notches (*ke*); they are gathered together into one day.[56] Within the twelve months, you perform the Fire phases for ten months. When the Yang is born, collect the Medicine from the palace of zi and cause it to ascend by inverting the course (*ni*). This is called "extracting

---

"branches of Lead" are the Yang born from the Yin. The petals stand for Original Spirit, and the branches stand for the Original Essence. They are associated with ji and wu, respectively, the Yin and Yang celestial stems that represent the two halves of the One (see table 5, p. 261).

[55] With reference to the Neidan practices, this refers to the "small celestial circuit" (*xiao zhoutian*) of the Fire phases. See Wang Mu, *Foundations of Internal Alchemy*, 71–86.

[56] See above, note 39.

Lead" (*chouqian*). When the Yin is born, withdraw the Fire from the position of WU, and cause it to descend by following the course (*shun*). This is called "augmenting Mercury" (*tianhong*).

As for the remaining two months, during the MAO month you increase Water and let Metal rest, and during the YOU month you circulate Fire and stop Water. You only perform the Water phases and do not perform the Fire phases. This is called "bathing" (*muyu*).[57] Since during the MAO month there is taking life within giving life, and during the YOU month there is giving life within taking life, you should avoid that Fire causes excessive heat, or you would be in danger.[58]

Excluding the 6,000 notches of those two months, in ten months there are 30,000 notches. Therefore it says, "altogether there are thirty thousand notches." If in the 30,000 notches of practice there is an error as fine as a hair, then Yin and Yang would miss the correct timing. You should not only avoid all dangers, but also know how to be careful and continuous, and "give your mind and bend your will" within an enclosure.[59] Manifest yourself in movement, and conceal yourself in quiescence. In the span of one year you will be able to nourish the Infant, and you will transcend the world as an immortal.

20

> When husband and wife conjoin,
> in the Cavern Chamber there are clouds and rain.
> In one year one infant is born;
> each of them can ride on a crane.

COMMENTARY

The "husband and wife" are the True Yin and the True Yang within yourself. When True Yin and True Yang find True Soil as a go-

---

[57] The MAO and the YOU months are the second and the eighth lunar months, respectively. "Water phases" (*shuihou*) is a synonym of "bathing."

[58] "Giving life" (*sheng*) and "taking life" (*sha*) represent the operation of the Yang and the Yin principles, respectively.

[59] The phrase "give your mind and bend your will" derives from *Mengzi*, 11.9 (see Legge, *The Chinese Classics*, vol. 2, p. 410).

between, they tie to one another as husband and wife. When they conjoin in the Cavern Chamber, "the clouds rise and rain falls."[60]

In one year, you are pregnant for ten months and bathe for two months. When the embryo is complete and the Breath is plenty, you give birth to the Infant, who exits from your Palace of the Muddy Pellet riding on a crane.[61] In nine years you generate nine infants; therefore it says "each of them." The myriads of transformation bodies are all one single body; therefore this does not mean that there are truly nine children.[62]

The Infant is a child (孩). When HAI 亥 and ZI 子 conjoin, they form the character "child" (孩). This is the essential in setting to practice in order to coalesce the embryo.[63]

---

[60] This phrase derives from the *Book of Changes*, "Commentary on the Judgment" ("Tuanzhuan") on the hexagram Qian ䷀ (no. 1; see Wilhelm, p. 370).

[61] The Palace of the Muddy Pellet (*niwan gong*) is the upper Cinnabar Field.

[62] The "transformation body" (*huashen*) is, in the first place, a body taken on by the Buddha in order to teach sentient beings.

[63] HAI 亥 and ZI 子 are the earthly branches associated with the hexagrams Kun ䷁ and Fu ䷗, respectively (see table 4, p. 260). Together, they represent the rebirth of Yang (the lower, initial line of Fu) from Kun (Pure Yin). This symbolic etymology of the character *hai* 孩 ("child") is also used in the *Duren shangpin miaojing neiyi* (Inner Meaning of the Wondrous Book of the Upper Chapters on Salvation), ch. 5.

7 Pointers to the Mystery

Zhixuan pian 指玄篇

Bai Yuchan 白玉蟾 (1194–1229?)

Bai Yuchan is one of the main figures in the history of Neidan. Despite his apparently brief earthly existence (he might have lived until 1289, but this seems improbable), he is ascribed with a remarkably vast literary production, which includes—in addition to anthologies, treatises, and a large number of poems—a noteworthy commentary to the *Daode jing* (Book of the Way and Its Virtue). Although he was the fifth master of the Southern Lineage (Nanzong), his works go beyond the boundaries of particular schools. In addition to Neidan, he was also a practitioner of the Taoist exorcist rituals known as Thunder Rites (*leifa*).

The two essays translated here are found in a collection entitled *Zazhu zhixuan pian* (Pointers to the Mystery: A Miscellany), which is attributed to Bai Yuchan and contains works by authors related to the Southern Lineage. The "Essay on Resolving Doubts in the Cultivation of Immortality" ("Xiuxian bianhuo lun") is presented as a dialogue between Bai Yuchan and his master, Chen Nan (?–1213, also known as Chen Niwan). The essay is especially concerned with the different levels of Neidan; what might at first appear to be the most difficult level is defined as "extremely easy to achieve," while the procedure most commonly followed is said to be "difficult to achieve." The text also shows that the same terms take on different senses according to the different levels (or stages) of Neidan. The second selection, entitled "Essay on 'The Spirit of the Valley does not Die'" ("Gushen busi lun"), consists of a commentary on one of the passages of the *Daode jing* most frequently quoted in Neidan texts.

109

ESSAY ON RESOLVING DOUBTS
IN THE CULTIVATION OF IMMORTALITY

Bai Yuchan, who came from Hainan, had been a disciple of Chen Niwan since his young age. All of a sudden, nine years had already passed. One day, they were both under a pine on the cliff of a mountain. The wind was clear and the moon was bright; the night was calm and the air was cool. Thinking of the great matters of life and death, and of the fast pace of impermanence, Yuchan bowed down twice and asked: I have not been your disciple for a long time, and I reckon that my fortune and destiny are flimsy and shallow. Yet, I dare ask you: Is my destiny to become an immortal in this life?

Chen Niwan said: Anyone can do it, and this is even more true of you.

Yuchan said: I cannot avoid the obligation of showing respect to you, but I will ask a presumptuous question. How many gateways are there to the cultivation of immortality? How many methods are there to refine the Elixir? I am like one who cannot distinguish jade from ordinary stones, but I wish to attain realization[1] through your word.

Chen Niwan said: Come here, I will tell you. In the cultivation of immortality there are three degrees, and in refining the Elixir there are three accomplishments.

In the Way of Celestial Immortality, one can undergo transmutation and ascend in flight to Heaven. Superior persons can study this Way. Lead is the body (*shen*) and Mercury is the mind (*xin*); Water is concentration (*ding*) and Fire is wisdom (*hui*). In the blink of an eye, one can coagulate [the Elixir], and in ten months, one achieves the birth of the embryo. This is the alchemical method of the higher degree. There are no trigrams and no lines, no pounds and no ounces. Its method is simple. Therefore it is transmitted through the Heart and is extremely easy to achieve.

In the Way of Water Immortality one can enter and exit the manifested and unmanifested domains. Median persons can study this Way.

---

[1] *Dianhua*, lit., "transformation." This term, which is also used in Buddhism, means attaining realization through an external influence, especially of a master.

Lead is Breath (*qi*) and Mercury is Spirit (*shen*); Fire is WU and Water is ZI. In one hundred days, one can attain the inchoate merging (*hunhe*) [of Yin and Yang], and in three years the image [of the Elixir] is formed. This is the alchemical method of the middle degree. Although there are trigrams and lines, there are no pounds or ounces. Its method gives importance to the subtle. Therefore it is transmitted by means of oral instructions, and it certainly can be achieved.

In the Way of Earthly Immortality one can preserve the [bodily] form and dwell in the world. Ordinary persons can study this Way. Lead is the essence (*jing*) and Mercury is the blood (*xue*); Water is the kidneys and Fire is the heart. In one year you can attain the coagulation [of Yin and Yang], and in nine years the practice is achieved. This is the alchemical method of the lower degree. Not only are there trigrams and lines, but there are also pounds and ounces. Its method is complex. Therefore it is transmitted in writing, but I am afraid that it is difficult to achieve.

In the alchemical method of the higher degree, the ingredients are Essence, Spirit, the *Hun*-soul, the *Po*-soul, and the Intention. The Fire phases are walking, standing, sitting, and lying down. The operation is spontaneity in clarity and quiescence.

In the alchemical method of the middle degree, the ingredients are liver, heart, spleen, lungs, and kidneys. The Fire phases are [established according to] the year, the month, the day, and the hour. The operation is embracing the Origin and guarding Unity.

In the alchemical method of the lower degree, the ingredients are essence, blood, marrow, breath, and the bodily juices. The Fire phases consist of closing, swallowing, striking, and rubbing. The operation is meditating on the ascent and descent [of Yin and Yang within the body].

Ultimately, the wondrous point does not lie in searching a clue in order to understand. Those who are mired in images and stuck in words become vain and arrogant. They will reach old age with no results.

Yuchan said: Reading the books on the Elixir requires many years and is like walking among thistles and thorns. Today, the dust has been cleared and the mirror is bright, the clouds have broken apart and the moon shines. The ten thousand phenomena have returned to unity, and the ten thousand illusions have returned to reality. Yet, I still do not know precisely where I should set to practice.

Chen Niwan said: This is a truly good question. To refine the Elixir, this is the essential:

- The altar, the furnace, the tripod, and the stove are the body (*shen*)
- The Spirit Chamber is the mind (*xin*)
- The collection is sitting straight and practicing concentration
- Circulating Fire is taking care and being attentive
- Advancing and withdrawing is action and cessation
- "Making dikes and embankments" is discontinuing the practice from time to time[2]
- Extracting and augmenting is the cyclical operation
- Bathing is the "fragrant vapor" of True Breath[3]
- Nourishing the Fire is ceasing thinking
- The "fight in the wild" is controlling and subduing the body and the mind[4]
- "Guarding the citadel" is coagulating the Spirit and gathering the Breath[5]

[2] This expression derives from the *Cantong qi* (The Seal of the Unity of the Three), 39:1 (translated above, p. 14).

[3] The expression "fragrant vapor" (*xunzheng*) also derives from the *Cantong qi*, 33:9–12: "When the Golden Sand enters the five inner organs, / a mist disperses like wind and rain, / a fragrant vapor extends to the four limbs, / and one's countenance grows pleasant, moistened and fair" (see Pregadio, *The Seal of the Unity of the Three*, p. 84).

[4] The expression "fight in the wild" (*yezhan*) derives from the *Book of Changes* (*Yijing*), hexagram Kun ☷ (no. 2), sixth line: "Dragons fighting in the wild. Their blood is black and yellow" (black and yellow denote Yang and Yin, respectively.). It is also used in the *Cantong qi*, 49:37–38 (see Pregadio, *The Seal*, p. 96) and in the *Wuzhen pian* (Awakening to Reality), "Jueju," poem 35 (see Cleary, *Understanding Reality*, p. 92). In the *Cantong qi*, this expression refers to the metaphoric fight between the Yin and Yang principles that takes place in the night of new moon, when the Yin principle has concluded its cycle and the Yang principle is ready to rise again.

[5] The expression "guarding the citadel" (*shoucheng*) derives from the *Wuzhen pian*, "Jueju," poem 35 (see Cleary, *Understanding Reality*, p. 127).

- Giving life and giving death is forgetting the mechanism and ceasing thoughts[6]
- The Mysterious-Female is the place where thought arises
- The conjunction is the merging [of the two into one]
- Achieving the Elixir is "reverting to the root" and "returning to the mandate"[7]
- "Shifting the Tripod" is moving Spirit[8]
- "Delivering the Embryo" is "having a body outside one's body"
- True Emptiness is returning to the fundament and reverting to the origin
- "Reaching completion" is "smashing Emptiness" (*dapo xukong*)

Therefore by being able to gather, one achieves form; and by being able to disperse, one achieves Breath (*qi*).[9] Coming and going without obstruction, one freely roams everywhere in a spontaneous way.

Yuchan asked: If one is diligent but has not encountered an accomplished person, one will certainly encounter that person; if one has encountered that person but is not diligent, one will forever be an inferior ghost. This being so, what are the signs that verify the method of cultivating the Elixir?

Chen Niwan said: When you begin to cultivate the Elixir, your Spirit is clear and your Breath is limpid; your body and mind are in

---

[6] "Giving life and giving death" refers to nourishing the precelestial Yang Breath and eliminating the postcelestial Yin breaths, respectively.

[7] These two expression derive from the *Daode jing* (Book of the Way and Its Virtue), sec. 16, and are also found in the *Wuzhen pian*, "Jueju," poem 51; see above, p. 83.

[8] "Shifting the Tripod" (*huanding*) is the name of one of the higher stages in several codifications of the Neidan practice; see Wang Mu, *Foundations of Internal Alchemy*, pp. 105–6. At that stage, spirit is moved from the middle to the upper Cinnabar Field.

[9] Bai Yuchan seems to refer here to what other Neidan texts express in terms of "coagulation" and "dispersion." The coagulation (of the Essence, of the five agents, etc.) results in the formation of the embryo, while its dispersion leads to the formation of Breath (*qi*).

harmony and at ease. All your lingering illnesses are extinguished, and your sleep is without dreams.[10] You can go without eating for one hundred days, and if you drink liquor you do not get drunk. When you arrive at that stage, your red blood changes into white blood, and your Yin breath is refined into Yang breath. Your body is as hot as fire, and you walk as though you were flying. You can dry water by holding it in your mouth, and you can cook meat by blowing on it. You do not use your mind to deal with the world of phenomena, you are "just so" (*ruru*) and do not move. You have demons and spirits at your service, and you conjure thunders and storms. With your ears, you can hear the Nine Heavens, and with your eyes, you can see ten thousand miles away. Your whole body is pure Yang, and your sinews and bones are made of gold and jade. As the Yang Spirit manifests itself in the realm of form, you enter and exit [the manifested and the unmanifested domains] in a spontaneous way.

When this occurs, the Way of long life without death has been completed. Unfortunately, the worldly people become stuck in discourses on the ingredients and the Fire phases. They think that those are things that have form and require "doing," but it is for this very reason that they cannot obtain the immediate awakening. How can they know that before the subdivision of the Inchoate [into the ten thousand things] there are no years, months, days, and hours? And that before one is generated by one's father and mother there are no essence, blood, breath, and bodily juices?

The Dao is fundamentally formless, but is represented by the Dragon and the Tiger; it is fundamentally nameless, but is symbolized by Lead and Mercury. For those who study Celestial Immortality, what is necessary is that "form and spirit are both wondrous," and that they join in their reality with the reality of the Dao. How can you become trapped by Yin and Yang within the five agents? You must leap outside of Heaven and Earth. Only then can you be called one who has attained the Dao.

---

[10] See *Zhuangzi*, ch. 6: "The True Man of ancient times slept without dreaming and woke without care; he ate without savoring and his breath came from deep inside"; trans. Watson, *The Complete Works of Chuang Tzu*, pp. 77–78.

Some people wonder, "This method and the method of Chan Buddhism are more or less the same." They just do not know that talking,
lecturing, and holding question-and-answer sessions all day long is
only dried wisdom; and that being withered and murky throughout
the years is only idle emptiness.[11] Instead, the learning of Celestial
Immortality is like a pearl in a plate of crystal: round and radiant, it
turns around, lively and incessantly. What we call a Celestial Immortal
is a Golden Immortal.[12] Yet, this is something so wondrous that it
cannot be conveyed in words. Who is able to know this, and who is
able to practice it? If one comprehends the *Jingang jing* (Diamond
Sutra) and the *Yuanjue jing* (Sutra of Complete Enlightenment), the
meaning of the Golden Elixir becomes clear.

What need is there of discriminating on what is different or the
same between Laozi and the Buddha? "In the world there are no two
Ways, and the sage does not have two minds."[13] Even more important:
"All human beings have it complete in themselves: it is entirely
achieved in everybody."[14] And moreover: "Wherever there is a green
poplar, you can tie your horse there," and "The road leading to the
capital Chang'an begins from the threshold of every house." Just take
the way that is shorter for you, and that is all.

Yuchan said: In the world, many are those who study immortality. Just
because they study but have no attainment, or because they have
attainment but do not put it into practice, or because they put it into
practice but are not assiduous, until old age they are content with
going towards death under the Nine Springs.[15] Is this not sad? Now I
intend to carve wood in order to transmit the oral instructions of my

[11] These two statements refer to Buddhism and Taoism, respectively. The
first one alludes to the dialogues between masters and disciples made of
"questions and answers" (*wenda*, Jpn. *mondō*), recorded in several Chan
Buddhist texts. "Withered" (*ku*) and "murky" (*hun*) are two terms used in the
Zhuangzi (ch. 15) and the *Daode jing* (sec. 15 and 20) to define the Taoist
saint. Here, however, both terms are used in a negative sense.
[12] "Golden Immortal" (*jinxian*) is a honorific designation of the Buddha.
[13] This statement derives from the *Xunzi*, ch. 21.
[14] This famous Chan Buddhist saying is found in the *Biyan lu* (Blue Cliff
Record), where it refers to the Buddha-Nature.
[15] The Nine Springs (*jiuquan*) are the netherworld.

Master to the world.[16] But if I do it, I would disclose much of the celestial mechanism. Shall I not be punished for this?

Niwan said: We would be teaching divine immortality to the world. If we were punished, Heaven would not be Heaven! The books say: "My destiny is in me, it is not in Heaven." What punishment could there be?

Yuchan said: Our Ancestral Master, Zhang Pingshu (Zhang Boduan), gave three times the transmission to a wrong person and incurred three times into troubles. How could that happen?[17]

Niwan said: He momentarily made an error of judgment, and in addition, his motives were not ordinary ones. Alas! As the saying goes, the Master is on the shores of Heaven, and the disciple is in a corner of the ocean. It is extremely difficult to understand someone who operates in the midst of defilement.

If today we publish this text and distribute it to the world, so that those who cultivate immortality can follow it and figure out the meaning, the wondrous principle would become clear. But all of this is given by Heaven. How could it be transmitted by means of a written essay or a spoken speech?

As long as you are able to be at rest and quiescent, to be without thoughts within your thoughts, and to make your practice pure, you will attain Unity. If you are for the whole day like a hen hatching her eggs, then Spirit will return, Breath will be restored, and you will spontaneously see the One Opening of the Mysterious Barrier. It is so great that there is nothing outside it, so small that there is nothing inside it. Thus, you should collect the precelestial One Breath and use it as the mother of the Golden Elixir. "Assiduously practice it,"[18] and in a short time you will be on a par with Zhongli Quan and Lü Dongbin. This is a result that has been verified.

[16] "Carving wood" is a metaphor for "writing a book." In other words, Bai Yuchan tells Chen Niwan that he intends to put his teachings in writing and to publish them.

[17] In his biographies and in several prefaces to the *Wuzhen pian*, Zhang Boduan is said to have given illicit transmissions of Internal Alchemy to three persons. After that, he repented and wrote his *Wuzhen pian*.

[18] *Daode jing*, sec. 41: "A superior person hears of the Dao, and assiduously practices it."

Thinking of those who study immortality without a guide, I have respectfully collected the main points of our questions and answers, and have entitled them "Essay on Resolving Doubts in the Cultivation of Immortality."

ESSAY ON "THE SPIRIT OF THE VALLEY DOES NOT DIE"

Translator's note: This essay is a commentary on *Daode jing* (Book of the Way and Its Virtue), sec. 6: "The Spirit of the Valley does not die: it is called the Mysterious-Female. The gate of the Mysterious-Female is called the root of Heaven and Earth. Unceasing and continuous, its operation never wears out."

The Valley is the Celestial Valley. Spirit is the Original Spirit within each person.

The Celestial Valley harbors creation and transformation and comprises Emptiness and Void. A valley on the Earth comprises the ten thousand things and contains mountains and rivers. As the human being shares its endowment with both Heaven and Earth, it also has a valley. That valley stores True Unity and houses Original Spirit.

Thus the head has nine palaces, which correspond on high to the Nine Heavens. The palace in the center is called Muddy Pellet (*niwan*). It is also called Yellow Court, Mount Kunlun, and Celestial Valley; its names are many. As for the palace in which the Original Spirit resides, it is as void as a valley. Since Spirit resides there, it is called Spirit of the Valley.

If Spirit is preserved, one lives; if it leaves, one dies. During the day, one is attached to objects, and during the night, one is attached to dreams; therefore Spirit cannot secure its residence. It is like the dream of the yellow millet that was not yet cooked,[19] or like the dream of

---

[19] In the "dream of the yellow millet" (of which several variants exist) Lü Dongbin falls asleep in a tavern while his yellow millet is cooking. Zhongli Quan is also there. Lü dreams that he passes the imperial examinations and begins an official career that eventually leads him to become a vice minister. He gets married twice with women from rich families, has children, and later is appointed prime minister. Things, however, take a wrong turn when he is

Nanke.[20] All the glories, disgraces, riches, and honors of a whole
lifetime, and all the miseries, sorrows, pleasures, and joys of a hundred years, are only a continuous single dream. This causes Spirit to
leave without returning and to wander around without coming back.
Thus the roads of life and death part from one another, and the paths
of obscurity and light are cut off from each other.

This shows that you cannot live by yourself—it is only Spirit that
makes you live; and you cannot die by yourself—it is only Spirit that
makes you die. If Spirit resides in that Valley and does not die, how
could you ever die?

However, it is only owed to the Mysterious-Female that "the Spirit
of the Valley does not die." The Mysterious is Yang and Heaven;[21] the
Female is Yin and Earth. Thus the two Breaths (*qi*) of the Mysterious
and the Female have a profound meaning. But unless one encounters
an accomplished person (*zhiren*) and receives the oral instructions,
one cannot understand this.

The *Lingshu neijing* (Inner Book of the Numinous Pivot) says:
"The Original Spirit of the Celestial Valley: if you are able to guard it,

falsely accused of corruption, his wife betrays him, and his children are
murdered. On his way to exile he finds himself in a thunderstorm and is close
to dying. In that moment, he wakes up. The yellow millet has not yet finished
to cook. Zhongli Quan explains to him that ordinary life is like that dream.
Lü Dongbin takes him as his master, and together they create the Zhong-Lü
school of Neidan.

[20] In the Nanke dream, Chunyu Fen falls asleep under a tree after heavy
drinking, and dreams that he visits an imaginary kingdom where he marries
the king's daughter. Long time later, he is appointed Governor of Nanke and
enjoys power and fame, together with his dearest friends in real life. One day,
however, Nanke is invaded by a neighboring kingdom, and shortly thereafter,
Chunyu's wife dies. The king orders him to go back home, where he wakes up
in his own bed. When he sees an ants' nest under the tree where he had fallen
asleep, he realizes that the wonderful places he had visited were nothing but a
formicary. That night, even the formicary is destroyed by a storm. Then
Chunyu finds out that his friends have died. He becomes aware of the vacuity
and the impermanence of the world and converts to Taoism.

[21] The text has *yuan*, "origin," which here stands for *xuan*, "mystery" or
"mysterious."

you will become a realized person (*zhenren*) of your own."[22] This means that within the human being, above there is the Muddy Pellet of the Celestial Valley, which is the mansion that stores Spirit; in the center there is the Crimson Palace of the Responding Valley, which is the mansion that stores Breath; and below there is the Origin of the Barrier of the Numinous Valley, which is the mansion that stores the Essence.[23]

The Celestial Valley is the Original Palace and the Chamber of the Original Spirit. It is what preserves the numinous Nature (*xing*), and is the essential of Spirit. The saintly persons are the essential of Heaven and Earth; they know the origins of transformations. Their Spirit is guarded in the Original Palace, and their Breath floats in the Mansion of the Female.[24] When Spirit and Breath conjoin, one spontaneously attains realization, becoming one with the Dao and entering the domain where there is no birth and death. Therefore [the *Daode jing*] says: "The Spirit of the Valley does not die: it is called the Mysterious-Female." The sage operates within the Mysterious-Female, and creation and transformation occur at the center of the "indistinct and vague."[25]

When the Breath of the Mysterious-Female enters its own roots, excessive idleness strays into anxiety, while attending to it strays into agitation. If you want it to be "unceasing and continuous," you should never interrupt it. To let it be continuous, maintain it by complying with its being-as-it-is (*ziran*). After a long time, your Spirit of its own becomes peaceful and your breathing of its own becomes stable. Your Nature enters what-is-as-it-is. In the wondrous operation of non-doing, it will never be wearied or exhausted. Therefore [the *Daode jing*] says: "Its operation never wears out."

From this, it becomes clear that the Mysterious-Female is the correct path of the ascent and descent of the Mother of Breath

---

[22] The received version of the *Huangdi neijing lingshu* (Inner Book of the Yellow Emperor: The Numinous Pivot) does not contain this passage. It is unclear, however, whether Bai Yuchan refers precisely to this text.

[23] The Celestial Valley (*tiangu*), the Responding Valley (*yinggu*), and the Numinous Valley (*linggu*) are the upper, middle, and lower Cinnabar Fields, respectively.

[24] Mansion of the Female (*pinfu*) is another name of the lower Cinnabar Field.

[25] For this expression, see above, page 95 note 23.

through its two sources, one above and one below.²⁶ The worldly people do not inquire into its roots and do not investigate its origin. Instead, they take the "mysterious" to be the nose, and the "female" to be the mouth. But if the nose and the mouth were the Mysterious-Female, then what would the Gate of the Mysterious-Female be? Nothing of this kind can ever fulfill the wonder of the Mysterious-Female. Unless one is a great saint, how can one inquire into these principles?

---

²⁶ The Mother of Breath (qimu) is the source of Original Breath (yuanqi). See Zhuangzi, ch. 6: "The Way has its reality and its signs but is without action or form. . . . Fu Xi got it and entered into the Mother of Breath" (trans. Watson, p. 81). Cheng Xuanying's (fl. 631–50) commentary adds: "The Mother of Breath is the Mother of Original Breath. It responds to the Dao. [Fu Xi] attained the highest Dao and therefore he was able to draw the eight trigrams and from them to develop the six lines, to harmonize Yin and Yang and to join with the Original Breath."

8 Model Images of the Golden Elixir

Jindan faxiang 金丹法象

Weng Baoguang 翁葆光 (fl. 1173)

Although the *Jindan faxiang*, or *Model Images of the Golden Elixir*, does not rank among the main Neidan texts, it is included in the present anthology as it contains one of the most comprehensive lists of synonyms and secret names found in the literature of Internal Alchemy.

The author, Weng Baoguang, wrote one of the main commentaries to the *Wuzhen pian* (Awakening to Reality), entitled *Wuzhen pian zhushu* (Commentary and Subcommentary to the *Wuzhen pian*). In addition, he composed the *Wuzhen zhizhi xiangshuo sansheng biyao* (Straightforward Directions and Detailed Explanations on the *Wuzhen pian* and the Secret Essentials of the Three Vehicles), which contains supplementary materials on the *Wuzhen pian*. The *Jindan faxiang* is the last part of the *Biyao*.[1] It is divided into seven sections, entitled "Yang" (92 synonyms), "Yin" (id.), "Yin within Yang" (88 synonyms), "Yang within Yin" (id.), "Central Palace" (96 synonyms), "External Medicine" (93 synonyms), and "Internal Medicine" (35 synonyms).

In this translation, I have arranged the synonyms of "Yin" and "Yang," and those of "Yin within Yang" and "Yang within Yin," into parallel columns, as the terms in each pair of synonyms perfectly match one another. The synonyms of the "Central Palace" are translated in a separate section. In the received text, the final two sections of the text ("External Medicine" and "Internal Medicine") contain errors and omissions. Reconstructing the correct sequences of synonyms appears to be impossible, and these sections are omitted from the present translation.

---

[1] The expression "Model Images" (*faxiang*) in the title of Weng Baoguang's work derives from a sentence in the "Appended Sayings" ("Xici") of the *Book of Changes* (*Yijing*): "Among models and images, none is greater than Heaven and Earth" (A.11; see Wilhelm, *The I-ching or Book of Changes*, p. 319). This sentence is also found in the *Cantong qi* (The Seal of the Unity of the Three), 77:1 (see Pregadio, *The Seal of the Unity of the Three*, p. 115).

YIN AND YANG

Translator's note: With a few exceptions, terms related to "Yang" are in the left column, and terms related to "Yin" are in the right column.

Heaven	Earth
Sun	Moon
Shen	*Shang* [2]
Qian ☰	Kun ☷ [3]
Li ☲	Kan ☵ [4]
Father	Mother
Husband	Wife
Lord	Subject
Host	Guest
Wife	Husband [5]
Nature	Emotions
Breath	Essence
Spirit	Existence
Capping ceremony	Marriage ceremony [6]

[2] *Shen* and *Shang* are two of the twenty-eight lodges (*xiu*, constellations crossed by the apparent path of the Sun around the Earth) respectively belonging to the western and the eastern sectors of Heaven (see table 8, p. 264). *Shang* is usually called *xin* 心.

[3] Qian and Kun represent True Yang and True Yin, respectively.

[4] Li and Kan represent Yang containing True Yin and Yin containing True Yang, respectively.

[5] Note that, three lines above, these terms are inverted. There could be many reasons why, in a Neidan context, the "wife" is Yang and the "husband" is Yin; broadly, they derive from the view that Yin contains True Yang, and Yang contains True Yin.

[6] *Cantong qi*, 11:5: "The auras of the capping and the marriage ceremonies are tied to one another" (Pregadio, *The Seal*, p. 73). Traditionally, the "capping" ceremony (*guan*, for the coming of age) and the marriage ceremony (*hun*) marked the acquirement of social status for a male and a female, respectively.

Hun (celestial soul)	*Po* (earthly soul)
Eyes	Ears
Fire	Water
South	North
JIA	GENG [7]
WU	ZI [8]
BING	REN [9]
2	1 [10]
7	6 [11]
Heart	Kidneys
Flower	Wine [12]
Jade	Gold
Dragon	Tiger
Snake	Turtle
Masculine	Feminine
Male	Female
Empty	Full
Breath	Liquor [13]

[7] These celestial stems represent the East and West, respectively (see table 5, p. 261).

[8] These earthly branches represent the South and the North, respectively (see table 6, p. 262).

[9] These celestial stems represent the South and the North, respectively (see table 5, p. 261).

[10] These are the generation numbers of Fire and Water, respectively (see table 2, p. 258).

[11] These are the accomplishment numbers of Fire and Water, respectively (see table 2, p. 258).

[12] *Wuzhen pian* (Awakening to Reality), "Jueju," poem 33: "As soon as the eldest son drinks the wine of the West, the youngest daughter first opens the flower of the North."

[13] These terms usually refer to the "breath of the kidneys" and the "liquor of the lungs" ("liquor of the heart"), which represent Yang within Yin and

Above	Below
Hub	Axle
Ingredient	Medicine [14]
Vessel	Tripod [15]
Square	Compass
Tracing [the origin]	Flowing [to the end] [16]
Mercury	Lead
Light	Heavy
Floating	Sinking
Essence	Radiance [17]
Graphs	Chirping [18]
WU	JI [19]
Great	Small
Movement	Quiescence
Outward	Inward
Hare	Crow
Firm	Yielding

Yin within Yang, respectively.

[14] This pair of synonyms intends to show that the compound word *yaowu*, meaning "ingredients," refers to both the Yin and Yang ingredients of the Elixir: the word *yao* is assigned to the Yin principle, and the word *wu* is assigned to the Yang principle.

[15] In the Neidan use of the compound word *dingqi* 鼎器, *qi* 器 (lit., "vessel") usually stands for the furnace.

[16] Tentative translation.

[17] These terms refer to the "essence of the Moon" (*yuejing*, Yang within Yin) and the "radiance of the Sun" (*riguang*, Yin within Yang), respectively. See *Cantong qi*, sec. 7 (translated above, p. 5).

[18] Possibly an allusion to the graphs (*zi*) used to represent the six sounds emitted in certain breathing practices, which replace the "chirping" (*ming*) of breath produced by other practices. See *Cantong qi*, sec. 26, translated above, p. 11.

[19] These two celestial stems represent the Yang and Yin aspects of Unity, respectively (see table 5, p. 261).

Red	Black
Exhaling	Inhaling
Non-Being	Being
Odd	Even
Virtue	Punishment
Rites	Wisdom [20]
Joy	Anger
Reward	Penalty
Man	Woman
Daytime	Nighttime
Heat	Cold
Celestial *Hun*-soul	Earthly *Po*-soul
Qian ☰ emblem	Kun ☷ emblem
Sun's *Hun*-soul	Moon's *Po*-soul
Extension and Wings	Emptiness and Rooftop [21]
Fang-6	*Mao*-7 [22]
First moon quarter	Last moon quarter [23]
Mare of Qian ☰	Ox of Kun ☷
Zhen ☳ Dragon	Kan ☵ Tiger

[20] "Rites" (*li*) literally denotes the institutions, rules, and conventions that regulate social life. In a Neidan context, however, "rites" refers to the perfect operation of what is external, just like "wisdom" refers to the perfect operation of what is internal.

[21] Extension (*zhang*) and Wings (*yi*) are two lodges belonging to the southern sector of Heaven, and Emptiness (*xu*) and Rooftop (*wei*) are two other lodges belong to its northern sector (see table 8, p. 264).

[22] *Fang* and *mao* are two lodges respectively belonging to the eastern and the western sectors of Heaven (see table 8, p. 264).

[23] I.e., the waxing and the waning moon, respectively representing the first half of the month (ruled by the Yang principle) and its second half (ruled by the Yin principle).

Fusang tree	Mount Hua[24]
Mount Kunlun	Meandering River [25]
Lovely Maid	Infant
Eldest son	Youngest daughter [26]
Wood-son in law	Metal-married daughter
WU-Soil	JI-Soil
2-South	1-North
Earth-2	Heaven-1
Vermilion Sand	Black Lead [27]
Laminar malachite	Mountains and marshes
Green Dragon	White Tiger
Fire-Dragon	Water-Tiger
Dragon of the Sea	Tiger of the Mountain
Red Phoenix	Black Turtle
Qian ☰ Furnace	Kun ☷ Tripod
Jade Tripod	Gold Furnace
Jade pond	Western stream
Inferior virtue	Superior virtue
"Vague and indistinct"	"Dim and obscure" [28]

[24] *Wuzhen pian*, "Jueju," poem 19: "On the top of Mount Hua, the male Tiger roars; near the Fusang tree, at the bottom of the sea, the female Dragon howls." The Fusang tree and Mount Hua represent East and West, respectively.

[25] The Meandering River is said to be found on Mount Kunlun, at the center of the world.

[26] In the *Book of Changes*, the eldest son and the youngest daughter correspond to the trigrams Zhen ☳ and Dui ☱, respectively.

[27] Vermilion Sand (*zhusha*) is one of the common names of cinnabar. Cinnabar and black lead represent Yang containing True Yin and Yin containing True Yang, respectively.

[28] *Daode jing* (Book of the Way and Its Virtue), sec. 21: "Vague and indistinct! Within there is something. Dim and obscure! Within there is an essence." See also *Wuzhen pian*, "Jueju," poem 44: "Within the vague and

True Sand	True Mercury
Vermilion Sparrow	Dark Warrior [29]
Cinnabar Yang [30]	True Yin
Tripod of the Vermilion Sand	Furnace of the Supine Moon [31]
"What is generated at JIA-YI"	"What is generated at GENG-XIN" [32]

YIN WITHIN YANG AND YANG WITHIN YIN

Translator's note: With a few exceptions, terms related to "Yin within Yang" are in the left column, and terms related to "Yang within Yin" are in the right column.

Zhen ☳	Dui ☱
Li ☲	Kan ☵
Wife	Husband
Subject	Lord
Guest	Host
MAO	YOU [33]
JIA	GENG [34]
East	West

indistinct, seek for the image; within the dim and obscure, look for the true essence."

[29] Two of the main emblems of the South and the North, respectively.

[30] *Danyang* 丹陽 ("Cinnabar Yang") may be an error for *zhenyang* 真陽, "True Yang."

[31] *Wuzhen pian*, "Jueju," poem 4: "In the Furnace of the Supine Moon, the Jade Pistil is born; in the Tripod of the Vermilion Sand, the Water Silver is level."

[32] JIA and YI are the two celestial stems corresponding to the East; GENG and XIN are the two celestial stems corresponding to the West.

[33] These two earthly branches represent the East and the West, respectively (see table 6, p. 262).

[34] These two celestial stems represent the East and the West, respectively (see table 5, p. 261).

Qualities [35]	Nature
Humanity	Righteousness
Left	Right
3	4 [36]
8	9 [37]
Floating	Sinking
Liver	Lungs
Wood	Metal
Woman	Man
Ingredient	Medicine [38]
Father	Mother
Sun's *Hun*-soul	Moon's *Po*-soul
Crow's marrow	Hare's lard
Lovely Maid	Golden Old Man
People	Parents
Guest	Host
Green beauty [39]	Old gentleman [40]
Woman in Li ☲	Man in Kan ☵
True Mercury	True Lead
Liquor of Wood	Essence of Metal

[35] In the realized state, *qing* does not denote the ordinary "emotions," but the personal "qualities" (temperament, attitudes, etc.) that manifest externally one's inner nature.

[36] These are the generation numbers of Wood and Metal, respectively (see table 2, p. 258).

[37] These are the accomplishment numbers of Wood and Metal, respectively (see table 2, p. 258).

[38] See p. 124, note 14 above.

[39] *Wuzhen pian*, "Jueju," poem 33: "After you have him meet the Green Beauty, lock them at once in the Yellow House."

[40] *Wuzhen pian*, "Jueju," poem 26: "Coming back, she enters the Yellow Dame's dwelling, and marries the Lord of Metals making him an old gentleman."

Fire's Mercury	Water's Metal
Yellow Sprout	White Snow [41]
Jade Liquor	Golden Liquor
Spirit Water	Flowery Pond
Fire-Dragon	Water-Tiger
Female Dragon	Male Tiger
Golden Crow	Jade Hare
True Dragon	True Tiger
True Yin	True Yang
Feminine mother	Masculine father
Feminine Yin	Masculine Yang
Yin Fire	Yang Water
Breath of Yang	Essence of Yin
Flowing Pearl	Golden Flower [42]
Woman's green	Man's white
Feminine Fire	Masculine Metal
Red Lead	Black Lead
Vermilion Sand	Water Silver
"Joined pears"	"Fire jujubes"
East-2	West-4
Jade Mushroom	Knife-point [43]

[41] *Wuzhen pian*, "Lüshi," poem 11: "The Yellow Sprout and the White Snow are not difficult to seek; to attain them, you must rely on deeply virtuous conduct."

[42] *Cantong qi*, sec. 62:1–4: "The Flowing Pearl of Great Yang desires ever to leave you. When, at last, it finds the Golden Flower, it turns about, and the two rely upon each other" (Pregadio, *The Seal*, p. 104).

[43] The *zhi* is a "plant of immortality," whose name is impossible to translate into Western languages. Sometimes it is understood as "mushroom," and here I adopt this term. "Knife-point" (or "point of the spatula," *daogui*) is a term derived from Waidan, where it denotes a small quantity of the Elixir collected from the alchemical vessel by using this tool. In an extended sense, it

Foundation of the Elixir	Mother of the Elixir
True Fire	True Water
wu in the North	zi in the South
Dragon in the West	Tiger in the East [44]
Water Silver	Jade Pistil [45]
Woman in the Heaven's mystery	Man in the Earth's yellow [46]
Crow in the Sun	Hare in the Moon
Mother's blood	Father's essence
Breath of the Dragon's moon quarter	Breath of the Tiger's moon quarter
"The Dragon exhales onto the Tiger"	"The Tiger inhales the Dragon['s essence]" [47]
"Whiteness of the Yin Fire"	"Lead of the Yellow Sprout" [48]
Water within Fire	Fire within Water
"The Red enters the Black"	"The Black enters the Red"
Marrow of the Red Phoenix	Essence of the Black Turtle
Father of the Flowing Mercury	Mother of the Yellow Gold
Essence of Red Lead	Marrow of Black Lead

connotes the Elixir itself. The "Jade Mushroom" is the Yin Elixir, and the "knife-point" is the Yang Elixir.

[44] In these terms, the ordinary positions of the Dragon (East, Yang) and the Tiger (West, Yin) are inverted. Therefore the Dragon is an emblem of Yin within Yang (True Yin), and the Tiger is a emblem of Yang within Yin (True Yang).

[45] See p. 127, note 31 above.

[46] *Xuan* ("mystery") also denotes a dark color, which is an attribute of Heaven. Yellow is the color of the Earth. The "Explanation of the Sentences" ("Wenyan") appendix to the *Book of Changes* says about this: "Mysterious and Yellow means the mingling of Heaven and Earth: Heaven is Mysterious and Earth is Yellow" (sec. 4; see Wilhelm, p. 395).

[47] *Cantong qi*, 64:5–6: "The Dragon exhales onto the Tiger, the Tiger inhales the Dragon's essence" (Pregadio, *The Seal*, p. 106).

[48] *Cantong qi*, 82:17–18: "The whiteness of the Yin Fire, the lead of the Yellow Sprout: the Two Sevens gather together to support and assist man" (Pregadio, *The Seal*, p. 120).

Mercury in the Sand	Silver in the Water [49]
JI in Li ☲	WU in Kan ☵
Woman within Kun ☷	Man within Qian ☰
One Yin within Li ☲	One Yang within Kan ☵
"The Moon is white at the mountain's peak"	"The Sun is red at the pool's bottom" [50]
Flowing Pearl of Great Yang [51]	River Chariot of the North [52]
"JI in Li ☲ is the radiance of the Sun"	"WU in Kan ☵ is the essence of the Moon" [53]
Lady in green attire	Gentleman in white silk [54]
Foreign child with emerald eyes	Old child with white hair [55]
Woman-and-man's form	Man-and-woman's body
True Mercury in the Sand	True Silver in the Lead
Water taken within Breath	Breath taken within Water

[49] *Wuzhen pian*, "Lüshi," poem 4: "If in the Golden Tripod you want to detain the Mercury in the Vermilion, first from the Jade Pond send down the Silver in the Water" (see above, p. 69). One of the most common Chinese names of cinnabar is *zhusha*, or Vermilion Sand. Therefore what the *Wuzhen pian* calls "the vermilion" is the same as what Weng Baoguang calls "the sand."

[50] *Wuzhen pian*, "Lüshi," poem 8: "The Sun is red at the pool's bottom, and Yin wondrously is exhausted; the Moon is white at the mountain's peak, and the Medicine puts forth new sprouts."

[51] See p. 129, note 42 above.

[52] *Cantong qi*, 22:7–10: "At the beginning of Yin and Yang, Mystery holds the Yellow Sprout; it is the ruler of the five metals, the River Chariot of the northern direction" (translated above, p. 9).

[53] These sentences are quoted from the *Cantong qi*, sec. 7 (translated above, p. 5).

[54] *Wuzhen pian*, "Wuyan siyun": "The lady is dressed in green attire, the gentleman dons white silk; if you see them you cannot use them, if you use them you cannot see them."

[55] The "foreign child with emerald eyes" and the "old child with white hair" are usually identified as Bodhidharma and Laozi, respectively. In Neidan, however, the first name is also used as synonym of True Mercury, and the second one, of True Lead.

"Inside the masculine is stored the feminine"	"Within the black there is the white"[56]
Eight ounces of Crow's liver	Half pound of Hare's marrow [57]
Mercury generated within the Sand	Sand produced inside Lead
"What is generated at BING-DING"	"What is generated at REN-GUI" [58]
Liquor generated within the Breath	Breath generated within the Liquor
Lovely Maid of 2 and 8	Gentleman of 9 and 3 [59]
"The dim and obscure essence"	"The vague and indistinct something" [60]
"Something within the vague and indistinct"	"Essence within the dim and obscure" [61]
Water Silver in the Tripod of the Vermilion Sand	Jade Pistil in the Furnace of the Supine Moon [62]
Half pound of Water of the last moon-quarter	Half pound of Metal of the first moon-quarter

[56] *Wuzhen pian*, "Jueju," poem 43: "Within the white there is the black: this is the Mother of the Elixir. The male harbors the female: this is the Embryo of Sainthood."

[57] In the traditional Chinese weight system, one pound (*jin*) is divided into sixteen ounces (*liang*). "Eight ounces" therefore is equivalent to "half pound." The two synonyms refer to the equal parts of Mercury (True Yin) and Lead (True Yang) that are required to form the Elixir.

[58] BING and DING are the two celestial stems corresponding to the South; REN and GUI are the two celestial stems corresponding to the North.

[59] *Wuzhen pian*, "Xijiang yue," poem 5: "To which family does the Lovely Maid of 2 and 8 belong, and where does the Gentleman of 9 and 3 come from?" In his commentary to these verses, Weng Baoguang says: "The numbers 2 and 8 are Yin; the Lovely Maid is one's own True Breath, also called Liquor of Wood. The numbers 9 and 3 are Yang; the Gentleman is one's own Yang Elixir, also called Essence of Metal" (*Wuzhen pian zhushu*, ch. 7).

[60] See p. 126, note 28 above.

[61] See p. 126, note 28 above.

[62] See p. 127, note 31 above.

"Mercury is the Water within the Sand"	"Metal is the Sand within the Water" [63]

CENTRAL PALACE

Soil

center

5 [64]

10 [65]

Messenger [66]

Intention

Spleen

Forefather

True Soil

Virtue of Soil

Earthenware crucible

Original Spirit

Divine Treasure [67]

Mysterious Barrier

Mysterious Gate

True Lead

Metal Mother

Metal Queen

Metal Tripod

[63] These sentences are found in Peng Xiao's *Zhouyi cantong qi fenzhang tong zhenyi* (The True Meaning of the *Cantong qi*, with a Subdivision into Sections), commentary to sec. 68.

[64] This is the generation number of Soil (see table 2, 258).

[65] This is the accomplishment number of Soil (see table 2, p. 258).

[66] This name alludes to the mediating function of Soil, which arbitrates between Yin and Yang and allows them to join one another. *Xin*, however, also means "trustworthiness."

[67] Or: Spirit Treasure.

Metal Embryo
Tripod of Lead
Tripod of Mercury
Mount Kunlun
Great Regulator
Palace of Qian ☰
Position of Kun ☷
Flowery Pond
Divine Embryo [68]
Divine Hut [69]
Mother's dwelling
WU and JI
Numinous Root
Embryo of Sainthood
Numinous Door
Great Abyss
Center of the compass
Pole star
"The inchoate"
Room of the Elixir
Mansion of Breath
Origin of the Barrier
Cinnabar Field
Crimson Palace
Yellow Court
Yellow Dame
Yellow Path
Original Center
Mysterious Opening

[68] Or: Spirit Embryo.
[69] Or: Spirit Hut. This term usually denotes the upper Cinnabar Field.

Mother of the Medicine

Foundation of the Elixir

Iced Pot

"Holding the Three" [70]

Star officer

Mother's Embryo

Northern Ocean

Empty Mystery

Yellow House [71]

Opening of going back to the root

Barrier of returning to the mandate

Furnace of the Supine Moon

Tripod of the Suspended Womb

Gate of the Mysterious-Female

Gate of WU and JI

Furnace of Creation and Transformation[72]

Mechanism of Creation and Transformation

Cavity of Conjunction

Furnace of the Great One

Cavity of Spirit and Breath

Altar for guarding Unity

Palace of the Central Yellow

Mansion of the Cinnabar Origin

Cinnabar Hinge

Mother of the Yellow Metal

[70] Probably an abbreviation of *hansan weiyi*, "holding the Three into One," or "that which holds the Three as One," with reference to the unity of Essence, Breath, and Spirit.

[71] See p. 128, note 39 above.

[72] *Wuzhen pian*, "Jueju," poem 49: "The one ingredient, the fine ghee of the Snowy Mountains, pours into the Eastern Sun's Furnace of Creation and Transformation."

Mansion of the "inaudible and invisible"[73]
"Gate of all marvels"[74]
Palace of Great Tenuity
Gate of the Inchoate
Dwelling of giving and taking life
Virtue of the Yellow Emperor's Soil
"The Yellow Center spreads through the veining"[75]
Divine Tripod of the Lord of Soil
"Born before Heaven and Earth" [76]
Golden Tripod of the Inchoate
"The white and the black tally with one another"[77]
Tripod and Vessel of Jiji ☰
"Heaven and Earth, the model images"[78]
His Majesty's Virtue of Earth
Precelestial Metal Embryo
Spirit Water and Flowery Pond
"Similar in kind to a hen's egg"[79]
Root of exhaling and inhaling

[73] *Daode jing*, sec. 14: "Watching, you do not see it: it is called invisible. Listening, you do not hear it: it is called inaudible. Grasping, you do not get it: it is called imperceptible."

[74] *Daode jing*, sec. 1: "Mystery and then again mystery, gate of all marvels."

[75] *Cantong qi*, 19:1–2: "From the Yellow Center it gradually spreads through the veining: moistening and impregnating, it reaches the flesh and the skin" (Pregadio, *The Seal*, p. 77).

[76] This phrase is found in several texts, including the *Daode jing*, sec. 25 ("There is something inchoate and yet accomplished, born before Heaven and Earth"); the *Zhuangzi*, ch. 6 (see Watson, *The Complete Works of Chuang Tzu*, p. 81); and the *Cantong qi*, sec. 24 (Pregadio, *The Seal*, p. 79).

[77] *Cantong qi*, 56:1–4: "Similar in kind to a hen's egg, the white and the black tally with one another. But one inch in size, yet it is the beginning" (Pregadio, *The Seal*, p. 101).

[78] See p. 121, note 1 above.

[79] See note 77 above.

9 Questions and Answers on the Golden Elixir

Jindan wenda 金丹問答

Xiao Tingzhi 蕭廷芝 (fl. 1260–64)

The *Jindan wenda*, or *Questions and Answers on the Golden Elixir*, is one of several works found in the *Jindan da chengji* (A Great Anthology on the Golden Elixir). It is entirely made of short explanations of several dozen terms and sentences found in Neidan texts, often with the support of quotations from earlier works.

The author, Xiao Tingzhi, was a second-generation disciple of Bai Yuchan (1194–1229?) through his master, Peng Si (fl. 1217–51), and as such belonged to the Southern Lineage (Nanzong) of Neidan. His work, however, shows that he also drew from texts belonging to the Zhong-Lü lineage. Other works in the *Jindan da chengji* include commentaries to the *Ruyao jing* (Mirror for Compounding the Medicine) and to the *Qinyuan chun* (Spring at the Qin Garden), one of the main Neidan poems attributed to Lü Dongbin.

This translation contains about one third of the text (thirty-two of the original ninety-three entries). It is based on the version found in the *Xiuzhen shishu* (Ten Books on the Cultivation of Reality), a vast anthology of materials mainly related to the Southern Lineage. Another edition is found in the *Yangsheng bilu* (Secret Records on Nourishing Life). I have added titles and short notes to almost all translated entries.

137

THE REVERTED ELIXIR OF THE GOLDEN LIQUOR

Question: Why is [the Elixir] called Reverted Elixir of the Golden Liquor (*jinye huandan*)?

Answer: Golden Liquor means Metal and Water. "Metal is the mother of Water—the mother is hidden in the embryo of her son." Therefore it is called Reverted Elixir.

A worthy man of the past said: "Elixir (*dan*) means the Cinnabar Field (*dantian*), Liquor means the liquor of the lungs." Since the liquor of the lungs reverts to the Cinnabar Field, it is called Golden Liquor reverted to the Cinnabar [Field].

Xiao Tingzhi gives two explanations of the term "Reverted Elixir of the Golden Liquor." Both are based on the sense of the word *jin* in the system of the five agents, where this word does not mean "gold," but "metal." According to the first explanation, "gold" and "liquor" respectively refer to Metal and Water, and "reverted Elixir" means the inversion of the generative sequence of these two agents that occurs in the alchemical process. Ordinarily, Water is the child of Metal, but in alchemy Metal is the child of Water; therefore Metal is found in the womb of Water. The quotation from the *Cantong qi* (The Seal of the Unity of the Three), sec. 23 (translated above, p. 11), refers to this inversion.

To make sense of the second explanation, the term *jinye huandan* requires a different translation. Here *dan* does not mean Elixir, but is an abbreviation of *dantian*, the lower Cinnabar Field. The Golden Liquor is the essence ("liquor") of the lungs (associated with the agent Metal) that returns to the Cinnabar Field.

THE FIRE

Question: What is Fire (*huo*)?

Answer: Fire is the True Breath of Great Yang; it is the Yang within Kan ☵. This is what the Realized Man Ziqing (Bai Yuchan) meant when he said: "Fire is kindled within Kan."

Bai Yuchan (1194–1229?) is the fifth patriarch of the Southern Lineage. See Chapter 7 above.

THE PHASES

Question: What are the phases (*hou*)?

Answer: Five days make one phase, because with them a sexagesimal cycle is complete: in one day there are twelve [double] hours, in five days there are sixty [double] hours, and they complete a sexagesimal cycle.

Ziyang (Zhang Boduan) said: "The work of one notch (*ke*) contains the nodal phases of a whole year." When you kindle the fire, a whole celestial circuit occurs in a short while (*qingke*).

In this entry, Xiao Tingzhi gives two examples of the meaning of "phase" (*hou*). The first paragraph refers to the sixty combinations of celestial stems and earthly branches that are used to define a complete time cycle (see table 7, p. 263). The actual length of the cycle varies according to the basic time unit. When the basic unit is the "double hour" (*shi*), a "phase" consists of five days, which contain sixty "double hours."

In the second paragraph, Xiao Tingzhi adds another definition. Here the time unit is the nodal phases (*jiehou*, more commonly called "nodal breaths," *jieqi*), i.e., the twenty-four periods of fifteen days that form one "celestial circuit," or one year. As the next entry shows in more detail, these longer stages are reproduced in a time as short as one "notch" (*ke*), the smallest time unit in premodern Chinese reckoning.

The sentence attributed to Zhang Boduan is found in the preface to the *Jindan sibai zi* (Four Hundred Words on the Golden Elixir), in *Xiuzhen shishu*, ch. 5.

THE FIRE PHASES

Question: How should the Fire phases (*huohou*) be used?

Answer: For the year use the month, for the month use the day, for the day use the [double] hour, for the [double] hour use the notch (*ke*).

This famous statement derives from the *Zhong Lü chuandao ji* (The Transmission of the Dao from Zhongli Quan to Lü Dongbin: An Anthology), sec. "Lun sishi" (On The Four Seasons) and "Lun chaoyuan" (On Having Audience at the Origin), which, however, does not mention the "notch."

Each time period corresponds to—and therefore can be represented by—a shorter time period. This is the principle at the basis of the Fire phases performed in the first stage of the Neidan practice. The last term mentioned here, *ke* or "notch," is the time unit lower than the *shi*, or "double hour." In premodern China, the day was divided into 100 *ke*, equivalent to the notches there were marked on a water clepsydra. While each *ke* formally corresponds to about 15 minutes in modern reckoning, the expression "one *ke*" essentially means "a short while," but sometimes is also used in the sense of "one instant" in an inner time scale. (This is the sense in which the word *ke* in used in the last entry translated in the present chapter.)

TRUE UNITY

Question: What is True Unity (*zhenyi*)?

Answer: If you are able to take the Celestial Reality that is in yourself and to secure it within the Celestial Valley, this is the Way of guarding True Unity. This is what Jindong zhu (Lord of the Golden Cavern) meant when he said: "The True One resides within the Great Abyss of the North Pole."

Each of the three Cinnabar Fields is called a "valley": the lower one is the Numinous Valley (*linggu*), the middle one is the Responding Valley (*yinggu*), and the upper one is the Celestial Valley (*tiangu*).
    The sentence attributed to Jindong zhu—one of the mythical Three Emperors of antiquity—is probably based on a passage in the *Baopu zi neipian* (Inner Chapters of the Master Who Embraces Spontaneous Nature), ch. 18, which states: "The One resides in the North Pole, in the midst of the Great Abyss."

MOVEMENT AND QUIESCENCE

Question: What are movement and quiescence (*dongjing*)?

Answer: Yang rules on movement, Yin rules on quiescence. Cuixu (Chen Nan) said: "Search for quiescence within movement; have activity within quiescence. The application of movement and quiescence is transmitted by word of mouth."

The sentences attributed to Chen Nan (?–1213, fourth patriarch of the Southern Lineage) are not found in his extant works.

THE FURNACE

Question: What is the furnace (*lu*)?

Answer: In the alchemical methods of the higher degree, the furnace is Spirit, the medicine is Nature (*xing*), Water is concentration (*ding, samādhi*), Fire is wisdom (*hui, prajñā*).

In the alchemical methods of the middle degree, the furnace is Spirit, the medicine is Breath, Fire is the Sun, Water is the Moon.

In the alchemical methods of the lower degree, the furnace is the body, the medicine is Breath, Fire is the heart, Water is the kidneys.

In addition, there are the Furnace of the Supine Moon (*yanyue lu*) and the Jade Furnace (*yulu*).

The main point of this entry is to show that different terms—such as furnace, medicine, Fire, and Water—take on different meanings according to the different stages or types of Neidan. (Other examples of the same principle are found in Chapters 7 and 11 below.)

THE TRIPOD

Question: What is the tripod (*ding*)?

Answer: It is what the Realized Man Bao meant when he said: "The Golden Tripod is close to the Muddy Pellet." This is where the Yellow Emperor cast the Nine Tripods.

The Muddy Pellet (*niwan*) is the upper Cinnabar Field. The last sentence refers to the legend of the Yellow Emperor, who cast a tripod on the shores of a lake and then ascended to Heaven as an immortal. In other versions of the legend, he used the tripod to compound an elixir, or the "nine elixirs." According to the passage attributed to the Realized Man Bao (whose identity is unknown to me), this occurred by means of inner practices.

THE THREE BARRIERS

Question: What are the Three Barriers (*sanguan*)?

Answer: The head is the Barrier of Heaven. The feet are the Barrier of Earth. The hands are the Barrier of Man.

These definitions of the Three Barriers ultimately derive from the early Taoist meditation practices, where the upper barrier is represented, however, by the mouth. See the *Huangting jing* (Book of the Yellow Court), "Inner" version, poem 18: "The mouth is the Barrier of Heaven, the pivot of Essence and Spirit, / the feet are the Barrier of Earth, the doors of life and destiny, / the hands are the Barrier of Man, they handle flourishing and decay."

THE THREE INNER ESSENTIALS

Question: What are the three inner essentials (*nei sanyao*)?

Answer: The first essential is the great Abyssal Pond (*yuanchi*). The second essential is the Crimson Palace (*jianggong*). The third essential is the Door of the Earth (*dihu*).

These three terms refer to the upper, middle, and lower Cinnabar Field, respectively. The Door of the Earth is otherwise identified either as "the space between the kidneys" or as the nose.

THE THREE OUTER ESSENTIALS

Question: What are the three outer essentials (*wai sanyao*)?

Answer: The mouth and the nose are altogether three openings. They are the gates through which Spirit and Breath come and go. During the practice, you harmonize respiration with your nose, seal the breath with your tongue, and close the cavity.

This passage derives in part from the preface to the *Jindan sibai zi* (Four Hundred Words on the Golden Elixir) in *Xiuzhen shishu*, ch. 5. For the meaning of "cavity," see the next entry.

THE CAVITY

Question: What is the "cavity" (*dui*)?

Answer: Zhenyi zi (Peng Xiao) said: "The cavity is the mouth."

Peng Xiao's sentence is found in his commentary to the *Cantong qi*, sec. 20.

THE INFANT AND THE LOVELY MAID

Question: Where exactly are the Infant (*ying'er*) and the Lovely Maid (*chanü*)?

Answer: The Infant is in the kidneys, the Lovely Maid is in the heart.

The Infant (Yang) in the kidneys (Yin) is an image of True Yang within Yin. The Lovely Maid (Yin) in the heart (Yang) is an image of True Yin within Yang. See also the next entry.

THE KIDNEYS AND THE HEART

Question: The kidneys pertain to Water and are Yin, but the Infant pertains to Yang. The heart pertains to Fire and Yang, but the Lovely Maid pertains to Yin. What is the reason?

Answer: The kidneys pertain to Kan ☵, but within Yin there is Yang, and this is the True Yang. The heart pertains to Li ☲, but within Yang there is Yin, and this is the True Yin.

THE MUDDY PELLET

Question: Where exactly is the Palace of the Muddy Pellet (*niwan gong*)?

Answer: In the head there are nine palaces. The central one is called Muddy Pellet.

The upper Cinnabar Field as a whole is often called Muddy Pellet. However, when this Field is represented as nine palaces arranged on two rows,
the Muddy Pellet is more precisely the third palace of the lower row, i.e,
the innermost palace. The *Xiuzhen shishu*, ch. 18, gives this description:
"The head contains nine palaces, which are images of the Nine Heavens
above and the Nine Earths below. . . . If, starting from the space between
the eyebrows, one penetrates one inch inside the head, one reaches the
Palace of the Hall of Light (*mingtang gong*), the residence of the Lord of
Great Unity (Taiyi jun). . . . If one penetrates two inches, one reaches the
Palace of the Cavern Chamber (*dongfang gong*). . . . If one penetrates
three inches, one reaches the Palace of the Cinnabar Field (*dantian gong*);
four inches, the Palace of the Flowing Pearl (*liuzhu gong*); and five inches,
the Palace of the Jade Emperor (*yudi gong*). One inch above the Hall of
Light there is the Palace of the Celestial Court (*tianting gong*); one inch
above the Cavern Chamber there is the Palace of Ultimate Truth (*jizhen
gong*); one inch above the Cinnabar Field there is the Palace of the Mysterious Cinnabar (*xuandan gong*); and one inch above the Flowing Pearl
there is the Palace of the Great August One (*taihuang gong*)."

THE YELLOW DAME

Question: What is the Yellow Dame (*huangpo*)?

Answer: Yellow is the color of Soil, and its position pertains to Kun
☷. The name derives from this. Ziqing (Bai Yuchan) said: "The Lord
of Metals is speechless and the Lovely Maid dies; the Yellow Dame
does not grow old and becomes pregnant."

Yellow Dame is a common alchemical name of Soil, the central agent that
makes the conjunction of Yin and Yang possible. The sentences attributed
to Bai Yuchan are found in *Xiuzhen shishu*, ch. 1.

ZI AND WU

Question: What are ZI 子 and WU 午?

Answer: ZI and WU are the center of Heaven and Earth. In Heaven,
they are the Sun and the Moon. In the human being, they are the

heart and the kidneys. In time, they are the ZI and WU hours. Among the trigrams, they are Kan ☵ and Li ☲. Among the directions, they are the South and the North.

This entry describes some of the main meanings of the earthly branches zi and WU. See table 6, p. 262.

THE MYSTERIOUS-FEMALE

Question: What is the Mysterious-Female (*xuanpin*)?

Answer: What is above is called Mysterious, what is below is called Female. In the One Opening of the Mysterious Barrier (*xuanguan yiqiao*), what is on the left is called Mysterious, what is on the right is called Female.

See the note to the next entry.

THE GATE OF THE MYSTERIOUS-FEMALE

Question: What is the Gate of the Mysterious-Female (*xuanpin zhi men*)?

Answer: The nose communicates with the Breath of Heaven and is called the Mysterious Gate. The mouth communicates with the Breath of the Earth and is called the Female Door. Therefore the mouth and the nose are called the Gate and Door of the Mysterious and the Female.

This entry and the previous one are two of many examples showing that *xuanpin* should not be translated as "mysterious female," where "mysterious" is an adjective of "female." Instead, *xuan* and *pin* are two nouns, and the compound *xuanpin* means the conjunction of Yin and Yang, or the active and the passive principles. *Xuan*, "mysterious," denotes Heaven, or the Yang principle. *Pin*, "female," refers to the Yin principle.

THE FIRE-DRAGON AND THE WATER-TIGER

Question: What are the Fire-Dragon (*huolong*) and the Water-Tiger (*shuihu*)?

Answer: The Tiger is the Metal of the West. Metal generates Water, but instead it stores its form within Water. The Dragon is the Wood of the East. Wood generates Fire, but instead it is conquered by Fire. This is what the True Master Taibai meant when he said: "When the five agents do not follow their course, the Tiger is born within Water. In the art of the reversal of the five agents, the Dragon comes forth from Fire."

This entry again refers to the inversion of the generative sequence of the agents that occurs in the alchemical process: Metal is born from Water, and Wood is born from Fire. Therefore the Tiger (an emblem of Metal) is said to "be born within Water," and the Dragon (an emblem of Wood) is said to "emerge from Fire." The passage attributed to Master Taibai (possibly Wang Fanggu, ca. 800) is found in Peng Xiao's *Jin yaoshi* (The Golden Key; *Yunji qiqian*, ch. 70).

THE THREE BARRIERS IN THE BACK

Question: What are the Three Barriers in the back (*beihou sanguan*)?

Answer: The one behind the brain is called Barrier of the Jade Pillow (*yuzhen*). The one in the Spinal Handle is called Barrier of the Pulley (*lulu*). The one at the junction of Water and Fire is called Barrier of the Caudal Funnel (*weilü*).

On this passage see Wang Mu, *Foundations of Internal Alchemy*, pp. 34–36: "The Barrier of the Caudal Funnel is located in the lowest section of the spine. The Barrier of the Spinal Handle is in the back, across from the heart. The Barrier of the Jade Pillow is behind the head, below the identically-named acupuncture point, across from the mouth."

THE THREE FLOWERS GATHER AT THE SUMMIT

Question: What is the meaning of "the Three Flowers gather at the summit" (*sanhua juding*)?

Answer: It means that Spirit (*shen*), Breath (*qi*), and Essence (*jing*) merge and become one. The One Opening of the Mysterious Barrier is the cavity of Spirit, Breath, and Essence.

The two famous sentences "the Three Flowers gather at the summit" and "the Five Breaths have audience at the origin" (found in the next entry) are first found in the *Zhong Lü chuandao ji*, sec. "Lun riyue" (On the Sun and the Moon).

THE FIVE BREATHS HAVE AUDIENCE AT THE ORIGIN

Question: What is the meaning of "the Five Breaths have audience at the origin" (*wuqi chaoyuan*)?

Answer: It means that the True Breaths of the five viscera rise to have audience at the Origin of Heaven.

See the note to the previous entry.

JOINING THE FOUR IMAGES IN HARMONY

Question: What is the meaning of "joining the four images in harmony" (*hehe sixiang*)?

Answer: When the eyes do not see, the *Hun* (celestial soul) resides in the liver. When the ears do not hear, the Essence resides in the kidneys. When the tongue does not move, the Spirit resides in the heart. When the nose does not smell, the *Po* (earthly soul) resides in the lungs. Essence, Spirit, *Hun*-soul, and *Po*-soul gather themselves in the Soil-Intention.

This passage derives from the preface to the *Jindan sibai zi* (Four Hundred Words on the Golden Elixir) in *Xiuzhen shishu*, ch. 5.

THE RIVER CHARIOT

Question: What is the River Chariot (*heche*)?

Answer: The True Breath of the North is called River Chariot. The wheel on the left is called the wheel of the Sun, and the wheel on the right is called the wheel of the Moon. [The River Chariot] carries the True Breath and revolves and stores the Original Yang. It follows its course by responding to the nodes [of time]. When you set to practice, you cannot do without the force of this chariot.

In Neidan, the basic meaning of River Chariot is the circuit formed by the conjunction of the Control and the Function vessels (*dumai* and *renmai*), which run along the back and the front of the body, respectively. This circuit is represented as a river. Since the circuit transports the Essence (*jing*) that is to be refined by Breath (*qi*), it is also likened to a chariot.

THE CLEAR AND THE TURBID

Question: What are the clear and the turbid (*qingzhuo*)?

Answer: The Yang is clear and the Yin is turbid. The clear floats, the turbid sinks. When you cultivate the Elixir, you keep the clear and remove the turbid. Essentially, the clear pertains to Yang, and the turbid pertains to Yin.

Qingzhuo, here rendered as "clear and turbid," can also be translated as "pure and impure."

THE FIVE AGENTS CONQUER EACH OTHER

Question: What is the meaning of "the five agents conquer each other" (*wuxing xiangke*)?

Answer: The *Jinbi jing* (Book on Gold and Jade) says: "Metal and Wood attack each other, Water and Fire conquer each other, and Soil flourishes in the village of Metal. When these three things disappear, the spokes converge in the Four Seas, and Great Peace is attained." All of this is due to the efficacy of the virtue of Soil in the Central Palace.

This entry refers to Soil as an emblem of the Center, which gives birth to the four external agents, and to which the four external agents return by means of the alchemical process. The sentence "the five agents conquer each other" is found in the *Cantong qi*, 66:5 (Pregadio, *The Seal of the Unity of the Three*, p. 107). *Jinbi jing* (Book on Gold and Jade) is the ancient title of a text, later also known as the *Longhu jing* (Book of the Dragon and the Tiger), that paraphrases the first part of the *Cantong qi*. The verses quoted in this entry are found in *Guwen longhu jing zhushu* (Commentary and Subcommentary to the Ancient Text of the *Book of the Dragon and the Tiger*), sec. 10.

THE EMBRYO OF SAINTHOOD

Question: What is the Embryo of Sainthood (*shengtai*)?

Answer: What has no substance generates substance and coalesces into the Embryo of Sainthood. It is carefully protected for ten months, as does a woman who is pregnant for the first time, or a little dragon that learns how to nourish its pearl. Indeed, when Spirit and Breath begin to coalesce, it is extremely easy to make errors due to carelessness.

THE FOUR CARDINAL POINTS

Question: What are the four cardinal points (*sizheng*)?

Answer: ZI, WU, MAO, and YOU are the four cardinal points. The One Opening of the Mysterious Barrier is the palace of the four cardinal points.

This entry refers to the four main earthly branches, respectively related to the North, the South, the East, and the West (see table 6, p. 262). The last sentence indicates that the four cardinal points return to unity in the One Opening of the Mysterious Barrier.

THE YELLOW COURT

Question: Where exactly is the Yellow Court (*huangting*)?

Answer: It is above the bladder, below the spleen, in front of the kidneys, left of the liver, right of the lungs.

Rather than a definition of its precise location, this is a reminder that the Yellow Court is the Center.

THE GOLDEN CROW AND THE JADE HARE

Question: What are the Golden Crow (*jinwu*) and the Jade Hare (*yutu*)?

Answer: The crow in the Sun is a simile for the Liquor in the heart. The hare in the Moon is a simile for the Breath in the kidneys.

The Golden Crow and the Jade Hare are the Yang and Yin ingredients of the Elixir, respectively. The *Wuzhen pian* (Awakening to Reality), "Jueju," poem 1, says: "First take Qian and Kun as the tripod and the furnace, / then catch the Crow and the Hare and boil the Medicine" (see above, p. 77).

THE WORK WITHIN TIME
AND THE WORK WITHIN THE INSTANT

Question: What is the meaning of "in order to set to practice wait for the [right] time, and start only then"?

Answer: There are the work within the time (*shi*) and the work within the instant (*ke*). Piling (Xue Daoguang) said: "To refine the Elixir you do not need to seek the winter solstice: the birth of the initial Yang occurs of its own within yourself." Ma Ziran said: "Distinguish zi and wu within the time that has no divisions; determine Qian and Kun within the trigrams that have no lines." These are examples of the work within the instant.

This entry says that the timing of the Neidan practice should not be determined by external factors, but only by internal ones. The zi "hour," in which the Yang principle is reborn, has nothing to do with ordinary time, but occurs within oneself.

The first quotation in this entry is drawn from Xue Daoguang's *Huandan fuming pian* (Returning to Life through the Reverted Elixir). Several texts in the Taoist Canon attribute the second quotation to Ma Ziran, who was a contemporary of Zhang Boduan.

10 Fifteen Essays to Establish the Teaching

Chongyang lijiao shiwu lun 重陽立教十五論

Wang Chongyang 王重陽 (1113–70)

Wang Chongyang was the founder of the Northern Lineage (Beizong) of Neidan. Also known as Wang Zhe, he apparently led a rather turbulent life until 1159, when he is said to have met Zhongli Quan and Lü Dongbin (see above the introduction to Chapter 4) and to have become an ascetic. From 1167, he begun preaching with his followers in the northeastern province of Shandong. In the strict sense, the Northern Lineage consists of Wang Chongyang and his seven main disciples, among whom Qiu Chuji (1148–1227) is the most important for the later history of Neidan.

The Northern lineage is the original nucleus of Quanzhen (Complete Reality), which continued to develop and is in the present day, with Tianshi dao (Way of the Celestial Masters), one of the two main branches of Taoism, headquartered in the Baiyun guan (Abbey of the White Cloud) in Beijing. Within Neidan, the Northern Lineage is especially important for its teachings on inner Nature (*xing*) and Existence (*ming*), on the equivalence between inner Nature and the Golden Elixir, and on the practice of "clarity and quiescence" (*qingjing*). As we read in the present text, "Nature and Existence are the root and foundation of self-cultivation." In another work, Wang Chongyang states that "the original True Nature is called Golden Elixir," and that "the only important things are the words 'clarity and quiescence,' which are found within one's heart. Nothing else is a practice of self-cultivation."[1] These and several other statements, some of which reveal a clear relation to Buddhism,

---

[1] *Chongyang quanzhen ji* (Complete Reality: A Collection by Wang Chongyang), ch. 2 and 10, respectively. The expression "clarity and quiescence" (*qingjing*) derives from the *Daode jing* (Book of the Way and Its Virtue), sec. 15.

reflect the main points of distinction between the Northern and the Southern lineages.

While there are reasons to doubt that the *Chongyang lijiao shiwu lun*, which combines doctrinal teachings and advice on lifestyle, is actually Wang Chongyang's own work, it is nevertheless deemed to be an original Beizong/Quanzhen document. The text is entirely translated below. Section numbers and titles are found in the original Chinese.

1: LIVING IN A CLOISTER

All those who leave their families should first seek shelter in a cloister. A cloister is a dwelling place on which one can rely. When there is a place on which one can rely, the mind gradually attains peace. When Breath (*qi*) and Spirit are in harmony and at ease, one enters the True Way.

In anything you do, you should not strain yourself: if you strain yourself, this will decrease your Breath. But you should not be motionless: if you are motionless, your Breath and blood will become stagnant. It is essential that movement and quiescence are balanced: only then can you embrace constancy and be secure in all circumstances. This is the way to reside in peace.

2: WANDERING IN THE CLOUDS

There are two ways of traveling. One way is to look at mountains and rivers, beautiful sceneries, and the red and green colors of flowers and plants. Some enjoy bustling and lively towns and cities, others admire the buildings and pavilions of temples and monasteries; some visit friends at random, others are absorbed in clothes and food. Those who are like this may travel ten thousand miles but will only exert and wear out themselves. They may see all the sights in the world, but their minds will be confused and their energy will wane. They are people who travel in vain.

The second way is to look for the principles of one's Nature and Existence, climbing perilous high mountains to seek the subtle and the mysterious, tirelessly searching for enlightened masters, crossing stormy waters of distant rivers, never weary of inquiring about the Dao. When there is agreement at a single sentence,[2] a radiance comes forth from within; one understands the great matter of life and death and becomes a person of complete realization. Those who are like this are true "travelers in the clouds."[3]

3: STUDYING FROM BOOKS

In the Way of studying from books, you should not confound your eyes by pursuing the words. You should, instead, extract the meaning and accord with it in your heart. Then put the book aside and investigate the meaning in order to extract the principles. Then put aside the principles in order to extract the true import. When you have been able to extract the true import, you can absorb it in your mind.

After a long time, the radiance of the mind will naturally overflow and the spirit of wisdom will leap; you will comprehend everything and understand everything. If you arrive to this point, you should foster it. Do not be in a rush, or you will lose hold of your inner nature and life.

If you do not thoroughly understand the meanings of books, and you just want to read and memorize a large quantity of things in order to have discussions with other people and show off your expertise, this will be of no advantage for your practice and will harm your life force. You may read many books, but what is the advantage with regard to the Dao?

When you have understood the meaning of a book, you can deeply store it within you.

[2] A single sentence, or even "a half sentence," is said to be sufficient for transmission from master to disciple.
[3] The expression "traveling in the clouds" (*yunyou*), which also gives its title to this section, refers to the constant wandering of some Taoist and Buddhist adepts who do not have a permanent dwelling place.

4: COMPOUNDING HERBAL MEDICINES

Herbal medicines embody the finest breaths (*qi*) of mountains and rivers, the pure essences (*jing*) of plants and trees. Some are warm, others cold: they can serve to supplement or to drain. Some are thick, others thin: they can be used externally or internally.

Those who become skilled in their study enliven the other people's inner natures and lives; the mindless healers, instead, only damage the other people's bodies. Those who study the Dao should be competent in this: without this competence, there is no way to assist the Dao. However, one should not become attached to this pursuit, as this would cause harm to one's hidden merit. Coveting wealth and property outside causes a loss in the cultivation of Reality within. Not only would this be a source of faults in this life, it would also cause retribution in future lives. My advanced disciples should carefully reflect on this.

5: ON BUILDING

A reed-thatched hut or a grass-thatched hut is needed to protect the body: spending the night outdoor or sleeping in a field is an affront to the Sun and the Moon. Sumptuous mansions and high buildings, instead, are not fit for a superior person. How could a large palace or a tall residence be the livelihood of a person of the Way?

Cutting down trees breaks the flow of the fluids in the Earth's vessels, just as asking for goods or money when giving teachings on the Dao takes away from the people's blood vessels.[4] If you only cultivate your outward operation and do not cultivate your inner practice, it is like painting a cake to satisfy hunger or collecting snow to serve as provisions. You spend much effort vainly, and at the end there is no result.

Those who have determination should hasten to seek the precious palaces within themselves: one may incessantly repair and restore the vermilion towers outside one's body, but sooner or later they will collapse. An intelligent person should examine this closely and in detail.

---

[4] I.e., it takes away from their means of support.

6: JOINING COMPANIONS IN THE DAO

The people of the Way join together as companions. They do so in the first place because they want to assist one another in sickness and disease: "If you die, I will bury you; if I die, you will bury me."

However, you should first select someone and then join that person as a companion; you should not first join some companions and then select one person. You should not be attached to one another; if you are, it would bind your hearts. But you should neither be unattached; if you are, your feelings would be disjoined. Between attachment and unattachment, you should take a middle course.

There are three kinds of people that one should join and three other kinds that one should not join. The first three are those with an enlightened mind, wisdom, and determination. The other three are those who are not enlightened and are attached to the external phenomena; those who lack wisdom and whose nature is foolish and turbid; and those who lack determination and always cause annoyances.

When you establish yourself in a spiritual community, always depend on your mind and your determination. Do not follow other people's emotions and do not rely on appearances. Only choose the wise ones. This is the superior method.

7: SITTING

"Sitting" does not mean sitting with the body upright and the eyes closed. That is false sitting.

In true sitting, during the twelve [double] hours, whether you are standing, walking, sitting, or lying down, and in all states of movement or quiescence, your mind should be like Mount Tai: motionless and unshaken. Shut the four gates—eyes, ears, mouth, and nose—and do not let any external condition enter. If there is even the slightest thought of movement and quiescence, it cannot be called "sitting in quiescence."

Those who can do this may dwell with their bodies in the world of dust, but their names are already recorded among the ranks of the Immortals. They do not need to call on far-away people, as they are worthies and sages within themselves. In one hundred years, when their work is completed,[5] they will shed their shells and ascend to Reality. When they achieve the pill of the Elixir, their Spirit will roam throughout the eight poles.

8: SUBDUING THE MIND

With regard to the Way of the mind, if it is constantly deep and profound, the mind does not move. Inchoate and silent, it does not see the external things; dim and obscure, it is neither inside nor outside. There is not even the slightest thought. This is the stable mind, and it does not need to be subdued.

If, instead, the mind is aroused by complying with the phenomena, it becomes disturbed and deranged as it looks for heads and tails. This is the confused mind, and it should quickly be brought to an end. You should not indulge in it, as it spoils your way (*dao*) and your virtue (*de*), and it damages your Nature (*xing*) and your Existence (*ming*). In standing, walking, sitting, or lying down, constantly strive to subdue it: hearing and seeing, knowing and perceiving are sources of sickness and trouble.

9: REFINING ONE'S NATURE

Regulating one's Nature (*xing*) is like tuning the string of a zither: if it is too tight it will snap, if it is too loose it will not respond. When tightness and looseness are balanced, the zither can be tuned. It is also like casting a sword: too much steel will cause it to break, too much tin will cause it to bend. When steel and tin are balanced, the sword can be cast.

If you embody these two methods when you tune and refine your Nature, it will be wondrous of its own.

---

[5] Or: "when their merit is completed."

10: MATCHING THE FIVE BREATHS

The Five Breaths gather in the Central Palace, the Three Origins collect in the sinciput. The Green Dragon emits a red mist, the White Tiger exhales a black smoke. The ten thousand spirits arrange themselves in rows, and the hundred channels flow and stream. Cinnabar and its Powder will be brilliant and shining, Lead and Mercury will coagulate and be clear. The body may still depend on the human world, but the spirit already roams in the heavens above.

11: MERGING NATURE AND EXISTENCE

Nature (*xing*) is Spirit, Existence (*ming*) is Breath. When Nature meets Existence, it is like a bird finding the wind: it soars lightly, saving strength and succeeding with ease. As the *Yinfu jing* (Book of the Hidden Agreement) says, "The command of birds lies in Breath."[6] Those who cultivate Reality should comprehend this, but should not divulge it to inferior persons; the spirits would otherwise send down their reproval.

Nature and Existence are the root and foundation of self-cultivation: they should be refined with attention and care.

12: THE WAY OF THE SAGES

In order to enter the Way of the sages, one should work hard and be determined for several years, accumulating merit and piling up practice. Only then can the wise and the worthy enter the Way of the sages.

Then you may dwell in an ordinary house, but your inner Nature will fill Heaven and Earth.[7] The host of sages throughout Heaven will silently protect you, and the Immortal Lords of the Great Ultimate will obscurely surround you. Your name will be recorded in the Purple Prefecture (Zifu) and you will attain the rank of Immortal. Your

---

[6] See above, p. 41.

[7] Lit., "will fill Qian ☰ and Kun ☷," the trigrams that represent Heaven and Earth.

bodily form will temporarily dwell in the dust, but your mind will be already enlightened beyond all things.

13: TRANSCENDING THE THREE WORLDS

The worlds of Desire, of Form, and of Formlessness are the Three Worlds. When the mind forgets pondering and thinking, it transcends the world of Desire; when it forgets all phenomena, it transcends the world of Form; when it is not attached to the vision of Emptiness, it transcends the world of Formlessness.

When you leave these Three Worlds, Spirit dwells in the village of the immortals and the sages, and inner Nature resides in the realm of Jade Clarity.

14: THE METHOD OF NOURISHING ONESELF

The dharma-body is a representation of formlessness.[8] It is neither emptiness nor existence, it has neither front nor back, it is neither low nor high, it is neither long nor short. When it operates, there is nothing it does not pervade; when it is stored, it is inchoate and silent and it does not leave any trace.

If you obtain this Way, you can nourish it. The more you nourish it, the more are your merits; the less you nourish it, the less are your merits. Neither desire to go back [to the Origin] nor be attached to this world: then you will leave or stay, and this will occur naturally.

15: LEAVING THE ORDINARY WORLD

Leaving the ordinary world does not mean leaving it with one's body: it refers to the mind ground (*xindi*). The body is like a lotus root, the mind is like a lotus blossom: the root is in the mud, the blossom is in the open air. For one who attains the Dao, the body is in the ordinary world, but the mind is in the realm of the sages.

[8] On the dharma-body see p. 246, note 16 below.

Nowadays, people want to avoid death forever and leave the ordinary world. They are truly foolish: they do not understand the principle of the Dao.

I have written these fifteen essays in order to admonish the disciples of strong determination. If you examine them deeply and in all details, you will understand them.

11   The Harmony of the Center

Zhonghe ji 中和集

Li Daochun 李道純 (fl. 1288–92)

Li Daochun is one of the great masters of the Mongol Yuan dynasty (1279–1368), an extremely important period in the history of Neidan. The reunification of the Chinese empire after the division into the Jin and the Southern Song dynasties (in the north and the south, respectively) had the indirect consequence of encouraging several attempts to "merge" the Northern and Southern lineages (Beizong and Nanzong), which had independently developed in the previous two or three centuries. Li Daochun is the creator of one of the most remarkable of these attempts. As a major example of the Neidan gift of "crossing boundaries," his works also incorporate Buddhist and Neo-Confucian concepts.

The *Zhonghe ji* (The Harmony of the Center: An Anthology), compiled by one of his disciples, is Li Daochun's most important work. "The Harmony of the Center" may serve to render its title into English, but is not a precise translation of the term *zhonghe*. This expression derives from the *Zhongyong* (The Middle Course), one of the main early Confucian texts, where *zhong* denotes the state in which "emotions" (*qing*, defined in this work as pleasure, anger, sorrow, and joy) do not emerge, and *he* denotes the state in which, after they emerge, they follow proper degrees or rhythms. "Centrality and Harmony" or "The Center and its Harmony" might therefore be more precise translations of the title of Li Daochun's work.

The selections translated here show that Li Daochun establishes two main levels of Neidan, summarized by the terms Internal Medicine and External Medicine. The higher level, inspired by the principles of the Northern Lineage, is reserved to those who have an innate comprehension of the Dao. The lower level, which substantially corresponds to the principles and practices of the Southern Lineage, is addressed to all other adepts. The first way focuses on the cultivation of inner nature (*xing*); the second one gives initial priority to the cultivation of individual existence (*ming*). The first way is said to lead to the "immediate awakening"; the second one follows the gradual process of the Southern Lineage with its

163

classical subdivision into three stages. Both ways, however, are said to lead
to the same result.

THE GOLDEN ELIXIR[1]

Ding'an asked:[2] When the Golden Elixir is achieved, can it be seen?
    The Master answered: Yes, it can be seen.
    He asked: Does it have a form?
    The Master answered: No, it has no form.
    He asked: If it has no form, how can it be seen?
    The Master answered: "Golden Elixir" is only a name used by
necessity:[3] how can it have a form? When I say that it can be seen, it
cannot be seen with the eyes.

The Buddhists say: "In not seeing, you see it closely; in seeing closely,
you do not see it."[4] The *Book of the Way [and its Virtue]* says:
"Watching, you do not see it; listening, you do not hear it."[5] This is
what we call the Dao: watching, you do not see it—but never are you
not seeing it; listening, you do not hear it—but never are you not
hearing it.
    When I say that it can be seen and heard, I do not mean that it is
within the reach of the eyes and the ears. It can be seen only with the
Heart (*xin*), and it can be heard only with the Intention (*yi*). It is like
the blowing of a strong wind that shakes the trees on a mountain or
rouses the waves on the water: could you say that the wind is not
there? But listening, you do not hear it, and grasping, you do not get
it: could you say that the wind is there?
    The same is with the foundation (*ti*) of the Golden Elixir. There-
fore at the beginning of its refining, Being and Non-Being operate

---

    [1] Title added by the translator.
    [2] Zhao Ding'an was one of Li Daochun's main disciples.
    [3] See above, p. 55 note 27.
    [4] These sentences derive from the commentary to the *Heart Sutra* by the
Chan Master Dadian Baotong (732–824).
    [5] *Daode jing* (Book of the Way and Its Virtue), sec. 14: "Watching, you do
not see it: it is called invisible. Listening, you do not hear it: it is called
inaudible. Grasping, you do not get it: it is called imperceptible."

with one another, and movement and quiescence attend one to the other. When the work comes to achievement, all illusory conditions instantaneously cease, and all the ten thousand phenomena are empty. Movement and quiescence are both forgotten, and Being and Non-Being are both removed. "As the Mysterious Pearl achieves its image, the Great Unity returns to reality."[6] Nature (*xing*) and Existence (*ming*) are both complete, form and spirit are both wondrous. You exit from Being and enter Non-Being, freely roam among the clouds, and realize the "golden immortality."

Therefore the scriptures and the books on the Elixir use many different names to lead students from the coarse to the subtle, so that they may gradually enter a blissful realm and come to see their Nature and to awaken to Emptiness. However, the truth of all this is not on paper. It is like a boat that ferries people across a river: after they have reached the other shore, the boat becomes useless. This is what an ancient sage meant when he said: "Once you've gotten the hare, forget the snare; once you've gotten the fish, forget the trap."[7]

THE EXTERNAL MEDICINE AND THE INTERNAL MEDICINE[8]

The External Medicine (*waiyao*) allows you to cure illnesses, and to "prolong your life and have enduring presence."[9] The Internal Medicine (*neiyao*) allows you to transcend the world, and to exit from Being and enter Non-Being.

In general, those who study the Dao should begin from the External Medicine; then they will know the Internal Medicine by themselves. Superior persons have already planted the root of virtue, and

---

[6] This sentence is quoted from Zhang Boduan's preface to his *Wuzhen pian* (Awakening to Reality).

[7] *Zhuangzi*, ch. 26; see Watson, *The Complete Works of Chuang Tzu*, p. 302.

[8] In the original text, this section is entitled "Explanation of the Charts of the External and Internal Medicines of the Golden Elixir." The two charts are reproduced on the next page.

[9] This phrase derives from the *Daode jing*, sec. 59: "This is called 'planting the root deep and making the base firm': it is the Way of long life and enduring presence."

know it by birth;[10] therefore they do not refine the External Medicine, and directly refine the Internal Medicine.

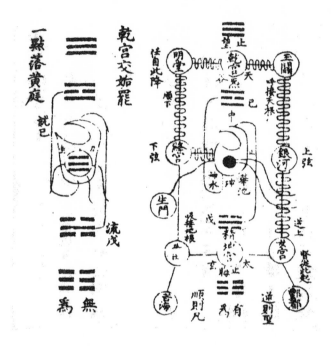

Fig. 2. The External Medicine (*waiyao*, right) and the Internal Medicine (*neiyao*, left).

With the Internal Medicine "there is no doing, yet nothing is not done"; with the External Medicine "there is doing, and something whereby it is done."[11]

The Internal Medicine is devoid of form and substance, but has actuality; the External Medicine has a foundation and an operation, but is devoid of actuality.

---

[10] This sentence alludes to a passage of the *Lunyu* (Sayings of Confucius), 16:9: "Those who know by birth are superior; those who know by study are next." See Legge, *The Chinese Classics*, vol. 1, pp. 313–14.

[11] *Daode jing*, sec. 48 and sec. 38, respectively.

The External Medicine is the superior undertaking of the physical body (*seshen*); the Internal Medicine is the superior undertaking of the dharma-body (*fashen*).[12]

The External Medicine is the way of the Earthly Immortality; the Internal Medicine is the way of the Water Immortality. When the two Medicines are complete, this is the way of Celestial Immortality.[13]

The External Medicine brings one's Existence to fulfillment; the Internal Medicine brings one's Nature to fulfillment. When the two Medicines are complete, form and spirit are both wondrous.

The External Medicine

Initial barrier: Refining the Essence to transmute it into Breath. You should first of all recognize the time of birth of the Celestial GUI, and quickly collect it.[14]

Middle barrier: Refining the Breath to transmute it into Spirit. Harmonize the true breathing[15] and let it flow in cycles through the six empty spaces. Starting from the Great Mysterious Barrier, invert its course and let it flow to the cavity of the Celestial Valley, so that the conjunction [of Yin and Yang] may occur. Then let it descend to the Yellow Room and enter the Central Palace. When the conjunction of Qian ☰ and Kun ☷ pauses, one particle [of Original Breath] falls into the Yellow Court.[16]

---

[12] On the dharma-body see p. 246, note 16 below.

[13] "Earthly," "Water," and "Celestial Immortality" are traditional designations of three degrees of transcendence, from the lowest to the highest. For another example, see the "Essay on Resolving Doubts in the Cultivation of Immortality" translated above, Chapter 7.

[14] This alludes to a verse in the *Wuzhen pian*, "Lüshi," poem 7: "When Lead meets the birth of GUI, quickly you should collect it" (translated above, p. 72).

[15] That is, the breathing of the Original Breath, and not the common breath of inspiration and expiration. See Wang Mu, *Foundations of Internal Alchemy*, pp. 55–63.

[16] The expression "flowing in cycles through the six empty spaces" derives from the "Appended Sayings" ("Xici") of the *Book of Changes* (B.7; see Wilhelm, *The I-ching or Book of Changes*, p. 348), and is also found in the

Upper barrier: Refining the Spirit to return to Emptiness. You purify your thoughts by means of the Heart; this is called "the 7 returns." Your emotions (*qing*) return to your nature; this is called "the 9 reverts."[17]

The Internal Medicine

The Internal Medicine is the essential of refining Spirit. Form and spirit are both wondrous, and you join your truth with the truth of the Dao.

The Internal Medicine is the one particle of precelestial True Yang. It is likened to the inner line of the trigram Qian ☰, which conjoins with Kun ☷ and forms Kan ☵, that is, Water. The inner line [of Kan ☵] is the Metal within Qian ☰; it is also called Metal within Water, and its common name is "perfect Essence."

When the perfect Essence is firm, it returns to the Ancestral Breath (*zuqi*). The Ancestral Breath is the Precelestial Original Breath of Empty Non-Being and True Unity; it is not the breath of exhalation

Cantong qi (The Seal of the Unity of the Three), 4:8 (Pregadio, *The Seal of the Unity of the Three*, p. 71). In both texts, the "six empty spaces" (*liuxu*) are the six lines of the hexagrams, which can be filled by Yin (--) or Yang (—) signs. In this paragraph, instead, "six empty spaces" refers to six points in the back and six points in the front of the body along the route through which the Essence is circulated in the first stage of the Neidan practice. The Great Mysterious Barrier (*tai xuanguan*), the Celestial Valley (*tiangu*), and the Yellow Room (*huangfang*) are three of these points. Both Central Palace (*zhonggong*) and Yellow Court (*huangting*) refer to the lower Cinnabar Field. — This paragraph describes in an extremely synthetic way the practice of the River Chariot (*heche*); see Wang Mu, *Foundations of Internal Alchemy*, pp. 71–74.

[17] The two sentences are quoted from the *Cantong qi*, 55:7 (Pregadio, *The Seal*, p. 101), and appear in many Neidan texts where they take on different meanings according to the context. As they are used here, 7 and 9 are the "accomplishment numbers" of the agents Fire and Metal, respectively (see table 2, p. 258). Fire represents the Heart and the Original Spirit, and Metal represents the emotions (*qing*). In the conditioned state, thoughts and emotions become separated from the Original Spirit and the inner nature, respectively. Through the Neidan practice, thoughts (7) "return" to one's Original Spirit, and emotions (9) "revert" to one's inner nature.

and inhalation. When the inner line of Qian ☰ conjoins with Kun ☷ and forms Kan ☵, at the same time the Yin [line] within Kun ☷ enters Qian ☰ and forms Li ☲. The Yin [line] within Li ☲ is originally Kun ☷, the Earth; therefore it is also called Mercury in the Sand.[18]

"The Dao generates the One, the One generates the Two, the Two generate the Three, the Three generate the ten thousand things."[19] The Void transmutes itself into Spirit, Spirit transmutes itself into Breath, Breath transmutes itself into Essence, and Essence transmutes itself into form.[20] This is called "following the course" (*shun*).

The ten thousand things hold the Three, the Three return to the Two, the Two return to the One. When the ten thousand things are refined into the perfect Essence, Essence transmutes itself into Breath, and Breath transmutes itself into Spirit. This is called "inverting the course" (*ni*). (*Note by Li Daochun*: The books on the Elixir say that "following the course" forms the human being, while "inverting the course" forms the Elixir.)

ESSENCE, BREATH, SPIRIT[21]

Transmitted to All Disciples

The disciples of Complete Reality (*quanzhen*) should practice the Way of Complete Reality. Complete Reality means keeping the fundamental reality complete.[22] Keeping the Essence complete, keeping the

---

[18] "Sand," *sha*, is an abbreviation of *dansha* ("cinnabar sand") or *zhusha* ("vermilion sand"), two common names of cinnabar. In Neidan, the term "mercury in the sand" means the True Yin (True Mercury) found within the Yang (cinnabar).

[19] *Daode jing*, sec. 42.

[20] The last stage corresponds to the generation of the "ten thousand things," i.e., the world of form, which occurs through the conjunction of the essences of Yin and Yang.

[21] In the original text, this section is entitled "The Way of Life of Complete Reality" ("Quanzhen huofa").

[22] "Complete" (*quan*) here should be understood in the sense of "intact," i.e., undamaged by the postcelestial world in which we live.

Breath complete, keeping the Spirit complete: this is Complete Reality. As soon as something is lacking, it is not complete; as soon as a single spot is defiled, it is not real.

By keeping the Essence complete, you can protect the body (*shen*). To keep the Essence complete, first the body must be at rest and stable. When it is at rest and stable, there are no desires, and thus the Essence is complete.

By keeping the Breath complete, you can nourish the mind (*xin*). To keep the Breath complete, first the mind must be clear and quiescent. When it is clear and quiescent, there are no thoughts, and thus the Breath is complete.

By keeping the Spirit complete, you can return to Emptiness. To keep the Spirit complete, first the Intention must be sincere. When the Intention is sincere, body and mind join one another, and you return to Emptiness.

Therefore Essence, Breath, and Spirit are the three original ingredients; and body, mind, and Intention are the three original essentials.

Studying the methods of divine immortality does not require much doing. It is sufficient to refine the three treasures of Essence, Breath, and Spirit so that they are the matrix of the Elixir. When the three treasures meet in the Central Palace, the Golden Elixir is achieved. How could this be difficult to understand? How could it be difficult to practice? What is difficult to practice or difficult to understand is evil, false, and deceptive.

The essential of *refining the Essence* consists in the body. When the body does not move, "the tiger roars and the wind blows," the dark turtle withdraws and conceals, and the Original Essence coagulates.[23]

The essential of *refining the Breath* consists in the mind. When the mind does not move, "the dragon howls and the clouds rise," the vermilion sparrow spreads its wings, and the Original Breath breathes.[24]

---

[23] This paragraph refers to the conjunction of emotions (*qing*, represented by the Tiger) and Original Essence (represented by the Dark Turtle).

[24] This paragraph refers to the joining of inner nature (represented by the Dragon) and Original Spirit (represented by the Vermilion Sparrow). The

The essential of *refining the Spirit* consists in the Intention. When the Intention does not move, the two things conjoin, the three origins merge into one, and the Embryo of Sainthood is achieved.[25]

Qian ☰ and Kun ☷, which are the tripod and the furnace, Kan ☵ and Li ☲, which are the ingredients, as well as the eight trigrams, the three origins, the five agents, and the four images—none of them lies outside of these three words: Essence, Breath, and Spirit. And the culmination of Complete Reality is not outside of the two words "body" and "mind." Anything separate from body and mind is an external path (*waidao*). Yet, you should not become attached to your body and mind: as soon as you are attached to them, you are tied to them. You should let them operate, but you should be detached from their operation.

What I call "body" and "mind" are not the illusory body and the heart made of flesh.[26] They are the invisible body and mind. Let's see—what are the invisible body and mind?

The clouds from the top of the mountain,
the moon towards the heart of the waves.[27]

This body is the body that has been clear and quiescent for countless eons: it is the wondrous Being within Non-Being. This mind is the

sentences "the tiger roars and the wind blows" and "the dragon howls and the clouds rise" are found in several Taoist texts. They derive in the first place from the "Explanation of the Sentences" ("Wenyan") appendix to the *Book of Changes*: "The clouds follow the dragon, the wind follows the tiger" (see Wilhelm, p. 382)

[25] The "two things" are Yin and Yang. The "three origins" are Original Essence, Original Breath, and Original Spirit.

[26] "Mind" and "heart" are both called *xin* in Chinese.

[27] These verses are inspired by analogous Chan Buddhist sayings or "public cases" (*gongan*, in Japanese *kōan*). Li Daochun seems to mean here that the clouds that appear to be on the top of a mountain disappear when they are seen from the top of the mountain; this is an example of "true" Non-Being hidden by "illusory" Being. Vice versa, the moon reflected on the waves of the sea appears to be an unreal phenomenon, but the reflection is only possible because there is a moon in the sky; this is an example of "true" Being hidden by "illusory" Non-Being.

foundation that has been numinous and wondrous "apparently since before the time of the [Celestial] Emperor":[28] it is the true Non-Being within Being.

Being within Non-Being is represented by Kan ☵. Non-Being within Being is represented by Li ☲. Our Patriarch (Zhang Boduan) said:

> Gather the solid [line] from the center in the position of Kan ☵,
>
> and transmute by projection the innermost Yin in the palace of Li ☲.
>
> Thus it alters itself and forms the strong body of Qian ☰:
> withdrawing and concealing or leaping into flight depends entirely on the mind.[29]

Can there be any doubt that the two words "body" and "mind" are the culmination of Complete Reality?

The essential of refining the Elixir consists only in the words Nature (*xing*) and Existence (*ming*). Anything separate from Nature and Existence is a "side gate" (*pangmen*).[30] If you cling only to Nature or to Existence, this is called being unbalanced. This is what one of our Masters meant when she said:

> Spirit is one's Nature, and Breath is one's Existence.[31]

Refining Breath consists in preserving the body, and refining Spirit consists in protecting the mind. When the body does not move, "the

---

[28] This expression derives from the *Daode jing*, sec. 4, which says of the Dao: "I do not know whose child it is; it seems to be earlier than the [Celestial] Emperor." — In Neidan, the "invisible body and mind" described here by Li Daochun are often called "dharma-body" (*fashen*) and "celestial mind" (*tianxin*), respectively.

[29] *Wuzhen pian*, "Jueju," poem 16 (translated above, p. 80).

[30] This term, very common in Neidan texts, denotes teachings or practices that are deemed to be ineffective or even harmful for true realization.

[31] This verse is quoted from the *Lingyuan dadao ge* (Song of the Great Dao, the Numinous Source) by Cao Wenyi (ca. 1125), a female Neidan adept.

tiger roars"; when the mind does not move, "the dragon howls."[32] When the tiger roars, Lead seizes Mercury; when the dragon howls, Mercury seizes Lead. Lead and Mercury are different names for Kan ☵ and Li ☲.

The Yang within Kan ☵ is the perfect Essence within the body; the Yin within Li ☲ is the original Breath within the mind. In order to refine the Essence to transmute it into Breath one must first "protect the body"; in order to refine the Breath to transmute it into Spirit one must first "protect the mind." When the body is stable, one's bodily form (xing) is firm, and when the bodily form is firm, one brings one's Existence to fulfillment. When the mind is stable, one's Spirit is complete, and when the Spirit is complete, one brings one's Nature to fulfillment. When body and mind are united, when Nature and Existence are complete, when form and spirit are wondrous—this is called "achieving the Elixir."

However, transmuting the Essence into Breath, and the Breath into Spirit, is nothing exceptional. Why? Because there is also the wondrousness of refining Spirit, and this is something not easy to talk about in a simple way.

What I said above is a general approximation of the Golden Elixir. Just by looking at this, you will trust that the great undertaking is not on paper. Otherwise, you should know where to set to practice. Once you know where to set to practice, start there and go ahead. Begin by refining the Essence; only when the Essence is settled can you refine the Breath; only when the Breath is stable can you refine the Spirit; and only when the Spirit has coagulated can you return to Emptiness. Emptiness and then again Emptiness: the Way and its Virtue will join one another.

Refining the Essence consists in knowing the time. What I call "time" does not mean the time of the hours: if you are attached to that time, you are in error. But if I said, "there is no time," how could you begin [to practice]? What would you do, ultimately? Alas! One of the ancients said: "When the time comes, the Spirit knows it."[33] And

[32] See above, note 24.

[33] This statement is attributed to Chen Nan, but is not found in his extant works.

our Patriarch said: "When Lead meets the birth of GUI, quickly you should collect it."[34] These words say all that needs to be said.

Refining the Breath consists in harmonization (*tiaoxie*). "Harmonization" means balancing the true breathing and stabilizing the true Origin.[35] Laozi said:

> The gate of the Mysterious-Female
> is called the root of Heaven and Earth.
> Unceasing and continuous,
> its operation never wears out.[36]

Is this not the essential point of "harmonization"?

Nowadays, people point to the mouth and the nose and say that they are the Gate of the Mysterious-Female (*xuanpin zhi men*). This is wrong. The Mysterious-Female is the hinge of the opening and closing of Heaven and Earth. The "Appended Sayings" of the *Book of Changes* says:

> Closing the gates is called Kun ☷, opening the gates is called Qian ☰. One opening, one closing, this is called change.[37]

"Closing and opening" is the same as "movement and quiescence." This is what Laozi meant when he said that "its operation never wears out."

A book on the Elixir says:

> Exhaling touches onto the root of Heaven, inhaling touches onto the root of Earth. On exhaling, "the dragon howls and the clouds rise"; on inhaling, "the tiger roars and the wind blows."[38]

"Exhaling touches onto the root of Heaven, inhaling touches onto the root of Earth" has the same meaning as "Closing the gates is

---

[34] *Wuzhen pian*, "Lüshi," poem 7 (translated above, p. 72).

[35] "True breathing" is the breathing of the Original Breath, and not the breathing of ordinary inhaling and exhaling.

[36] *Daode jing*, sec. 6.

[37] *Book of Changes*, "Appended Sayings," sec. A.10 (see Wilhelm, p. 318).

[38] This passage is quoted, without attribution, in the *Jindan wenda* (Questions and Answers on the Golden Elixir). See also note 24 above.

called Kun ☷, opening the gates is called Qian ☰." And "On exhaling, 'the dragon howls and the clouds rise'; on inhaling, 'the tiger roars and the wind blows'" has the same meaning as "One opening, one closing, this is called change" and "its operation never wears out."[39]

How could taking the mouth and the nose as the Mysterious-Female not be an error? When we speak of exhaling and inhaling, we mean the inexhaustible coming and going of the true breathing.

Oral Instructions

When the external Yin and Yang come and go, this is the External Medicine. When the internal Kan ☵ and Li ☲ converge their spokes, this is the Internal Medicine.[40] Externally there is operation; internally there is "being as it is" (ziran). In their operation, Essence, Breath, and Spirit are two, but in their foundation they are one.[41]

With regard to the External Medicine: First of all, the essence of the intercourse (jiaohe zhi jing, semen) should not be wasted; the breath of exhaling and inhaling should be subtle until there is no breathing; and concerning the spirit of the thinking mind, the main thing consists in being "serene and quiescent."[42]

With regard to the Internal Medicine: *Refining the Essence* means refining the Original Essence, and extracting the Original Yang within Kan ☵. When the Original Essence is firm, the essence of intercourse of its own will not be wasted.

Refining the Breath means refining the Original Breath, and replenishing the Original Yin within Li ☲. When the Original Breath is settled, the breath of exhaling and inhaling of its own will neither enter nor exit.

Refining the Spirit means refining the Original Spirit. Kan ☵ and Li ☲ join their bodies and form Qian ☰. When the Original Spirit

---

[39] This passage means that the breathing of the Original Breath is modeled on, and equivalent to, the operation of the Breath of the Dao in the cosmos.

[40] *Cantong qi*, 8:6 (see Pregadio, *The Seal*, 72).

[41] They are two because each of them has an "external" and an "internal" aspect. Despite this, they are fundamentally one.

[42] *Cantong qi*, 18:2 (translated above, p. 6).

coagulates, the spirit of the thinking mind enters the state of stability and concentration.

Above this there is the stage of refining Emptiness. It is not easy to talk about it in simple words. The most important thing consists only in understanding in silence and comprehending by the Heart. Come on! Come on!

NATURE AND EXISTENCE

Nature (*xing*) is what we call the perfect precelestial Spirit and the One Numen. Existence (*ming*) is what we call the perfect precelestial Essence and the One Breath. Essence and Spirit are the roots of Nature and Existence.[43]

The creations and transformations brought about by Nature pertain to the mind. The creations and transformations brought about by Existence pertain to the body. Understanding and cognition emerge from the mind: with thoughts and cogitations, the mind yokes one's Nature. Responses and reactions emerge from the body: with speech and silence, with sight and hearing, the body burdens one's Existence.

It is because one's Existence is burdened by the body that there are birth and death. It is because one's Nature is yoked by the mind that there are coming and going.[44]

Thus we know that these two words, "body" and "mind," represent the dwellings of Essence and Spirit, and that Essence and Spirit are the foundations of Nature and Existence. Nature cannot be established without Existence, and Existence cannot be preserved without Nature. The names are two, but the principle is one.

Alas! The Buddhist and the Taoist disciples of the present day divide Nature and Existence into two, taking one side and criticizing the other. They just do not know that neither the "lone Yin" (*guyin*, i.e., Nature or *xing*) nor the "solitary Yang" (*guayang*, i.e., Existence or *ming*) can bring the great undertaking to fulfillment. If those who

---

[43] The *Daozang* text erroneously omits the character 「神」 in the last sentence.

[44] I.e., the "coming and going" of thoughts.

cultivate their Existence do not realize their Nature, how can they
escape the cycles of kalpas? If those who see their Nature do not understand their Existence, how can they finally revert [to the Origin]?[45]
An immortal master said:

> Refining the Golden Elixir without realizing one's Nature
> is the first sickness of self-cultivation.
> Cultivate only your true Nature without cultivating the Elixir,
> and for ten thousand kalpas your soul can hardly enter
> sainthood.[46]

How truthful are these words!

The superior persons jointly attain Nature and Existence. First, by
observing the precepts and by concentration and wisdom they empty
their minds.[47] Then, by refining Essence, Breath, and Spirit they
protect their bodies. When the body is tranquil and stable, the basis of
Existence is permanently firm; when the mind is empty and clear, the
foundation of Nature is entirely illuminated. When one's Nature is
entirely illuminated, there is no coming and going; when one's Existence is permanently firm, there is no death and birth.

As one reaches the inchoate, complete, and immediate awakening,
one directly enters the state of non-doing: Nature and Existence are
both intact, and form and spirit are both wondrous.

However, neither can we say that Nature and Existence are fundamentally two, nor can we speak of them as one. The reason is that
they are fundamentally one, but their operation is twofold. Those who

---

[45] A common reciprocal accusation between Buddhists and Taoists was
that Buddhism gives too much emphasis on the cultivation of Nature (*xing*)
and the mind, and Taoism gives too much emphasis on the cultivation of
Existence (*ming*) and the body. Therefore, to make his point clearer, Li
Daochun here uses two expressions that typify Buddhism and Taoism, saying
that only by realizing Nature can Taoist adepts also "escape the cycles" of
kalpas, and only by knowing Existence can Buddhist adepts also "revert" to
the origin.

[46] These verses are quoted from the *Qiaoyao ge* (Songs Metered on the
Hexagram Lines), a work attributed to the immortal Lü Dongbin.

[47] Precepts (*jie*), concentration (*ding*), and wisdom (*hui*) respectively
correspond to the Buddhist practices of *śīla*, *samādhi*, and *prajñā*.

have attachments and prejudices take them as separate gateways; this is because they do not comprehend Nature and Existence. As they do not comprehend Nature and Existence, they separate them into two. If Nature and Existence do not guard one another, how could one ascend to the Truth and climb up to Reality?[48]

THE MYSTERIOUS BARRIER[49]

The Mysterious Barrier (*xuanguan*) is an extremely mysterious and extremely wondrous mechanism. Many of the present-day students are mired in their bodily form. Someone says that the Mysterious Barrier is between the eyebrows; someone says that it is in the wheel of the navel; someone says that it is in the space between the kidneys; someone says that it is before the kidneys and behind the navel; someone says that it is in the gallbladder; someone says that it is in the Cinnabar Field. Someone says that in the head there are nine palaces, and that the central one is the Mysterious Barrier. Someone refers to the Gate of Birth (*chanmen*, the vagina) as "the place where one comes to life,"[50] or to the mouth and the nose as the Mysterious-Female.

All of this is wrong. If the Mysterious Barrier is situated in the bodily form, it is entirely incorrect; yet, it cannot be separated from the person and cannot be searched outside of the person. Why does no book on the Elixir exactly say where it is found? Because it is something difficult to frame in writing or in speaking, and it is something that words cannot attain; and this is precisely why it is called Mysterious Barrier. Therefore the sages showed it only by writing the character 中 (*zhong*, "center"), because this character illustrates the Mysterious Barrier.

What I call center is not the center between "internal and external," is not the center of "the center of the four directions and above and below," and is not the center that is within.

---

[48] "Ascend to the Truth" and "climb up to Reality" translate *dengzhen* and *niejing*, two other expressions that hint at Taoism and Buddhism, respectively.
[49] Title added by the translator.
[50] See *Wuzhen pian*, "Lüshi," no. 9 (translated above, p. 73).

THE THREE VEHICLES OF THE GRADUAL METHODS

In the lower vehicle:

- The tripod and the furnace are body (*shen*) and mind (*xin*)
- The ingredients are essence and breath
- Water and Fire are heart and kidneys
- The five agents are the five viscera
- Dragon and Tiger are liver and lungs
- The True Seed is the essence
- The Fire phases are [established according to] the year, the month, the day, and the hour
- Bathing is swallowing saliva in order to irrigate [the viscera][51]
- The three essentials are the mouth and the nostrils
- The Mysterious Barrier is before the kidneys and behind the navel
- Achieving the Elixir is the inchoate merging of the five agents

This is the method for being serene and untroubled; its practices include more than one hundred items. If one is able to forget one's emotions (*qing*), it can nourish one's Existence (*ming*).[52]

In the middle vehicle:

- The tripod and the furnace are Qian ☰ and Kun ☷
- Water and Fire are Kan ☵ and Li ☲
- The ingredients are the Crow and the Hare[53]
- The five agents are Essence, Spirit, the *Hun*-soul, the *Po*-soul, and Intention (*yi*)

[51] On the practice of "bathing" (*muyu*) in Neidan see Wang Mu, *Foundations of Internal Alchemy*, pp. 102–5. In the earlier Taoist meditation practices of the *Huangting jing* (Book of the Yellow Court, "Inner" version, poem 2), saliva is swallowed in order to "irrigate (*guangai*) the Five Flowers and plant the Numinous Root." The Five Flowers are the five viscera.

[52] Note that in the "lower vehicle" there is no mention of extracting True Yin from Yang and True Yang from Yin.

[53] See *Wuzhen pian*, "Jueju," no. 1 (translated above, p. 77).

- Dragon and Tiger are body and mind
- The True Seed is breath
- The Fire phases are [established according the increase and decrease of] cold and heat during the year
- Bathing is "irrigating with dharma-water"[54]
- Sealing firmly is "the inner domain not going out and the outer domain not coming in"
- The three essentials are the Great Abyss, the Crimson Palace, and the Room of the Essence[55]
- The Mysterious Barrier is the Muddy Pellet[56]
- Achieving the Elixir is the inchoate merging of Essence and Spirit

This is the method of the middle vehicle for nourishing one's Existence; its practices include several dozen items. It is very similar the lower vehicle, differing only slightly from it. If it is performed without negligence, it can confer long life and enduring presence.

In the higher vehicle:

- The tripod and the furnace are Heaven and Earth
- Water and Fire are the Sun and Moon
- The "mechanism of transformation" (*huaji*) is Yin and Yang
- The five agents are lead, mercury, silver, cinnabar, and Soil
- Dragon and Tiger are Nature (*xing*) and emotions (*qing*)
- The True Seed is thought
- The Fire phases are the refining of thought by means of the Heart (*xin*)
- Nourishing the Fire is ceasing thinking
- Sealing firmly is "holding one's radiance"

[54] In Buddhism, the "dharma-water" (*fashui*) is the Buddha-truth that washes away illusion.

[55] Great Abyss (*taiyuan*), Crimson Palace (*jianggong*), and Room of the Essence (*jingfang*) are the upper, middle, and lower Cinnabar Fields, respectively.

[56] Muddy Pellet (*niwan*) is another name of the upper Cinnabar Field.

- The "fight in the wild" is submitting and subduing the inner demons[57]
- The three essentials are body, mind, and Intention
- The Mysterious Barrier is the Celestial Mind
- Achieving the Elixir is the return of the emotions (*qing*) to Nature (*xing*)
- Bathing is harmonizing one's breath into a "fragrant vapor"[58]

This is the way of the higher vehicle for extending one's life; it is in part similar to the middle vehicle, but the points of application are not the same. Again, it consists of several dozen items. If superior persons perform it steadily from beginning to end, they can experience the Way of Immortality.

THE SUPREME ONE VEHICLE

The Supreme One Vehicle is the Upmost Wondrous Way of Ultimate Truth.

- The tripod is the Great Void and the furnace is the Great Ultimate (*taiji*)[59]
- The foundation of the Elixir (*danji*) is clarity and quiescence
- The Mother of the Elixir (*danmu*) is non-doing
- Lead and Mercury are Nature (*xing*) and Existence (*ming*)
- Water and Fire are concentration (*ding*, *samādhi*) and wisdom (*hui*, *prajñā*)
- The conjunction of Water and Fire is ceasing desires and terminating anger
- "Metal and Wood pairing with each other" is Nature and emotions joining as one[60]

[57] On the expression "fight in the wild" (*yezhan*) see above, p. 112 note 4.
[58] On the expression "fragrant vapor" (*xunzheng*) see above, p. 112 note 3.
[59] The world, perceived in its state of Unity (*taiji*), becomes similar to a furnace that nurtures the Elixir refined in the tripod of Great Void, or Non-Being.
[60] See *Cantong qi*, sec. 72 (translated above, p. 19).

- Bathing is cleansing the mind and clearing away cogitation
- Sealing firmly is maintaining sincerity and concentrating the Intention
- The three essentials are precepts, concentration, and wisdom[61]
- The Mysterious Barrier is the center
- The "sign of response" is the enlightened mind[62]
- Coalescing [the Elixir] is seeing one's Nature
- The Embryo of Sainthood is the three origins merged into one
- Achieving the Elixir is Nature and Existence becoming one thing
- "Delivering the Embryo" is "having a body outside one's body"
- "Reaching completion" is "smashing Emptiness" (*dapo xukong*)[63]

This is the wondrousness of the Supreme One Vehicle. Accomplished persons can perform this. As their work is concluded and their virtue is flourishing, they directly advance to the complete and immediate awakening (*zhichao yuandun*). Form and spirit are both wondrous, and they join their truth with the truth of the Dao.

[61] See p. 177, note 47 above. In the Supreme One Vehicle, "precepts" does not only refer to morality, but to what the *Daode jing* calls "mysterious virtue" (*xuande*), what the *Cantong qi* calls "superior virtue" (*shangde*), and what the *Wuzhen pian* calls maintaining a "deeply virtuous conduct" (*dexing shen*): it means taking the operation of the Dao as a model of one's own operation. Any other "precept" is derived from this principle. See *Daode jing*, sec. 10, 51, and 55; *Cantong qi*, sec. 20 (translated above, p. 8); *Wuzhen pian*, "Lüshi," poem 11 (Pregadio, *Awakening to Reality*, p. 54).

[62] A "sign of response" (*yingyan*) is an external phenomenon or event that attests to, and therefore verifies, one's spiritual attainment. In the Supreme One Vehicle, the "sign of response" is the enlightened mind (*mingxin*) itself.

[63] Note that in the Supreme One Vehicle there are no Fire phases.

12 The Great Essentials of the Golden Elixir

Jindan dayao 金丹大要

Chen Zhixu 陳致虛 (1290-ca. 1368)

Like Li Daochun a few decades before him (see the previous chapter), Chen Zhixu was another Yuan-dynasty Neidan master who focused on merging the doctrines of the Northern and Southern lineages (Beizong and Nanzong). As a representative of the "Yin-Yang" branch (*yinyang pai*), his Neidan includes sexual conjunction among its practices, a feature that was emphasized by later exponents of the same trend and has lead some Western scholars to call him a "sexual alchemist" (a term that has no correspondence in Chinese).[1]

While it is affected by a rather personal style of writing, the *Jindan dayao*, or *Great Essentials of the Golden Elixir*, is a monumental compendium of Neidan. The three essays translated here can hardly testify to its width and complexity. "The Wondrous Operation of the Golden Elixir" contains one of the clearest explanations of the alchemical equivalence among Metal, Lead, and the Elixir. "The Wondrous Operation of the Medicine" deals, in terms similar to those used by Li Daochun, with the distinction between the Internal Medicine and the External Medicine. "The Wondrous Operation of the Transmutation of Spirit" is concerned with the last stages of the practice (i.e., "refining Spirit and returning to the Dao") and describes the "gestation" and birth of the alchemical embryo.

Section titles are found in the original Chinese text.

[1] The "Yin-Yang" branch is distinguished from the "pure cultivation" branch (*qingxiu pai*). Neither terms denotes a lineage, and defines instead a type of Neidan, especially with regard to the practices. Each branch subsumes several lineages and sublineages in the proper senses. In addition, certain Neidan lineages (e.g., the Southern Lineage) are sometimes subdivided into "pure cultivation" and "Yin-Yang" branches.

THE WONDROUS OPERATION OF THE GOLDEN ELIXIR

The *Jinbi guwen* (Ancient Text on Gold and Jade) says:

> Within the arts of the Elixir, nothing is greater in sending forth
> their light than Metal and Fire.[2]

Metal and Fire are the True Lead. It also says:

> When the Original Princess begins to refine Mercury,
> the Spirit Chamber holds the cavernous Void.
> The Mysterious and the White generate the Lord of Metals:
> it is eminent and lays the beginnings.[3]

It also says:

> Only when the function of the Spirit Chamber is at work
> can the Golden Elixir be achieved.[4]

The Realized Man Boyang (Wei Boyang) said:

> When Metal goes back to its initial nature,
> then you can call it Reverted Elixir.[5]

Shangyang zi said:[6] "Metal" is not what is [commonly] called metal:

---

[2] *Guwen longhu jing zhushu* (Commentary and Subcommentary to the Ancient Text of the *Book of the Dragon and the Tiger*), sec. 11. This sentence is a paraphrase of a passage in the *Cantong qi* (The Seal of the Unity of the Three), 8:2–3: "Among the suspended images that send forth their light, none is greater than the Sun and the Moon" (see Pregadio, *The Seal of the Unity of the Three*, p. 72). The *Cantong qi* in turn quotes this passage from the "Appended Sayings" ("Xici") of the *Book of Changes* (A.11; see Wilhelm, *The I-ching or Book of Changes*, p. 319). "Suspended images" means planets and asterisms, which appear to be hanging in the sky.

[3] *Guwen longhu jing zhushu*, sec. 12. Original Princess (Yuanjun) is usually the name of Laozi's mother. According to a passage found elsewhere in the *Jindan dayao* (ch. 6), Chen Zhixu understands the "mysterious" as meaning Yin within Yang, and the "white" as meaning Yang within Yin.

[4] *Guwen longhu jing zhushu*, sec. 20.

[5] *Cantong qi*, 41:13–14 (see Pregadio, *The Seal*, p. 90).

[6] Shangyang zi (Master of Highest Yang) is Chen Zhixu's own appellation (*hao*).

when we refer to Metal, we mean Lead. Since Lead is the forefather of all metals, we call it in general "the Metal."

Indeed, this is not the metal that is treasured in the world, namely gold, and it does not come forth from common soil and common stones. This Metal is the precelestial Ancestral Breath, but is generated in the postcelestial state. Those who practice the great cultivation intend to search for the body of the Great Ultimate (*taiji*) before its division, the true instant of the creation of the world. Therefore the exalted immortals and the highest saints search for the Breath prior to the generation of Heaven and Earth within the state posterior to Heaven and Earth, after the rise of form and matter. With this Breath they refine and achieve the Pure Yang. This is why we call it the Elixir.

Now, Pure Yang is Qian ☰, and Pure Yin is Kun ☷; the Yang within Yin is Kan ☵, and the Yin within Yang is Li ☲. To use the human being as a metaphor, it is as if Li takes the Yang line from the center of Kan and fills the Yin within itself, forming Qian. This is why it is called Pure Yang. And since the central line of Kan belongs to Metal, it is called Golden Elixir.[7]

You should search for the precelestial state, before the rise of form. In the state posterior to Heaven and Earth, after the rise of form, there are human beings and things, and not the Golden Elixir.

Moreover, this is not gold, it is not lead, and it is nor silver: it is their Breath. This is what my master Yuandu zi (Zhao Youqin) meant when he said: "The precelestial One Breath comes from within Empty Non-Being." The *Huangting jing* (Book of the Yellow Court) says:

> The revolving purple and the enfolding yellow enter the
> Cinnabar Field,
> the inner light of the Obscure Chamber illuminates the Yang
> Gate.[8]

---

[7] The word *jin* means both "metal" and "gold." Therefore the term *jindan*, usually rendered as "Golden Elixir," also means "Metal Elixir."

[8] *Huangting jing*, "Inner" version, poem 2. In this work, "the purple" and "the yellow" denote the Yin and Yang inner breaths (*qi*) that practitioners circulate within their bodies. The Yang Gate (*yangmen*), usually called Gate of Life (*mingmen*), is the lower Cinnabar Field, or a point located in its region. The Obscure Chamber (*youshi*) is the kidneys.

It also says:

> To search for immortality, exhale and inhale the Original
> Breath.[9]

The *Xiantian daxue shu* (Book on the Great Learning of the Precelestial) by Wei Shilü says:

> The saint is able to revert to the One Breath, "go back to the root, and return to his mandate."[10] Joined to the Dao through his Original Spirit, he generates without exhaustion and embraces the ten thousand images. This is called "obtaining Unity." If we are forced to give it a name, we call it Elixir.
>
> This is not a technique: "The Way of Qian ☰ produces transformations," and "Yin and Yang are unfathomable."[11] It is the wonder of the utmost Reality of the Great Ultimate, and it embraces the principles of Nature (*xing*) and Existence (*ming*). It is called the Way in which Metal and Liquor return to their true states, and in which form and spirit are both wondrous. It is extremely simple and extremely easy, and once it is obtained, it is obtained forever. By obtaining the oral instructions on this Way, even the most foolish of all the small men would immediately raise to the rank of a saint.[12]

---

[9] *Huangting jing*, "Inner" version, poem 20.

[10] *Daode jing* (Book of the Way and Its Virtue), sec. 16: "Going back to the root is called quiescence, and this is returning to the mandate."

[11] These sentences derive from two different passages of the *Book of Changes*. The first one is found in the "Commentary on the Judgment" ("Tuanzhuan") on the hexagram Qian ☰ (no. 1): "The Way of Qian produces transformations, and each thing receives its correct nature and destiny" (see Wilhelm, p. 371). The second sentence is found in the "Appended Sayings": "That in which Yin and Yang are unfathomable is called Spirit" (A.5; see Wilhelm, p. 301). On the Way of the Golden Elixir not being a "technique" (*shu*) see also this passage of the *Jindan dayao*, ch. 3: ". . . it has been said that the Way of cultivation consists of the techniques of the Yellow Emperor and Laozi. No more of this nonsense! This is the Great Way of the Golden Elixir, and it cannot be called a technique."

[12] This passage is quoted from the *Wuzhen pian* (Awakening to Reality) commentary found in *Xiuzhen shishu*, ch. 26. Wei Shilü's text is now lost.

The essential is that those whom we call divine immortals embrace Spirit and attain immortality by eliminating the Yin and returning to the Yang. The Gentleman Danyang (Ma Yu) said:

> When one's Nature is stabilized, the emotions are forgotten; when the body is emptied, the Breath circulates; when the mind dies, the Spirit lives; when the Yang is abundant, the Yin vanishes.[13]

As soon as they receive the sworn transmission from a true master, those who practice the great cultivation hasten to eliminate the Yin from within themselves and go back to the most true Yang. Yingchan zi (Li Daochun) said:

> For the common people, there is no death until the Yang part is not exhausted. For those who practice the great cultivation, there is no immortality until the Yin part is not exhausted.[14]

Indeed, when thinking ends, the Yin vanishes; and when the illusory conditions are emptied, the Yang grows. Therefore when the Yin is exhausted and the Yang is pure, the medicine of the Golden Elixir ripens; and when the Elixir ripens, one raises in flight to the domain of divine immortality. This is what we call a divine immortal.

THE WONDROUS OPERATION OF THE MEDICINE

The Yellow Emperor said:

> Man is the thief of the ten thousand things.[15]

He also said:

---

[13] This passage is quoted from the *Danyang zhenren yulu* (Recorded Sayings of the Realized Man Ma Danyang [Ma Yu]). Ma Yu's text has "mind" (*xin*) instead of "Nature" (*xing*).

[14] *Zhonghe ji* (The Harmony of the Center: An Anthology), ch. 4. In his quotation, Chen Zhixu inverts the two sentences.

[15] *Yinfu jing*, sec. 12 (translated above, p. 32). The *Yinfu jing* is traditionally attributed to the Yellow Emperor (Huangdi).

The Sun and the Moon have rules, the large and the small have laws. The efficacy of the sage comes forth from this, the Numinous Light comes forth from this.[16]

The *Jinbi jing* (Book on Gold and Jade) says:

Refine the Silver in the Lead,
and the Divine Substance (*shenwu*) will be born of its own.[17]

The *Cantong qi* (The Seal of the Unity of the Three) says:

Like kinds yield results with ease,
unlike types are a challenge to craft.[18]

The Patriarch Danyang (Ma Yu) said:

Spirit and Breath are Nature and Existence; Nature and Existence are Dragon and Tiger; Dragon and Tiger are Lead and Mercury; Lead and Mercury are Fire and Water; Fire and Water are the Infant and the Maid; the Infant and the Maid are True Yin and True Yang.[19]

The Gentleman Ziyang (Zhang Boduan) said:

Swallowing saliva and ingesting breath are human actions;
only when you have the Medicine can you form and transform.
If in the tripod there is no True Seed,
it is like using water and fire to boil an empty pot.[20]

He also said:

You should know that the source of the stream, the place
where the Medicine is born,
is just at the southwest—that is its native village.[21]

---

[16] *Yinfu jing*, sec. 15 (translated above, p. 36).
[17] *Guwen longhu jing zhushu*, sec. 28.
[18] *Cantong qi*, 80:11–12 (see Pregadio, *The Seal*, p. 119).
[19] This passage is quoted from the *Danyang zhenren yulu*.
[20] *Wuzhen pian*, "Jueju," poem 5 (translated above p. 77).
[21] *Wuzhen pian*, "Lüshi," poem 7 (translated above, p. 72).

Shangyang zi said: From the antiquity to the present day, the highest saints and the immortals of rank have bequeathed books on the Elixir, but have been unwilling to express themselves clearly. With regard to the ingredients, they refer to Metal and Wood, Water and Fire, Lead and Mercury, or Cinnabar and Silver. These are all metaphors. The common people devote themselves to calcinating and refining, thinking that the ingredients are ordinary lead, quicksilver, and sulphur. They are like the blind leading the blind, and one feels deep grief for them.

Now I will disclose something clearly to the world. With regard to the ingredients, one should know that this Medicine does not come forth from metals, stones, herbs, or plants of the ordinary world. It has no form and no substance, but is obtained within what has form. It looks like gold, but is not the worldly gold; it looks like water, but is not the ordinary water.

In addition, there are the Internal Medicine and the External Medicine. In the External Medicine, within Kan ☵ you search for the precelestial Water of True Unity; within Water you gather the precelestial undefiled Lead; and within Lead you collect the precelestial Breath of the Great Unity. This Breath is the white within the black, or Yang within Yin.[22] This is what the *Wuzhen pian* (Awakening to Reality) means when it says: "Gather the solid [line] from the center in the position of Kan."[23]

   Indeed, the Water of True Unity is the same as the Essence and the Breath of True Unity. This Breath is the mother of Heaven and Earth, the root of Yin and Yang, the foundation of Water and Fire, the ancestor of the Sun and the Moon, and the forefather of the ten thousand things.

---

[22] *Cantong qi*, 22:1–4: "'Know the white, keep to the black,' and the Numinous Light will come of its own. White is the essence of Metal, Black is the foundation of Water" (translated above, p. 9). The first sentence of this passage derives from the *Daode jing*, sec. 28: "Know the white, keep to the black, and be a mold for the world." In Neidan, all these passages refer to the collection of the precelestial True Yang found within the postcelestial Yin.

[23] *Wuzhen pian*, "Jueju," poem 16 (translated above, p. 80).

The *Qi bitu* (Secret Charts of the *Cantong qi*) says:

> Kan ☵ is Water and the Moon. In the human being it is the kidneys. The kidneys store the vital Essence; within the Essence there is the Breath of pure Yang, which blazes and rises upward. The Essence is Yin and the Breath is Yang, therefore Lead is yielding and Silver is firm. The nature of the Tiger belongs to Metal, and Metal can generate Water. Gather it by means of inversion, because "the mother is hidden in the embryo of her son." Therefore the Tiger comes forth from Water. The Tiger then matches Lead; this is called Yang within Yin.[24]

This refers to the External Medicine.

In the Internal Medicine, within Li ☲ you search for the precelestial Liquor of the True Unity; within the Liquor you put in motion the long-accumulated precelestial Cinnabar; and within Cinnabar you circulate the most true precelestial Mercury. This Mercury is the black within the white, or Yin within Yang. This is what the *Wuzhen pian* means when it says: "Transmute by projection the innermost Yin in the palace of Li."[25]

The *Qi bitu* says:

> Li ☲ is Fire and the Sun. In the human being it is the heart. The heart stores the vital Blood; within Blood there is the Liquor of the True Unity, which flows and descends downward. The Blood is Yang and the Liquor is Yin, therefore Cinnabar is Yang and Mercury is Yin. The nature of the Dragon belongs to

---

[24] This quotation, as well as the one found after the next paragraph, correspond to passages of the *Wuzhen pian* commentary contained in the *Xiuzhen shishu*, ch. 26. Here lead is meant as the native Yin lead (sometimes called "black lead," *heiqian*) which contains True Yang, here called "silver." The sentence "the mother is hidden in the embryo of her son" derives from the *Cantong qi* (The Seal of the Unity of the Three), 23:4 (translated above, p. 11).

[25] *Wuzhen pian*, "Jueju," poem 16 (translated above, p. 80). This paragraph is concerned with the True Yin (Mercury) found within Yang (Cinnabar).

Wood, and Wood can generate Fire. Gather it by means of inversion, because "the mother is hidden in the embryo of her son." Therefore the Dragon comes forth from Fire. The Dragon then matches Mercury; this is called Yin within Yang.[26]

This refers to the Internal Medicine.

Yingchan zi (Li Daochun) said:

> In general, those who study the Dao should begin from the External Medicine; then they proceed to the Internal Medicine. Superior persons have already planted the root of virtue, and know it by birth; therefore they do not refine the External Medicine, and directly cultivate the Internal Medicine.
>
> With the Internal Medicine "there is no doing, yet nothing is not done"; with the External Medicine "there is doing, and something whereby it is done."
>
> The Internal Medicine is devoid of form and substance, but has actuality; the External Medicine has a foundation and an operation, but is devoid of actuality.
>
> The External Medicine is the superior undertaking of the physical body (seshen); the Internal Medicine is the superior undertaking of the dharma-body (fashen).
>
> The External Medicine is the way of the Immortals of Earth; the Internal Medicine is the way of the Immortals of Heaven.
>
> The External Medicine brings one's Existence to fulfillment; the Internal Medicine brings one's Nature to fulfillment.[27]

It is only because the Dao is related to Yin and Yang that there are an Internal and an External Medicine. Wuming zi (Weng Baoguang) said:

> Li ☲ is Yang outside and Yin inside. Kan ☵ is Yin outside and Yang inside. By transmuting the Yin found inside [Li ☲] by means of the Yang found inside [Kan ☵], the trigram Qian ☰

---

[26] See p. 190, note 24 above.

[27] This passage is quoted from Zhonghe ji, ch. 2 (translated above, pp. 165 ff.), with minor variants reflected in my translation.

is formed; this is a metaphor of the Golden Elixir. The Breath of utmost Yang coalesces within the Yin Ocean. Gather it to transmute your own Yin Mercury, and you will transform yourself into a being of Pure Yang.[28]

Shangyang zi, feeling no embarrassment, his lips pronouncing one discourse after the other, has tirelessly left down instructions on the Elixir, so that the people of later times could thoroughly understand. The "Song of the Golden Elixir" ("Jindan ge") by the Gentleman Haichan (Liu Haichan) says:

> If you want to transcend the ordinary and enter the place of
>   sainthood,
> there is nothing outside the two Elixirs, one Yin and one Yang.
> For the Yang Elixir you must obtain the precelestial Treasure;
> within there are the five colors, and it embraces the supreme
>   Dao.
> For the Yin Elixir you must recognize the precelestial Breath,
> and constantly protect the stem of Existence with the root of
>   Nature.[29]

The Yang Elixir is the External Elixir, the External Medicine. "Creation and transformation occur within the Furnace of the Two Eights. It is born in less than half of a [double] hour, and it is immediately accomplished."[30] This is the Breath of True Unity prior to Heaven and Earth; its appellation is True Lead, and it is also called Flowery Pond (*huachi*), Spirit Water (*shenshui*), and True Metal. Therefore Zhenyi zi (Peng Xiao) said:

> Before the inchoate state, when there are not yet Heaven and
> Earth, True Lead obtains the One and is the first to take form.

---

[28] *Wuzhen pian zhushu*, ch. 5. Yin Ocean (*yinhai*) here is a name of the kidneys.

[29] This poem does not seem to be found in other extant Neidan texts.

[30] This passage is quoted from the *Wuzhen pian* commentary in *Xiuzhen shishu*, ch. 29, with variants. The "hour" mentioned in this passage is the zi hour, the symbolic time of the coagulation of the Elixir. The "half hour" is the first half of the zi hour, in which the True Yang is born.

Then it gradually gives birth to Heaven and Earth, Yin and Yang, the five agents, and the ten thousand things.[31]

Those who practice the great cultivation collect this True Lead, let it return to the Tripod of the Suspended Womb, and let it enter the Chamber in order to transmute [one's own] Mercury.[32] This is called the External Elixir.

The Yin Elixir is the Internal Elixir, the Internal Medicine. As soon as they obtain the External Elixir, those who practice the great cultivation place it in the Tripod. Then they practice the Matching Fires (*fuhuo*) of Yin and Yang,[33] cyclically extracting and augmenting (*choutian*)[34] in order to warmly nourish it. The Patriarch Danyang (Ma Yu) said:

> The Liquor of the heart descends, the Breath of the kidneys ascends. When they reach the Yellow Room, if their generative force is not dispersed, the Elixir coalesces.[35]

The Wuzhen pian says:

> Desist from guarding the furnace of the Medicine and from watching over the Fire phases:
> just watch the breathing of the Spirit and rely on the celestial spontaneity.[36]

[31] *Zhouyi cantong qi fenzhang tong zhenyi* (The True Meaning of the *Cantong qi*, with a Subdivision into Sections), commentary to sec. 25. Peng Xiao's words are also quoted in *Xiuzhen shishu*, ch. 29. True Lead is here a name of Pure Yang (*chunyang*), the state of unity prior to subdivision of the Great Ultimate (*taiji*) into Yin and Yang.

[32] On the Tripod of the Suspended Womb (*xuantai ding*) see above, p. 94 note 21. The Chamber is the lower Cinnabar Field.

[33] That is, the Fire phases, where the increasing stages of heating (Yang) in the first part of the cycle are matched (*fu*) by decreasing stages (Yin) in the second part.

[34] That is, extracting Lead and augmenting Mercury. The practice described here by Chen Zhixu is the same as the one described by Peng Haogu in his commentary to the *Jindan sibai zi*, poem 19; see above, p. 106.

[35] This passage is quoted from the *Danyang zhenren yulu*. On the Yellow Room, see p. 105 note 52.

[36] *Wuzhen pian*, "Lüshi," poem 13 (see Pregadio, *Awakening to Reality*,

The "breathing of the Spirit" (*shenxi*) is what Zhuangzi spoke about when he said, "the Realized Man breaths through the heels";[37] [it is also] what Guangcheng zi spoke about when he said:

> In the Stove of the Elixir, the River Chariot rests from its toils,
> in the crane's womb, the breathing like a turtle is unceasing.[38]

"Breathing like a turtle," "breathing through the heels," and "breathing of the Spirit" have different names, but their operation is the same. This is called the True Fire, and it is the Internal Medicine. After you have ingested the Elixir, without the True Fire you cannot nurture the Embryo of Sainthood; therefore you should sit and watch over the breathing of the Spirit.

Now, "Heaven is 1 and generates Water, which in the human being is the Essence; Earth is 2 and generates Fire, which in the human being is the Spirit."[39] In the human being, Essence and Spirit strengthen and guard the entire person. Circulate the Yin and the Yang and merge exhalation and inhalation. Let Spirit and Breath operate by means of exhalation and inhalation; gather Water and Fire by means of Spirit and Breath; and refine your embryonic breathing by means of Water and Fire. When your embryonic breathing is unceasing, this allows Kan ☵ and Li ☲ to drift freely. Kan and Li conjoin and generate the Golden Liquor. When the Golden Liquor reverts [to the Cinnabar Field], the Elixir is achieved.[40]

---

p. 60). For "watch" (*kan*), some editions of the *Wuzhen pian* have "settle" (*an*).

[37] *Zhuangzi*, ch. 6: "The Realized Man breaths through the heels, the common man breaths through the throat" (see Watson, *The Complete Works of Chuang Tzu*, p. 78).

[38] This passage too is quoted from the *Danyang zhenren yulu*. The expression *mianmian* ("unceasing") derives from *Daode jing*, sec. 6: "The gate of the Mysterious-Female is called the root of Heaven and Earth. Unceasing and continuous, its operation never wears out."

[39] *Wuzhen pian zhushu*, ch. 8.

[40] This paragraph is similar to another passage found in *Wuzhen pian zhushu*, ch. 8. For the last sentence, see the second meaning of "Reverted Elixir of the Golden Liquor" in the *Jindan wenda* (Questions and Answers on the Golden Elixir), translated above, p. 138.

THE WONDROUS OPERATION
OF THE TRANSMUTATION OF SPIRIT

The Patriarch Zhongli (Zhongli Quan) said:

> Seek the immortals, search for companions, and learn how to
> heat the Elixir;
> attentively collect the Red Sulphur, and make the Great
> Reversion.[41]

The Gentleman Haichan (Liu Haichan) said:

> The celestial circuit of the Fire phases according to the
> hexagrams is concluded;
> you are pregnant with an infant, locked in the Lower Field.
> One clap of thunder arises from the earth:
> the Door of Qian ☰ breaks open, its radiance unfolds over ten
> thousand miles.
> You set yourself free, and break through the Great Mysterious
> Barrier (tai xuanguan):
> in that very moment you become a true immortal child.[42]

The *Cantong qi* says:

> In sleep, embrace your Spirit;
> when awake, watch over existence and extinction.
>
> Gradually your countenance will moisten
> and your bones will grow solid and strong.
> Having completely removed the evil of Yin,
> you can establish pure Yang.
>
> Cultivate this unceasingly,
> and your plentiful breath will course like rain from the clouds,

[41] In the second verse, the Red Sulphur (*zhuliu*) is the "Cinnabar" produced by the drying of Mercury when the Internal Medicine is refined at the
end of the Neidan process. Chen Zhixu says below that this is the "Pure Yang
of the Reverted Elixir of the Golden Liquor." Great Reversion (*dahuan*)
stands for Great Reverted Elixir (*da huandan*).

[42] I have not identified the source of this poem. The Door of Qian is the
sinciput, from which the immortal embryo is said to come forth.

overflowing like a marsh in the spring,
pouring forth like ice that has melted.

It will stream from the head to the toes;
on reaching the end, it will rise once again.
In its coming and going, it will spread limitless,
pervading throughout and extending all around.[43]

Shangyang zi said: As soon as they have ingested one "knife-point,"
those who practice the great cultivation should circulate their own
Jade Mushroom in order to nourish it.[44]

Every time you circulate the Fire, you suddenly experience the True
Breath in the Spinal Handle surging up to the Muddy Pellet.[45] There is
a tickling sound, as if something in the head touches the brain. In one
instant, it becomes similar to small sparrow's eggs, and it descends
from the palate through the Storied Pavilion.[46] It has a fragrant flavor
similar to iced milk, and a taste of incomparable sweetness.

When you experience this, it is a sign that you have obtained the
Reverted Elixir of the Golden Liquor. Slowly swallow it and let it
return to the Cinnabar Field. From then onwards, do this constantly
and without interruption. Close your eyes, observe within, and pass
through your viscera as if you were holding a bright torch in your
hands. Gradually a golden radiance will surround your body.

The Gentleman Niwan (Chen Nan) said:

In the past I practiced for a whole year:
my six pulses (*liumai*) came to rest, and my Breath went back
to the root.[47]

Laozi said:

---

[43] *Cantong qi*, 59:7–12 and 60:1–8 (see Pregadio, *The Seal*, p. 103).

[44] On the terms "knife-point" and Jade Mushroom see above, p. 129 note
43.

[45] The Spinal Handle (*jiaji*) is located in the middle of the spinal column.
The Muddy Pellet (*niwan*) is the upper Cinnabar Field.

[46] The Storied Pavilion (*chonglou*) is the trachea.

[47] *Cuixu pian* (The Emerald Emptiness), sec. "Luofu Cuixu yin" (Chant of
Emerald Emptiness on Mount Luofu).

In concentrating your breath until it is at its softest,
can you be like an infant?[48]

All of this refers to "nourishing warmly" (*wenyang*). "Nourishing
warmly" means "shattering your limbs and your entire body, dismiss-
ing the sharpness of your hearing and the brightness of your sight,"[49]
and looking like a fool for the whole day. You cannot separate from
this for even an instant: similar to a hen hatching her egg, your warm
breath cannot stop for a moment.

When this happens, you are seeing the efficacy of "extracting and
augmenting" with your own eyes. In "extracting and augmenting,"
after you fix (*zhi*) Mercury by means of Lead, you circulate the Fire
day after day. Gradually augment Mercury, so that Mercury gradually
increases and Lead gradually decreases. In due time, Lead will be
exhausted and Mercury will dry. It will transform itself into Cinnabar.
Its appellation is Pure Yang of the Reverted Elixir of the Golden
Liquor.

Thus we know that form transmutes itself into Breath, and Breath
transmutes itself into Spirit.[50] This Spirit is called the Infant, and is
also called the Yang Spirit. The *Book of the Yellow Court* (*Huangting
jing*) says:

Watching respectfully the lad who sits relaxed
I asked: From which family comes the child who resides in
   me?[51]

The Gentleman Zhengyang (Zhongli Quan) said:

[48] *Daode jing*, sec. 10.
[49] For these sentences, see *Zhuangzi*, ch. 6: "I smash up my limbs and
body, dismiss perception and intellect (*lit.*, the sharpness of my hearing and
the brightness of my sight), cast off form, do away with understanding, and
make myself identical with the Great Thoroughfare" (see Watson, p. 90).
[50] Note the replacement of "Essence" (*jing*) with "form" (*xing*) to define
the first stage of the Neidan practice, usually called *refining the Essence to
transmute it into Breath*. Chen Zhixu's work is one of the Neidan texts that
use this different term. There is a close relation between "essence" and
"form," since the "essence" of the Dao is the seed that generates the world of
form.
[51] *Huangting jing*, "Inner" version, poem 19.

The child is young and has yet to grow:
he entirely relies on his mom who nurtures him with love.[52]

In the past, during the Jingding reign-period (1260–64) of the Song dynasty, the immortal Lan Yangsu refined the Great Reverted Elixir of the Golden Liquor. When he obtained the Elixir he retired on Mount Nanyue. After he had carried it in his womb for a long time, Li Yuxi delivered a message to him on behalf of Gentleman Haichan (Liu Haichan). Lan Yangsu burst into a loud laughter. On his sinciput there was a clap of thunder, and he departed. In our own time, he is known as the Elder of the Loud Laughter on Mount Nanyue.

The Patriarch Chunyang (Lü Dongbin) said:

The nine-year Fire phases are just concluded:
suddenly the peak of the Gate of Heaven breaks open.
The Realized Man appears, the Great Spirit is everywhere:
from now, you can be congratulated as a Celestial Immortal.[53]

When it comes to this, the great undertaking of the Golden Elixir is concluded.

---

[52] These verses are attributed to Zhongli Quan in several Neidan texts, some of which have "dad and mom" (*yeniang*) for "mom" (*niangniang*): "The child is young and has yet to grow: he entirely relies on his dad and his mom who nurture him with love."

[53] These verses are quoted from a poem entitled "Song of the Unbaked Brick in the Kiln" ("Yaotou pi ge"), attributed to Lü Dongbin, found in *Lüzu zhi* (Monograph on Ancestor Lü), ch. 6.

13 Rectifying Errors for the Seekers of the Golden Elixir

Jindan jiuzheng pian 金丹就正篇

Lu Xixing 陸西星 (1520–1606)

Lu Xixing (from Yangzhou, Jiangsu) is the beginner of the Eastern Branch (Dongpai) and, like Chen Zhixu (see the previous chapter), a representative of the "Yin-Yang" variety of Neidan. Almost all of his works are included in a collection entitled *Fanghu waishi* (The External Secretary of Mount Fanghu). One of them, the *Jindan jiuzheng pian*, or *Rectifying Errors for the Seekers of the Golden Elixir*, is translated here mainly in order to allow comparison with other Neidan texts.[1]

Although Lu Xixing distinguishes his Neidan from the ordinary "arts of the bedchamber" (*fangzhong shu*), the entire alchemical discourse and symbolism reflected in this work is focused on the physical body. Lu Xixing's Neidan, in addition, is clearly addressed to male practitioners: while the male adept supplies his own Mercury (True Yin within Yang), the other ingredient of the Elixir, namely True Lead (True Yang within Yin), should be collected by means of sexual conjunction with a female.

With the exception of the prefaces, this chapter contains a complete translation of Lu Xixing's text. The subdivision into three untitled parts is found in the original Chinese text.

---

[1] My translation of this title is somewhat free. The title derives from the *Lunyu* (Sayings of Confucius), 1.14: "When he eats, the noble man does not look for gratification of his appetite, and when he is in his dwelling place, he does not look for comfort. He is earnest in his activities and careful in his words; he seeks those who have the Way so that he may be rectified. Such a person may be said indeed to love to learn" (see Legge, *The Chinese Classics*, vol. 1, pp. 143–44).

I

Someone asked Qianxu zi:[2] The books on the Elixir say that the precelestial One Breath should be sought in what is "of the same kind" (*tonglei*). What does this mean?

I said: I heard my Master say that the Way of the Golden Elixir must rely on the conjunction of Yin and Yang in order to be achieved. Yin and Yang are the male and the female, Li ☲ and Kan ☵, Lead and Mercury. These are the ingredients of the Great Elixir.

Now, the True Breath of Kan is called Lead, and the True Essence of Li is called Mercury. The precelestial Essence is stored in "me"; the precelestial Breath is taken from the "other." Why? The "other" is Kan. Kan ☵ is Yin outside and Yang inside; among the images it is Water and the Moon, and among humans it is the female. "Me" is Li. Li ☲ is Yang outside and Yin inside; among the images it is Fire and the Sun, and among humans it is the male. Therefore in the Way of Yin and Yang of the male and the female, "following the course" generates other human beings, and "inverting the course" achieves the Elixir. Their principles are the same.

He said: The *Book of Changes* clearly says that Kan is the middle son and Li is the middle daughter. Why do you say instead that "I" am Li?[3]

I said: This discourse is based on the positions [of the trigrams] in the "precelestial chart" (*xiantian tu*).[4] Master Shao (Shao Yong) said: "The essences of Yin and Yang are hidden in each other's house."[5]

---

    [2] Qianxu zi (Master Secluded in Emptiness) is Lu Xixing's own appellation (*hao*).
    [3] This question is clearly asked from the perspective of a male. In the *Book of Changes*, the conjunction of Qian ☰ and Kun ☷ gives birth to three "male" and three "female" trigrams, called "elder," "middle," and "younger." The elder son is Zhen ☳, the middle son is Kan ☵, and the younger son is Gen ☶. The elder daughter is Xun ☴, the middle daughter is Li ☲, and the younger daughter is Dui ☱.
    [4] See table 3, p. 259.
    [5] This and other similar sentences (e.g., "The essences of Kan ☵ and Li ☲ are hidden in each other's house") are attributed to Shao Yong and other authors.

Now, when the Great Ultimate (*taiji*) divides itself there are the two principles; after the two principles there are the four images; and after the four images there are the eight trigrams. Therefore Li ☲ pertains to Qian ☰, and Kan ☵ pertains to Kun ☷. The trigrams Li and Kan are formed by the conjunction of Qian and Kun. The male and female material bodies are formed by the conjunction of Yin and Yang. Therefore when Qian and Kun conjoin, Qian inevitably becomes empty [in the middle] and forms Li, and Kun inevitably becomes full [in the middle] and forms Kan. And when male and female conjoin, the Yin inevitably contains the Yang, and the Yang inevitably is rooted in the Yin. This is the difference between Kan and Li, the "other" and "me."

He said: Thus within Li ☲ there is the Yin essence, and within Kan ☵ there is the Yang breath. Why are the essence and the breath not found in "me," and I must take them from the "other"?

I said: Actually you have them; I have not yet finished to explain. In the past, I had been drowning in the treatises of Old Yuwu, but now I have begun to awaken myself.[6] Please listen carefully, and I will try to explain this to you.

I heard my Master say: "Yin and Yang and the two fives wondrously join and coagulate with one another: this is how a human being is born."[7] At the beginning, it is like a great block of wood, still uncarved: an intact body, like the inchoate Great Ultimate. Laozi said: "Holding the fullness of virtue is similar to being an infant. . . . He does not know of the joining of female and male, but he is aroused: this is the culmination of the essence. He cries for the whole day, but his voice is not hoarse: this is the culmination of harmony."[8] These are

    [6] Yuwu is Yu Yan, the author of a commentary to the *Yinfu jing* (Book of the Hidden Agreement; translated above, Chapter 2) and of several other works on Neidan and cosmology. The criticism by Lu Xixing is owed to the fact that Yu Yan's works are concerned with a quite different form of Neidan, which does not involve sexual practices.
    [7] The "two fives" (*erwu*) are the two pairs of agents formed by Metal and Water (whose numerical values are 4 and 1, respectively) and by Wood and Fire (3 and 2). The values of both pairs is 5. (See table 1, p. 257.)
    [8] *Daode jing* (Book of the Way and Its Virtue), sec. 55.

Yin and Yang in their pure state. At that time, the precelestial body is still inchoate and strong: what need is there to borrow, and what need is there to supplement? If one obtains that body, what should one add to the superior virtue of non-doing (*wuwei*)? Yet, when sexual desire awakens and Yin and Yang conjoin for the first time, the precelestial Breath escapes and hides itself within Kun. Therefore the three lines of pure Qian ☰ are broken and it becomes Li ☲.[9] Li is the Sun; when the Sun inclines to the West, the signs of old age emerge.[10] How could it have an enduring presence?[11] This is why the alchemical practice takes from Kan ☵. "Taking from Kan" means replenishing the broken Qian, filling that empty line, and returning to the body of pure Yang. This is the explanation of the Reverted Elixir (*huandan*) of the divine immortals.

He said: "I" become Li since [my essence] escapes. Why does the "other" become Kan?

I said: This is a good question! At the beginning of the inchoate, the "other" definitely has the body of Kun ☷, but at the age of fourteen the Yang begins to move. Within the pure Kun suddenly the Yang moves: is this not Kan ☵? Therefore Kan is the Yang within the Yin: the quiescence within the Great Ultimate culminates and there is movement. What is so by itself is called "precelestial." When Heaven, which is 1, generates Water, the Breath of True Unity becomes stored in Kan: "The mother is hidden in the embryo of her son" and within Water there is Metal.[12]

If you wish to compound the Golden Elixir, you should take Kan as a model. This is "the place where the Medicine is born,"[13] and it is

---

[9] *Po* "to break" also means "to lose virginity." In the context of Lu Xixing's sexual practices, a male "loses virginity" when his semen is emitted for the first time. This is equated to Qian's loss of its central Yang line, and is at the basis of Lu Xixing's and other *yinyang pai* authors' views on alchemy.

[10] The Sun inclining to the West represents the beginning of sunset.

[11] *Daode jing*, sec. 59. See above, p. 165 note 9.

[12] *Cantong qi* (The Seal of the Unity of the Three), 23:2 (translated above, p. 11).

[13] *Wuzhen pian* (Awakening to Reality), "Lüshi," poem 7 (translated above, p. 72).

the ladder and the raft for ascending to Reality. Now, the Yang within the Yin is ruled by movement; therefore in order to determine the time of "taking from Kan" you should look into that movement. The Yin within the Yang is ruled by quiescence; therefore after you fill Li, you should cultivate yourself in quiescence.

One who knows both movement and quiescence, and does not miss the proper times, isn't he a sage? The sage is the one who "contemplates the Way of Heaven and holds to the operation of Heaven."[14] Therefore the plenitude and depletion of the Moon are images of the oldness and youngness of the Medicine; and the growth and decline Sun is the ebb and flow of the Fire phases. When the Medicine and Fire meet one another, the Elixir is achieved. When the Elixir is achieved, the embryo is delivered and the transformation of Spirit takes place.

Someone also said: Your explanation is entirely concerned with the postcelestial. May I also hear something about the precelestial?

I said: I have looked into what the *Book of Changes* says about this. It says: "Essence and Breath become the creatures; the dispersal of the *Hun*-soul becomes change."[15] Now, the Yang within the Yin is called Breath (*qi*), and the Yin within the Yang is called Essence (*jing*). These two attend to one another, and things are generated. What we ordinarily see is the Way of "following the course": when the essence arrives first and the breath follows later, the Yin embraces the Yang and forms a female. When the breath comes first and the essence follows later, the Yang embraces the Yin and forms a male. However, the distinction between the male Li ☲ and the female Kan ☵ is not established when they form their physical bodies, but when they first receive their breath. Moreover, the Way of the Golden Elixir is achieved by the conjunction of Yin and Yang. The Way of the humans

[14] *Yinfu jing* (Book of the Hidden Agreement), sec. 1 (translated above, p. 24).

[15] *Book of Changes*, "Appended Sayings" ("Xici"), sec. A.4 (see Wilhelm, *The I-ching or Book of Changes*, p. 294). According to the traditional Chinese view, the birth of a human being is owed to the conjunction of Essence (*jing*) and Breath (*qi*), provided by one's father and mother, respectively; and its death—here called "change" (*bian*)—to the dispersal of the "celestial" soul.

follows the course; the Way of the Immortals inverts the course: one collects the medicine in Kan, and makes the Elixir in Li. Can there be any doubt about this?

2

Someone asked: Our bodies, made of the four elements, are entirely Yin.[16] However, our bodies sometimes are in movement: should they not pertain to Yang?

I said: Li is Fire and is the Sun. Although movement pertains to the Yang, its root is actually in the Yin. Therefore it is said that Fire is Yang but has its roots in the Yin. Look at the numinous radiance that glitters and that no one can control: the Yang within ourselves is exactly like that. Thus, it is constantly in danger of fleeing. Knowing that, the sage takes the Water of True Unity from Kan in order to restrain it. Therefore, the emotions that blaze inside and the essence that escapes outside are like a fire burning below, and like water boiling in a pot. Taking the Breath of precelestial Unity from the "other" in order to subdue "my" essence that flees and easily escapes is like pouring spring water from a jar in order to help the water that boils in the pot. It will always be of benefit.

[He said:] Then could you tell me something about the method of "taking from Kan"?

I said: The celestial mechanism is extremely cryptic: unless one obtains the pointers of a master, who would dare to speak recklessly?

[He said:] I beg you to give me a clue. I am waiting for you to awaken me.

[I said:] In the *Book of Changes*, the Thunder ☳ within the Earth ☷ forms the hexagram Fu ䷗ (Return). Within the multiple Yin [lines], suddenly the Yang moves: this is the root of creation and transformation, and the point of conjunction of all categories of things. When Confucius pondered the *Book of Changes* and arrived to this hexagram, he could not refrain from sighing and said: "Fu indeed reveals

---

[16] In Buddhism, the four elements (*sida*) are Earth, Water, Fire, and Wind.

the Heart of Heaven and Earth!."[17] The *Cantong qi* also has this sentence, and in addition it says: "Therefore change encompasses the Heart of Heaven; the hexagram Fu ䷗ lays the initial buds."[18] It also says: "In issuing commands comply with the seasonal ordinances; never neglect the timing of the movement of the lines."[19] Indeed, this is what they mean. Therefore, if one understands that the Thunder within the Earth forms Fu, then one also understands that the Yang is born from the Yin, and the Breath of True Unity is stored in the "other." This is entirely clear!

Someone also said: Concerning the birth of the Medicine, all the books on the Elixir use a metaphor, saying: "On the third day it comes forth at GENG." May I hear about this?

I said: Kan is the Moon, and the Moon is the Great Yin; when it receives the radiance of the Sun, it generates light. On the third day, the Moon comes forth at GENG:[20] these are the "initial buds" of the Yang, equivalent to the hexagram Fu ䷗ (Return).[21] On the eighth day there is the waxing quarter, which results into the two Yang lines of Lin ䷒ (Approach). When the Moon is full in the East, the three Yang lines form Tai ䷊ (Peace). The waining quarter is the decline of the Yang, and the last day of the month is the exhaustion of the Yang. Bo ䷖ (Splitting Apart) and Fu ䷗ pursue one another, and after the end there is a new beginning.[22] Therefore on the third day [the Yang principle] is once again reborn.

[17] *Book of Changes*, "Commentary on the Judgment" ("Tuanzhuan") on the hexagram Fu ䷗ (no. 24; see Wilhelm, p. 505).

[18] *Cantong qi*, 12:1–2 (see Pregadio, *The Seal of the Unity of the Three*, p. 73).

[19] *Cantong qi*, 14:9–10 (see Pregadio, *The Seal*, p. 75).

[20] Compare *Cantong qi*, 13:1–2: "On the third day, it comes forth with its clear light, when Zhen ☳ and GENG match the western direction" (see Pregadio, *The Seal*, p. 74). GENG is the celestial stem associated with the first stage of the moon cycle. See table 5, p. 261.

[21] *Cantong qi*, 12:2 "The hexagram Fu ䷗ lays the initial buds" (see Pregadio, *The Seal*, p. 73).

[22] Bo ䷖ (Splitting Apart) is the hexagram that represents the final stage of the Yang principle before Kun ䷁, which in turn represents the dominion of the Yin principle. See table 4, p. 260.

The creation and transformation produced by the "other" are exactly like this. The alchemical practice takes this as a model in order to look into the oldness and youngness of the ingredient. My Master spoke of "the Medicine within the furnace in the 15th day of the 8th month."[23] He added: "When the shine of the snow in the deep pool of iced water terminates, and the new moon emerges beyond the top of the plum trees, the Medicine is born.[24] The celestial mechanism is mysterious and wondrous: here it is entirely revealed."

In the past, I followed these words, but I could not understand them. Then I suddenly awakened to their meaning, and I understood how deep was the grace of my Master. It was as bright as if he had exposed the Sun and the Moon to my view.

He said: How should one deal with the oldness and youngness of the ingredient?

I said: The creations and transformations of the Golden Elixir are formed by the Breath of precelestial Great Unity. In the precelestial Breath, the heavy and the light have not yet taken form: it is Yang within the Yang. Its beginning is extremely subtle, and its wondrousness is unfathomable. Therefore it must be quickly collected when it is born at GUI, and it must be used while it is still whole.[25] Even a small delay would cause it to produce dregs and to move into the postcelestial domain: the Yang would turn into the Yin. When a poem of the *Wuzhen pian* (Awakening to Reality) says: "What you see cannot be

---

[23] The 15th day of the 8th lunar month is the day of the Mid-Autumn festival (*zhongqiu*). Although this stage is dominated by the Yin principle, at this time the Yang principle prepares its rebirth, which occurs in the 11th lunar month. The 15th day of the 8th month is therefore an emblem of True Yang within Yin.

[24] This sentence establishes a parallel between the lunar cycle and the menstrual cycle.

[25] This sentence is based on a line of the *Wuzhen pian*, "Lüshi," poem 7 (translated above, p. 72): "When Lead meets the birth of GUI, quickly you should collect it." In the context of Lu Xixing's alchemy, GUI is understood as meaning *tiangui*, "menstruation": True Yang should be collected through intercourse with a female immediately after her menstruation.

used," it refers to the oldness.[26] When it says: "In one instant fire and smoke fly, and the Realized Man spontaneously emerges," it refers to the youngness.[27]

Alas! Except for a sage, who else can understand the wonder of creation and transformation? And who can put it into operation?

3

Someone asked: Unless one is a sage, one cannot put the wonder of creation and transformation into operation. We are not sages. If one wants to put it into operation, what are the essentials?

I said: Did not a Master say, "True Soil seizes True Lead, True Lead controls True Mercury"?[28] What is the True Soil? It is the Soil that is one's own "self" (jitu). If those who collect the Medicine do not refine the Soil that is one's own "self," then the numinous Mercury can be easily lost, and what they do would yield no result: they would face embarrassment and disgrace. When the books mention "laying the foundations for refining oneself" (zhuji lianji), they refer to this.

In the human being, the "self" is the Intention; it is also called "one's own Nature" (jixing). As it flows among the [other] four images and does not have a fixed position, it is called Soil.[29] The beginning and end of the Golden Elixir entirely depend on this. Therefore when you refine the Medicine and you seek Lead, you receive it by means of the "self"; when you gather the Fire and you place [the ingredients] in the tripod, you send it forth by means of the "self"; when you refine by heating and you "bathe," you guard this by means of the "self"; when you "nourish warmly" and you deliver the embryo, you achieve this by means of the "self." With a correct heart

---

[26] Wuzhen pian, "Wuyan siyun" (see Cleary, Understanding Reality, p. 127). Lu Xixing understands this sentence as meaning, "When you see it, it cannot be used."

[27] Wuzhen pian, id. (Cleary, p. 127).

[28] Jindan sibai zi (Four Hundred Words on the Golden Elixir), poem 1 (translated above, p. 88).

[29] The four images are the four external agents, i.e., Wood, Metal, Fire, and Water. Soil is the central agent.

and a sincere intention, the person can be cultivated, the kingdom can be governed, and the world can be in peace. These are the greatest essentials for refining the Elixir.

The *Cantong qi* says: "[Kan ☵ and Li ☲] spin the hub and align the axle."[30] It also says: "The Pole Star holds its correct position."[31] In bequeathing their words, the ancient immortals have given repeated warnings and admonitions. There are many cases like this one.

Moreover, it is through their emotions and desires that our father and mother have given us birth. Therefore whenever our material nature comes in contact with something, it gives rise to emotions.[32] If "refining oneself" has not yielded results, and the six senses are not yet stabilized,[33] when one enters the chamber the "great operation" (*dayong*) will appear in front of one's eyes: one's Nature will move, one's emotions will be set ablaze, and the Lovely Maid will flee.[34] If that happens, how could one catch the instant to steal the pearl under the chin of the black dragon? A saying goes: "If you pry into the tiger's lair and you pluck the tiger's whiskers, how can you escape the tiger's jaws?" Be careful! Be careful! Unless you are very wise, you will not succeed; unless you are very strong, you cannot make it.

My Master told me: "The mirror to enter the teaching lies in your mind; if your mind is not empty, the scene will not be true." Alas! Are the teachings on "emptying the mind" not the key for refining oneself? The *Qingjing jing* (Book of Clarity and Quiescence) says:

> He contemplates the mind within, and the mind is devoid of mind. He contemplates the forms outside, and the forms are devoid of form. He contemplates the objects from a distance,

[30] *Cantong qi*, 1:4 (translated above, p. 4).

[31] *Cantong qi*, 17:11 (see Pregadio, *The Seal*, p. 77).

[32] The "material nature" (*qizhi zhi xing*) is one's character or personality, as distinguished from one's "true nature."

[33] For the six senses (*liugen*) see below, p. 224 note 6.

[34] In the context of the sexual practices, "entering the chamber" (*rushi*) means entering the site of sexual conjunction. — In Neidan, the Lovely Maid (*chanü*) is a common image of True Yin within Yang. In the context of Lu Xixing's practices, instead, it represents the Yin essence within the Yang male, that is, his semen. Just like in the "arts of the bedroom," in Lu Xixing's practices the male semen should not be emitted.

and the objects are devoid of object. When one awakens to these three things, one sees them in their emptiness. . . . As in what is empty there is nothing, in nothingness there is nothing that is not.[35]

This is the meaning of "emptying the mind": it is the great liberation and the great emancipation of "refining oneself." Therefore [the *Qingjing jing*] continues by saying: "Constant quiescence, constant response."[36] Ah! "Constant quiescence" is the effect of refining oneself; and "constant response" is the operation of seeking Lead. When my Master spoke of "the Medicine within the furnace in the 15th day of the 8th month" he required me to give him a reply, but I was blank and could not answer. Then he replied by himself, saying, "Wind and flowers are dust on a chair." Those who are fascinated by a scenery always take wind, flowers, snow, and moon to be the four charming features. Facing a beautiful scenery generates so many emotions that they cannot deal with them. Yet, my Master compared all of this to dust on a chair. Is this not "forgetting the self," "forgetting things," and "forgetting forgetfulness"?

The principles of collecting the Medicine and the essentials of refining oneself are the most important things that my Master has taught me. In the past I followed his words; today I understand them.

Someone who had been listening to this quickly stood up and said: Were it not for your words, I would have never heard the essentials of the Great Way. Now please shut your mouth.[37] I will retire to practice "refining myself."

[35] The *Qingjing jing* is one of the main Taoist meditation texts. It states that the innate clarity and quiescence of the mind and the spirit are defiled by passion and desires. Only by comprehending that mind, forms, and individual objects are devoid of a substantial nature is it possible to awaken to their fundamental emptiness. This is attained by contemplation, and leads one to the recovery of the "clarity and quiescence" mentioned in the title of the work.

[36] The *Qingjing jing* has: "Constant response, constant quiescence: this is constant clarity and quiescence."

[37] However irreverent it might seem, this expression derives from the *Daode jing*, sec 52 and 56: "Shut the openings, close the gates." *Dui* ("openings") is sometimes understood as meaning "mouth."

14 Principles of the Conjoined Cultivation of Nature and Existence

Xingming guizhi 性命圭旨

Anonymous (ca. 1600)

The *Xingming guizhi*, or *Principles of the Conjoined Cultivation of Nature and Existence*, dates from around 1600 and is attributed to an anonymous disciple of an equally unknown Yin Zhenren (Realized Man Yin). Because of its renown and its wide circulation, it has sometimes been seen as a work that reflects the "popularization" of Neidan during the Ming and the Qing periods (1368–1644 and 1644–1912). While this is to some extent true, the *Xingming guizhi* also ranks among the main doctrinal treatises of this tradition.[1]

The work is broad and has a complex structure. It is divided into four main parts, with sections within each part made of an illustration followed by explanatory texts. The explanatory texts in the first part are called "Explanations" ("Shuo") and deal with general subjects. Those in the other three parts are arranged into nine sets of "Oral Instructions" ("Koujue") and follow the sequence of the Neidan practice, culminating with "The Egress of the Yang Spirit." Large portions in all sections are made of quotations from earlier works.

These selections consist of four sections of the first part. I translate both the text found in the illustration and the relevant "Explanation." Section titles are found in the original Chinese text.

---

[1] *Xing* and *ming*, which form part of the title of the *Xingming guizhi*, are two of the main terms in Neidan. *Xing* can be understood and translated as "nature," in the sense of "human nature," "inner nature," or "inborn nature." *Ming* is in several respects a more complex concept. In addition to the literal translations as "order, command, mandate," this term means "destiny," "fate," "existence," and has also been understood by some Western scholars as "vital force." Several works translated in the present anthology also deal with these subjects. — The third word in the title, *gui*, represents in Neidan the balance and conjunction of Yin and Yang.

THE FIRE-DRAGON AND THE WATER-TIGER

[*Text in fig. 3*]

In the art of the reversal of the five agents,
the Dragon comes forth from Fire.

When the five agents do not follow their course,
the Tiger is born within Water.[2]

Explanation

Translator's note: This section is based on the initial part of Peng Xiao's *Jin yaoshi* (The Golden Key), which also contains the lines translated above.[3]

The Water-Tiger, or Black Lead, is the root that gives birth to Heaven and Earth; it is provided with both substance and Breath (*qi*). The Fire-Dragon, or Red Lead, is the foundation that gives birth to Heaven and Earth; it is provided with Breath but is devoid of substance.

What is provided with substance is True Lead. This is the essence of the Great Yin, the Moon, which is the mother that nourishes the bodily forms of the ten thousand things in Heaven and Earth. What is devoid of substance is True Mercury. This is the radiance of the Great Yang, the Sun, which is the father that gives birth to the ten thousand things in Heaven and Earth. The bodies of Lead and Mercury procreate and reproduce one another, moving in a ring without interruption. They can be called the ancestors that generate Heaven, Earth, and the ten thousand things.

The accomplished men of antiquity knew that the Divine Substance (*shenwu*) is hidden within them. By adopting model images,[4] they collected the Essence of Great Yin, and by setting up the tripod and the

[2] Xiao Tingzhi quotes the same sentences in his *Jindan wenda* (Questions and Answers on the Golden Elixir), where they are attributed to the Realized Man Taibai. See above, p. 146.
[3] Peng Xiao (?–955) is better known as the author of the earliest extant Neidan commentary on the *Cantong qi* (The Seal of the Unity of the Three). The *Jin yaoshi* is found in the *Yunji qiqian*, ch. 70.
[4] "Model images" (*faxiang*) means all the emblems, symbols, and names that are used to frame and guide the alchemical process.

Fig. 3. The Fire-Dragon and the Water-Tiger.

furnace, they gathered the Breath of Great Yang. They caused them to return to the Spirit Chamber (*shenshi*), where they inchoately conjoin. Their conjunction is endless, and their fecundity is inexhaustible. Then the *Hun*-soul is born within Wood, and the *Po*-soul is born within Metal. The *Hun*-soul and the *Po*-soul coagulate and transform themselves. They become the Seed and coalesce the hundred treasures. This is called the Reverted Elixir of the Golden Liquor (*jinye huandan*).[5]

THE CROW IN THE SUN AND THE HARE IN THE MOON

[*Text in fig. 4*]

The Lovely Maid grabs the Crow
to ingest the Jade Hare.
The Infant chases the Hare
to inhale the Golden Crow.[6]

Within the Sun there is the Crow,
the Crow is Spirit,
Spirit is Fire,
Fire pertains to the mind,
the mind is Mercury,
and Mercury resides in Li ☲.

Within the Moon there is the Hare,
the Hare is Breath,
Breath is the Medicine,
the Medicine pertains to the body,
the body is Lead,
and Lead resides in Kan ☵.

[5] The *Hun*-soul here stands for True Yin, and the *Po*-soul stands for True Yang. The term used for "seed," *yin'e*, belongs to the vocabulary of the *Cantong qi*: "Steadily and orderly the seed is nourished; from the coagulation of Spirit the corporeal frame is formed" (10:10–11; see Pregadio, *The Seal of the Unity of the Three*, p. 73). See also below, p. 229.

[6] This stanza is drawn from the "Du *Cantong qi* zuo" (Written after Reading the *Cantong qi*) by Xiao Tingzhi, in *Xiuzhen shishu*, ch. 12.

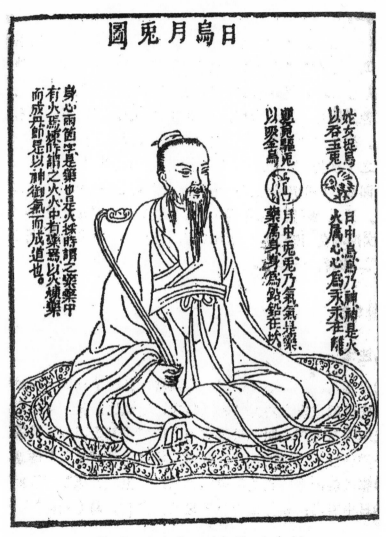

Fig. 4. The Crow in the Sun and the Hare in the Moon.

The two words "body" and "mind"
are the Medicine and the Fire.[7]
When you collect it, it is called Medicine:
within the Medicine there is the Fire.
When you refine it, it is called Fire:
within the Fire there is the Medicine.
Using Fire to refine the Medicine
and to attain the Elixir
is the same as using Spirit to master Breath
and attain the Dao.[8]

Explanation

The Sun is Yang. The Yang holds the Yin within, just like within cinnabar there is mercury. Without the Yin, the Yang could not make its *Hun*-soul shine. Therefore there is the name "feminine Fire" (*cihuo*), meaning that Yang holds the Yin within. In the Sun there is a crow; its trigram pertains to the South, and its name is "the Li ☲ woman." Therefore it has been said: "The Sun resides in the position of Li, but is a woman."[9]

The Moon is Yin. The Yin holds the Yang within, just like within lead there is silver. Without the Yang, the Yin could not make its *Po*-soul glow. Therefore there is the name "masculine Metal" (*xiongjin*), meaning that the Yin holds the Yang within. In the Moon there is a hare; its trigram pertains to the North, and its name is "the Kan ☵ man." Therefore it has been said: "Kan matches the palace of the Toad, yet is a man."[10]

---

[7] This stanza is drawn from the *Zhonghe ji* (The Harmony of the Center: An Anthology), ch. 3.

[8] This stanza and the previous one are drawn from Chen Xubai's (Yuan dynasty) *Guizhong zhinan* (Compass for Peering into the Center), ch. 2, sec. "Huohou" (The Fire Phases).

[9] This paragraph is concerned with the True Yin found within Yang. The quotation derives from the *Wuzhen pian* (Awakening to Reality), "Jueju," poem 15 (see Cleary, *Understanding Reality*, p. 73).

[10] This paragraph is concerned with the True Yang found within Yin. The quotation again derives from the *Wuzhen pian*, "Jueju," poem 15. The

Wuying zi said:[11]

> Lead seeks the essence in the brain of the Jade Hare,
> Mercury takes the blood in the heart of the Golden Crow.
> Just chase these two things, and coalesce the Elixir:
> the supreme Way is uncomplicated and devoid of artifices.

The *Wuzhen pian* (Awakening to Reality) says:

> First take Qian ☰ and Kun ☷ as the tripod and the furnace,
> then catch the crow and the hare and boil the Medicine.
> Once you have chased the two things and they have returned to
>   the Yellow Path,
> how could the Golden Elixir not be born?[12]

This means that the "two things" are one body.

"THE THREE FAMILIES SEE ONE ANOTHER"

[*Text in fig. 5*]

> Body, mind, intention:
> who made them into three families?
> Essence, breath, and spirit:
> through me they become one.
>
> The liver is green and is the father,
> the lungs are white and are the mother,
> the heart is red and is the daughter,
> the spleen is yellow and is the forefather.
> The kidneys are black and are the son,
> and the son is at the origin of the five agents.

"palace of the Toad" is the Moon.

[11] The *Xingming guizhi* here reads "Wulou." This could be Wulou zi (Master Without Contaminations), some of whose verses—not those translated below—are found in the *Panxi ji*, ch. 6. In my translation, however, I follow the reading of the *Yin zhenren Liaoyang dian wenda bian*, sec. 1, which attributes these verses to Wuying zi (Master Without Concealment).

[12] *Wuzhen pian*, "Jueju," poem 1 (translated above, p. 77).

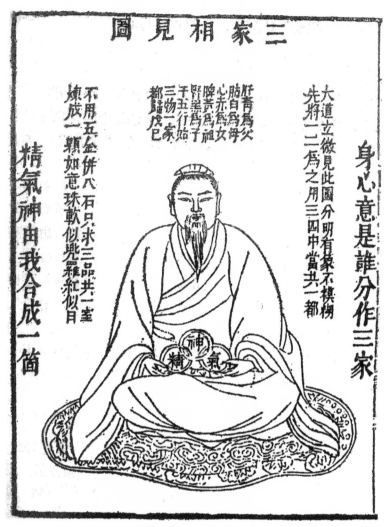

Fig. 5 "The Three Families See One Another."

The three things are one family:
all of them return to WU and JI.[13]

The mystery and subtleness of the great Dao are shown in this picture:
understand the image, and nothing is unclear.
First take 1 and 2; let them operate.
The 3 and the 4 correspond; join them in one lot.

Do not use the five metals and the eight minerals:
search for the three, and join them in one chamber.[14]
When you refine them, they become the Wish-Fulfilling Gem,
soft like the catkins of the *douluo* tree, and red like the Sun.

Explanation

Translator's note: Except for the first paragraph, this section derives from Li Daochun's *Zhonghe ji* (The Harmony of the Center: An Anthology), ch. 2. It contains an abbreviated version of Li Daochun's comments on the *Wuzhen pian* poem about "the three fives returning to oneness" ("Lüshi," poem 14, translated above, p. 75; for the numeric symbolism used in the passage below, see the notes on that poem).

Body, mind, and intention are called the three families (*sanjia*). "The three families see one another" means that the embryo is complete. Essence, Breath, and Spirit are called the three origins. "The three origins join as one" means that the Elixir is achieved.

Taking the three and causing them to return to unity consists in being empty and quiescent. By making one's mind empty, Spirit and Nature join with one another. By making one's body quiescent, Essence and emotions become silent. By bringing the Intention to a state of great stability, the three origins merge into one.

When the Emotions join with one's Nature, we say that "Metal and Wood pair with one another." When the Essence joins with one's Spirit, we say that "Water and Fire conjoin with one another." When

---

[13] This stanza is drawn from the *Cantong qi*, 72:9–16 (translated above, p. 19), with a few changes in the line sequence.

[14] The "three" are Essence, Breath, and Spirit.

the Intention is in a state of great stability, we say that "the five agents are whole."[15]

However, refining the Essence into Breath depends on the body not moving; refining the Breath into Spirit depends on the mind not moving; and refining the Spirit into Emptiness depends on the intention not moving. The mind does not move: this is the meaning of "East is 3, South is 2, together they make 5." The body does not move: this is the meaning of "North is 1, West is 4, they are the same." The Intention does not move: this is the meaning of "Wu and ji also follow, their birth number is 5."[16] Body, mind, and Intention join with one another: this is the meaning of "When the three families see one another, the Infant coalesces."

THE FIVE BREATHS HAVE AUDIENCE AT THE ORIGIN

Explanation

Translator's note: Except for the last paragraph, this section derives from the *Lingbao bifa* (Complete Methods of the Numinous Treasure), sec. 8. The last paragraph derives from the *Zhonghe ji*, ch. 3. See also the passage of the *Jindan wenda* (Questions and Answers on the Golden Elixir) translated above, p. 147.

When the One Breath divides itself for the first time, it arranges itself as the two principles. When the two principles establish their positions, they divide themselves into the five elders.[17] The five constancies pertain to different lands, and each of them guards it own direction.[18] The five directions pertain to different Breaths (*qi*), and each of them guards its own son.

[15] The sentence "the five agents are whole" (*wuxing quan*) is found in the *Wuzhen pian*, "Lüshi," poems 3 (translated above, p. 68) and 11, and "Jueju," poem 45.

[16] In the *Wuzhen pian*, this sentence usually reads, "Wu and ji dwell on their own, their birth number is 5." For the "birth number" (or "generation number"), see table 2, p. 258.

[17] The "two principles" are Yin and Yang. The "five elders" (*wuchang*) are the personifications of the five agents, called "emperors" in the following paragraphs.

[18] The "five constancies" (*wuchang*) are the five agents.

- The son of the Green Emperor is called Dragon Haze (Longyan). He receives the Breath of the virtue of Wood, [which corresponds to the celestial stems] JIA and YI, and [to number] 3.
- The son of the Red Emperor is called Cinnabar Origin (Danyuan). He receives the Breath of the virtue of Fire, [which corresponds to the celestial stems] BING and DING, and [to number] 2.
- The son of the White Emperor is called Dazzling Flower (Haohua). He receives the Breath of the virtue of Metal, [which corresponds to the celestial stems] GENG and XIN, and [to number] 4.
- The son of the Black Emperor is called Mysterious Darkness (Xuanming). He receives the Breath of the virtue of Water, [which corresponds to the celestial stems] REN and GUI, and [to number] 1.
- The son of the Yellow Emperor is called Constant Presence (Changcun). He receives the Breath of the virtue of Soil, [which corresponds to the celestial stems] WU and JI, and [to number] 5.[19]

Therefore when Metal finds Soil, it is born; when Wood finds Soil, it flourishes; when Water finds Soil, it stops; and when Fire finds Soil, it rests.[20] Only the saint knows the Way for inverting the mechanism (huiji) and finds the principle for returning to the Origin. In that moment, he gathers the five, causes the four to converge, brings the three together, conjoins the two, and returns to the One.

Indeed, when the body does not move, the Essence is firm and Water has audience at the Origin. When the mind does not move, the

[19] The names of the sons of the five emperors are not found in the *Lingbao bifa*. They derive instead from the *Huangting jing* (Book of the Yellow Court), where they are the appellations of the gods of liver, heart, lungs, kidneys, and spleen, respectively. — For the correspondences mentioned in these paragraphs, see table 1, p. 257.

[20] These sentences allude to the sequences of "generation" (*xiangsheng*) and "conquest" (*xiangke*) among the five agents, and intend to show that Soil, the central agent, exerts its influence on the other four agents. In these sequences, Metal is generated by Soil; Wood conquers Soil; Water is conquered by Soil; and Fire generates Soil.

Breath is firm and Fire has audience at the Origin. When the true Nature is silent, the *Hun*-soul is stored and Wood has audience at the Origin. When the errant motions are forgotten, the *Po*-soul is subdued and Metal has audience at the Origin. When the four elements are at rest and in harmony, the Intention is stable and Soil has audience at the Origin.[21] This is called "the five Breaths have audience at the Origin". They all gather at the summit.[22]

---

[21] In Buddhism, the four elements (*sida*) are Earth, Water, Fire, and Wind.

[22] If the word "summit" (*ding*) is intended in a literal sense and with regard to the human body, it denotes the sinciput, the point from which the alchemical embryo is delivered at the conclusion of the Neidan practice.

15 The Secret of the Golden Flower

Jinhua zongzhi 金華宗旨

Attributed to Lü Dongbin 呂洞賓

The *Taiyi jinhua zongzhi* is probably the best-known Neidan work outside China. The text, especially renowned for its teaching on "reversing the light" (*huiguang*, sometimes translated as "circulating the light"), probably dates from the late seventeenth century. Although, after Richard Wilhelm's translation, it has usually been called *The Secret of the Golden Flower*, its title actually means *Ancestral Teachings on the Golden Flower of Great Unity*.[1]

There are several versions of the *Jinhua zongzhi*, none of which can be considered as the "authentic" one. The selections below are translated from the version found in the *Daozang xubian* (Sequel to the Taoist Canon). This version belongs to the Longmen (Dragon Gate) lineage, and in particular to its Jingai branch, which regards the *Jinhua zongzhi* as the main text on the cultivation of inner Nature (*xing*).[2]

There are several differences between the selections published here and the corresponding portions in other published translations of the text. In particular, the first section is much longer and detailed compared to the version translated by Thomas Cleary, and certainly contains portions written by Min Yide (1748–1836, the main Jingai master) or by another author before him (possibly Tao Sixuan, ?–1692, another Jingai master).

Section titles and their numbers are found in the original Chinese text.

---

[1] Or, *Teachings of the Ancestor on the Golden Flower of Great Unity*. Compare this passage in section 1: "In our practice, we should only take the Great Unity as the root and the Golden Flower as the branch." The "ancestor" is Lü Dongbin, who revealed this work through "spirit writing."

[2] Richard Wilhelm's translation, which includes a "psychological commentary" by C.G. Jung, is based on an edition published by Zhan Ranhui in 1921. Thomas Cleary's translation (also entitled *The Secret of the Golden Flower*) is based on the edition in the *Daozang jiyao* (Essentials of the Taoist Canon), first published by Jiang Yuanting in ca. 1800.

I: THE CELESTIAL HEART

Our Patriarch (Lü Dongbin) said: The Celestial Heart (*tianxin*) is the Heart with which the Three Powers are equally endowed.[3] This is what the books on the Elixir call the Mysterious Opening.[4] Everyone has it, but in the worthy and the wise ones it is open, in the foolish and the deluded ones it is closed. If it is open, one lives a long life; if it is closed, one dies prematurely.

All of us can see that the years of our lives are counted. We all wish to search for life, but we are all going towards death. As we have a body, could it be otherwise?[5] The six senses entice it and the six defilements distress it.[6] The years decrease quickly, and in the blink of an eye we meet our end.

Feeling concern for all this, the men of greatest attainment have transmitted the Way of greatest attainment. However, "I taught you with assiduous repetition, and you listened to me with contempt."[7] Why? Essentially, because people do not understand the foundation (*ti*) and the operation (*yong*) of the Great Dao, and they injure and harm one another. Searching for life in this way is like turning south when one intends to go north. How can they know that Emptiness and Non-Being are the foundation of the Great Dao, and that the

---

[3] The Three Powers (*sancai*) are Heaven, Earth, and Man. — To appreciate the sense of this and the next section of the *Golden Flower*, it should be considered that the term *xin* literally means "heart," but in several instances it can more appropriately be rendered as "mind." A third meaning, namely "center," also applies in several cases, including the present one. In other words, *tianxin* can be rendered in at least three ways: "Heart of Heaven" (i.e., Celestial Heart), "Mind of Heaven," and "Center of Heaven."

[4] The Mysterious Opening (*xuanqiao*) is the same as the One Opening of the Mysterious Barrier (*xuanguan yiqiao*). The *Golden Flower* also calls it Celestial Heart.

[5] For "body," the text uses the expression "lungs and intestines" (*feichang*), an expression drawn from the poem "The Young Mulberry Tree" ("Sangrou") in the *Book of Poems* (*Shijing*).

[6] In Buddhism, the six senses (*liugen*) are eye, ear, nose, tongue, body, and mind. The "six defilements" (*liuchen*) are the respective fields: form, sound, scent, flavor, the physical domain, and the mental domain.

[7] This sentence is made of two verses from the poem "Outward Demeanor" ("Yi") in the *Book of Poems*.

unseen and the manifest are its operation? This is why one should neither dwell in Being nor in Non-Being, and should allow the mechanism of Breath (*qiji*) to flow all around.

In our practice, we should only take the Great Unity as the root and the Golden Flower as the branch, so that root and branch can support one another and we can live a long life free from death. Since ancient times, immortals and realized ones have sealed this teaching: it has been transmitted and has been received in the same way. After the manifestation of the Most High, it was bequeathed to Eastern Florescence (Donghua), and finally it reached the Lineages of the North and the South.[8]

Fundamentally, the Way is not hidden, but the transmission from Heart to Heart is extremely secret. And it is not only secret: if it is not transmitted from the Heart and received by the Heart, it can be neither transmitted nor received. The oral transmission is assuredly wondrous, but the understanding can hardly be complete. How much more could this be true if it is displayed in writing? Therefore the Great Way of the Most High upholds the transmission from Heart to Heart: it is transmitted and received in an invisible way. The understanding occurs unexpectedly. Neither can the master fix a time to transmit it to a disciple, nor can the disciple fix a time to receive it from a master. If one is truly faithful and utterly pure, as soon as the opportunity arises the spirits [of the master and the disciple] merge with one another and [the transmission] occurs clearly and unexpectedly. Sometimes they look at each other and smile together, other times one receives it in tears.

Entering the Way and awakening to the Way are one and the same thing. Some disciples enter the Way when they awaken to it, others awaken to the Way when they enter it. There has never been, however,

---

[8] "Most High" ("Taishang") is an appellation of Lord Lao (Laojun, the deified aspect of Laozi). Eastern Florescence, whose full name is Imperial Lord of Eastern Florescence (Donghua dijun), is the first patriarch of the Quanzhen lineage, or the second one when Laozi is counted as the first one (as does the present passage). The emphasis given to this deity is explained by the fact that Longmen was the foremost Quanzhen lineage when the *Secret of the Golden Flower* was written.

someone who has entered the Way and has obtained it without first realizing the unity of the Heart and the authenticity of the Heart. Without that unity there is dispersal, and without that authenticity there is instability. With dispersal, the Light cannot coalesce, and with instability, it cannot coagulate.

If one cannot see one's own Heart, how can one join the Heart transmitted by the Most High? This why Confucians value inner observation (*neixing*) and Taoists value inner contemplation (*neiguan*). Moreover, the Buddhist *Sutra in Forty-Two Sections* (*Sishier zhang jing*) says: "Fix your Heart on one point, and nothing will be impossible."[9]

Indeed, it is only through the supreme Great Way that we can entirely obtain the complete foundation of the One Heart.[10] How is this complete foundation? It is empty, pure, and unmixed: such is the wondrous foundation of the ancestral teaching (*zongzhi*). As for its wondrous operation, it lies only in "fixing one's Heart on one point."

Inner contemplation consists in the instructions for fixing one's Heart: this is the secret teaching in the transmission from Heart to Heart. Not only can this be known by the Heart, but it can also be transmitted by oral teaching; and not only can it be transmitted by oral teaching, but it can also be displayed in writing. [However,] only when the practice reaches culmination, and when the Heart is empty and all contaminations come to an end, is it possible to instantaneously comprehend the mysterious and wondrous teaching. Not only cannot this be displayed in writing, but it cannot be obtained even by oral teaching. It is true emptiness, true silence, true purity, true Non-Being.

The transmission of the Mysterious Pearl from Heart to Heart is extremely secret. It can be entirely manifested only after one has awakened [to the Way] and has entered [the Way]: there is no other means, because [at that time] the Celestial Heart opens itself like a cave. Nowadays, those who seek the Way are like people crossing a great watercourse devoid of banks. When they reach the other shore,

---

[9] This sentence is not found in the *Sutra in Forty-Two Sections*; it appears to be quoted from the *Fo yijiao jing* (Sutra of the Buddha's Bequeathed Teaching), sec. 3.

[10] *Yixin* (One Heart) can also be understood as One Mind.

they should forego the method, just like in the simile of the raft.[11] But if they do not know where to go, how could one not provide them with a raft? I now take on me the responsibility of being an Ordination Master, and I will provide them with that raft.[12]

Now, the One Opening of the Celestial Heart is neither within nor outside the body. It cannot be opened by fumbling around it, and can only be silently maintained (*cun*) in order to tend to it. If you want to know how to maintain it, there is nothing beyond these words: "Form is emptiness, emptiness is form."[13] It is what the books on the Elixir refer to as "so" (*na me*), saying that it is not "so" and yet it is "so." It is just "thus" (*ruru*).[14] Once it is opened, it remains open forever. As for the practice, it consists only in two words: "maintaining sincerity" (*cuncheng*).

In your wondrous use of "maintaining sincerity," there are instructions within the instructions.[15] Therefore when the time comes to cast away the ten thousand conditions (*wanyuan*), you only use the character 丶 (*yi*) of the Brahmā Heaven. Maintain the central dot in the point between the eyebrows, the left dot in the left eye, and the right dot in the right eye. Then your eyes will emit a spiritual light, which collects itself in the point between the eyebrows.

The point between the eyebrows is the Celestial Eye (*tianmu*), the door through which the Three Luminaries enter and exit joined to one another.[16] If you can use the three eyes[17] like the character 伊 (*yi*) of

[11] The raft is a common metaphor in Buddhist texts. It represents, first of all, the "vehicle" (*yāna*) that allows one to "cross over to the other shore." In many cases, it also stands for that vehicle as a device that plays an indispensable function, but is not needed after it has served its purpose.

[12] The Ordination Master (*dushi*) formally ordains disciples into monkhood or priesthood. Note that the word *du* ("ordination") primarily means "crossing over," and thus fits the image of the "raft."

[13] This famous statement comes from the Buddhist *Heart Sutra*.

[14] *Ruru* is one of the Chinese terms that translate Sanskrit *tathatā*, the state of "suchness" or of "being as it is."

[15] That is, there are two levels of teaching, the second of which is more important and secret than the first one.

[16] According to Min Yide's commentary, the Three Luminaries (*sanguang*) are the Sun, the Moon, and Celestial Net (*tiangang*), i.e., the Northern

the Brahmā Heaven,[18] and if, by means of the Intention, you subtly circulate [the Light] as if you were polishing a mirror, the Three Luminaries will coalesce at once in the point between the eyebrows. Their light will glow like a Sun in front of you. Then, by means of the Intention, you lead that light and fix it in the point behind the heart and in front of the Barrier.[19] That point is the Gate of the Mysterious-Female. As you lead it by means of the Intention, the light will at once fix itself there.

As long as you do not forget the mysterious meaning of the two words *ruo* ("like that") and *ru* ("thus"), the Celestial Heart will certainly open itself like a cave. Later, I will explain its mysterious operation again in detail.[20] My urgent advice is: From beginning to end, never be led by [the transformations of] the Origin.[21]

All of you should abide by this and practice it: besides purifying your thoughts in this way, there is no other method to progress. The *Lengyan jing* (Śūraṅgama sūtra) says: "With pure thoughts you will fly and will be certainly born in Heaven." This Heaven is not the deep blue sky: it means to be born in the Palace of Qian ☰.[22] After a long time, you will naturally obtain a Heaven outside yourself.

Dipper. These represent Yang, Yin, and Unity, respectively.

[17] The central, left, and right eyes.

[18] Instead of the three-dot character, found in the previous paragraph, here the text has an ordinary Chinese character, which however is only meant to indicate the pronunciation of the three-dot character, namely, *yi*.

[19] The "barrier" (*guan*) mentioned here is the Spinal Handle (*jiaji*), located in the middle of the spinal column, across from the heart.

[20] It is not clear whether this sentence refers to the entire *Secret of the Golden Flower* or to a particular section or passage. In an appendix to the present chapter (pp. 236–237), I translate the passage of the *Golden Flower* that contains the most detailed explanation on the Celestial Heart.

[21] This sentence is translated in accordance with Min Yide's commentary: "The Origin (*yuan*) is transformed and made illusory by the mechanism of [postcelestial] breath (*qi*) . . . If you are led by this, you fall into the Māra Lair" (i.e., into hell).

[22] In other words, it means having a "rebirth" in the state of Unity, which is represented by the trigram Qian ☰.

Indeed, the body is like a kingdom, and Unity is its ruler. The Light is the Heart and the Intention of the ruler, and it is also similar to the ruler's edicts and decrees. Therefore, once the Light is reversed, all the breaths (*qi*) of the entire body rise to have audience with the ruler. It is like a saintly king establishing the capital and ascending to the throne: at that time, the ten thousand kingdoms offer jade and silk. It is also like a ruler whose ministers have the same mind as him, and whose subjects spontaneously obey his orders: each of them performs their function.

All of you should entirely focus only on reversing the Light: this is the supreme wondrous Truth. After you reverse it for a long time, this Light will coagulate and become a spontaneous dharma-body (*fashen*), which will be filled by it.[23] This is what our lineage calls the "seed" (*yin'e*), and what the Western teaching calls the Citadel of the King of the Dharma (*fawang cheng*).[24]

If the ruler receives support, Essence and Breath live day by day, and Spirit becomes increasingly flourishing. In one instant your body and your Heart will merge and transform themselves. Does this not mean that there is a Heaven beyond the Heaven, and a body beyond the body?

Therefore the Golden Flower is the Golden Elixir. The transformations of the spiritual light depend on each person's Heart. The wondrous instructions found here are not different to any extent [for different persons] but are exceedingly versatile and adaptable. They require understanding and clarity,[25] and they demand deep quiescence. Without extreme understanding and clarity, it would be impossible to practice this. Without extremely deep quiescence, it would be impossible to guard it.

---

[23] On the "dharma-body" see p. 246, note 16 below.

[24] For the term "seed" see above, p. 214, note 5. The Western Teaching is Buddhism, and the King of the Dharma is the Buddha.

[25] Lit., "sharpness of hearing (*cong*) and brightness of sight (*ming*)"; but the compound *congming* is also used to mean "intelligence."

3: REVERSING THE LIGHT AND GUARDING THE CENTER

Our Patriarch (Lü Dongbin) said: What is the origin of the term "reversing the Light" (*huiguang*)? It originated with the Realized Man Wenshi.[26] When we reverse the Light, all the Yin and Yang Breaths (*qi*) of Heaven and Earth coagulate. This is what we call "refining thought," "purifying Breath," or "purifying thinking."

According to the instructions to begin the practice, Non-Being [at first] seems to be within Being. In due time, when the practice is completed and outside one's body there is another body, Being is born within Non-Being.[27] The Light becomes true only with one hundred days of focused practice: at that time, it becomes the Spirit-Fire (*shenhuo*). After one hundred days, it spontaneously coalesces, and the one particle of True Yang suddenly generates the Pearl, sized as a grain of millet.[28] This is just like when husband and wife conjoin and there is an embryo. In order to attend to it, you must be in the state of quiescence. The reversion of the Light is the same as the Fire phases (*huohou*).

Within the transformations of the Origin,[29] the Yang Light is the ruler. In the [world of] form, it is the Sun; in the human being, it is the eyes. The contaminations of the cognitive faculty of Spirit (*shenshi*) are owed in the first place to "following the course" (*shun*). Therefore the Way of the Golden Flower thoroughly uses the method of "inverting the course" (*ni*). Reversing the Light does not only reverse the essential radiance (*jinghua*) of a single body; it directly reverses the True

---

[26] Wenshi is the appellation (*hao*) of Yin Xi, the Guardian of the Pass to whom, according to the Taoist tradition, Laozi handed over the *Daode jing* (Book of the Way and Its Virtue). A work entitled *Wenshi zhenjing* (True Book of Master Wenshi), dating from the thirteenth century, does contain the expression *huiguang*, "reversing the Light."

[27] At the beginning, one seeks Non-Being within Being; at the end, Being is seen as a manifestation of Non-Being. "Outside one's body there is another body" is a frequent expression that refers to the birth of the embryo generated through the Neidan practice, or one's immortal body.

[28] See above, p. 94 note 21.

[29] I.e., the phenomena that are generated as transformations of the original state of Non-Being. See also above, note 21.

Breath of [the entire] creation and transformation. It does not only stop the momentary errant thoughts; it directly empties the transmigration throughout thousands of eons. Therefore one breath is equivalent to one year in human time, and to one hundred years in the long night of the nine paths of reincarnation.

After ordinary people emit their first cry,[30] they follow the course of life by adapting to their surroundings, and until old age they never invert their vision. When the Yang Breath withers and becomes extinct, there is the world of the Nine Obscurities.[31] Therefore the *Lengyan jing* says: "With pure thoughts, you fly; with pure emotions, you fall."[32]

If those who study the Way have few thoughts and too many emotions, they sink into the inferior paths. Only through careful contemplation and through stillness and quiescence can one attain the correct awakening (*zhengjue*). This is where one uses the method of inverting the course. When the *Yinfu jing* (Book of the Hidden Agreement) says, "The mechanism is in the eyes,"[33] and when the *Huangdi suwen* (Plain Questions of the Yellow Emperor) says, "All the essential radiance in the human body concentrates above in the empty opening," this is what they mean.[34] If you understand this point, having a long life lies in it, and transcending life also lies in it. This practice is the thread that joins the Three Teachings to one another.[35]

The Light is neither within the body nor outside the body. Mountains and rivers, the Sun and the Moon, and the whole great Earth are nothing but this Light. Therefore it is not only within the body. Understanding and clarity, knowledge and wisdom in all of their workings are also nothing but this Light. Thus it is also not outside

---

[30] I.e., immediately after birth.

[31] *Jiuyou*, i.e., the hells.

[32] In the *Lengyan jing*, this sentence refers to ascending to Heaven or falling into hell.

[33] *Yinfu jing*, sec. 18 (translated above, p. 39).

[34] There seems to be no sentence corresponding to this one in the *Huangdi neijing suwen* (Inner Book of the Yellow Emperor: The Plain Questions). However, the *Lingshu* (Numinous Pivot) version of the *Huangdi neijing*, sec. 80, says: "The Essence and Breath of the five viscera and the six receptacles concentrates above in the eyes."

[35] The Three Teachings are Taoism, Buddhism, and Confucianism.

the body. The radiance of Heaven and Earth fills a great chiliocosm,[36] and the radiance of a single body also pervades Heaven and covers the Earth. Therefore as soon as one reverses the Light, Heaven and Earth and mountains and rivers all reverse it.

The essential radiance of the human being concentrates above in the eyes, which are the great "barrier and lock" of the body.[37] Reflect on this: If you do not sit in quiescence for only one day, this light flows and roams away, and "no one knows where it stops."[38] If you can sit [in meditation] even for a short while, the ten thousand eons and the thousand births are all brought to an end.

The return of the ten thousand phenomena (*wanfa*) to quiescence is truly unconceivable: this is the wondrous Truth. However, when you start the practice you should go without interruption from the superficial to the deep, from the gross to the subtle, in order to attain that wonder. The practice should be consistent from beginning to end; "one knows for oneself whether the water is hot or cold."[39] You should return to the emptiness of heaven and the vastitude of the ocean; only when the ten thousand phenomena are just as they are (*ruru*) can there be attainment.

What the saints have transmitted to one another is nothing but inverting the radiance (*fanzhao*). It was called "knowing where to stop" (*zhizhi*) by Confucius, "contemplation of the mind" (*guanxin*) by the Buddha, and "inner contemplation" (*neiguan*) by Laozi, but all of them are this method. However, although people can pronounce the words "inverting the radiance," they cannot attain it: they do not know the meaning of these words. "Inverting" means that the knowing, conscious mind returns to the initial point in which neither form nor spirit are yet manifested. Within one's own six-feet [body], one

---

[36] In Buddhism, a "great chiliocosm" (*daqian shijie*) is equivalent to one billion "small worlds."

[37] The term *guanjian* often denotes a "crucial point," but in this sentence can also be understood literally as "barrier and lock."

[38] This expression is drawn from the poem "Minister of War" ("Qifu") in the *Book of Poems (Shijing)*.

[39] A Chan Buddhist saying.

turns around and seeks the body before the birth of Heaven and Earth. People nowadays sit idly for a couple of hours, glance back at their own selves, and call this "inverting the radiance." How can they have results?

The two patriarchs of Buddhism and Taoism[40] taught that watching the tip of the nose does not mean to fix one's thoughts on it, or to contemplate it with the eyes and at the same time concentrate one's thoughts on the Central Yellow (zhonghuang).[41] Since "wherever the eyes go, the Heart also goes, and wherever the Heart goes, the Breath (qi) also goes,"[42] how could one of them go above and the other at the same time go below? How could one all of a sudden rise and the other, at the same time, all of a sudden descend? That would be like taking the finger for the Moon.[43]

Ultimately, what did the two patriarchs mean? The words "tip of the nose" are extremely wondrous. The nose is only used as a measure for the eyes:[44] they did not mean the nose itself. Indeed, you might keep the eyes too open, so that you would look too far and not see the nose; or you might keep them too closed, so that your eyes would shut and again you would not see the nose. If the eyes are too open, you would stray by moving towards the external and would easily enter dispersion and confusion. If the eyes are too

[40] The Buddha and Laozi.

[41] Central Yellow means the "center" (yellow is the color assigned to the center in the system of the five agents). In this part of the Secret of the Golden Flower, this term refers to the center of the human being.

[42] See above, p. 39 note 41.

[43] In other words, it would be impossible for the eyes to concentrate on the nose ("above") and at the same time for the mind to concentrate on the Yellow Center ("below"). Min Yide's commentary says: "Here it says that one should not 'contemplate the nose with the eyes and at the same time concentrate one's thoughts on the Central Yellow.' This is in order to instruct the beginners that they should coagulate their Spirit on one point in order to collect the Light. The reason is that it is not possible to divide one's mind between two places. When they have succeeded in making [the Light] penetrate within, then the point of the nose becomes the finger, and the Central Yellow becomes the Moon."

[44] I.e., as a "reference point," as explained in the present paragraph.

closed, you would stray by going rapidly towards the internal and would easily enter haze and daze. You should "lower the curtains" as appropriate, to a point suitable to see the tip of the nose.[45] Therefore taking the tip of the nose as a measure is only done in order to "lower the curtains" to a suitable point. The Light will naturally spread through, and you will not need to toil either to concentrate it or not concentrate it.

Watching the tip of the nose is only used at the initial stage of entering the state of quiescence. You open your eyes to have a brief look, establish a point of reference, and then leave it aside. It is just like a mason who uses a plumb-line: he uses it at the beginning of his job, but then he continues to work in accordance with it, with no need to look at it again.

"Cessation and contemplation" (*zhiguan*) are Buddhist methods, which originally are not secret.[46] With your eyes, you carefully contemplate the tip of your nose; keeping your body straight while you sit relaxed, you collect your mind in the center of conditions (*yuanzhong*). In Taoism this is called the Central Yellow (*zhonghuang*), and in Buddhism it is called the "center of conditions"; but they are the same thing.[47] There is no need to speak of the center of the head: when you begin to learn [the method], it is sufficient to collect your thoughts in the point that lies midway between the eyes.

---

[45] "Lowering the curtains" (*chuilian*) is a metaphor for "closing the eyelids" sometimes used in Neidan texts.

[46] "Cessation and contemplation" (*zhiguan*) is also translated as "concentration and insight." "Cessation" (*zhi*) corresponds to Sanskrit *śamatha*, and "contemplation" (*guan*) corresponds to Sanskrit *vipaśyanā*. The first practice serves to calm the mind; the second one, to obtain insight into the nature of reality.

[47] In Buddhism, "conditions" (*yuan*) generally denotes the principle of cause and effect that rules over the conditioned world. The "center of conditions" is emptiness. Min Yide's commentary clarifies that this center is equivalent to what Taoism calls Mysterious Barrier, or One Opening of the Mysterious Barrier: "What the Buddhists call 'center of conditions' is what our lineage calls Gate of the Mysterious-Female. It is the Mysterious Opening that gives birth to Heaven, Earth, humans, and things. The foundation for cultivating reality and attaining the Dao lies here."

The Light is extremely lively; by collecting your thoughts in the point between the eyes, it will naturally spread through with no need for you to fix your thought on the Central Yellow.

The above words contain the entire essential teaching. Other details about entering and exiting the state of quiescence can be verified by means of the *Xiao zhiguan shu* (Small Book on Cessation and Contemplation).[48]

The term "center of conditions" is exceedingly wondrous: there is no place that is not the Center, and a whole great chiliocosm is within it. In general, "center of conditions" means that this point is the gateway to the mechanism of creation and transformation. Yet, although one can take it as an initial point, it is not determined and fixed. The meaning of this term is extremely flexible and extremely wondrous.

At the origin, the words "cessation" and "contemplation" cannot be separated. They mean concentration (*ding, samādhi*) and wisdom (*hui, prajñā*). Later, when an ordinary thought arises, you will not need to sit again like before. You should [instead] examine where that thought is, where it rises, and where it extinguishes itself. After you inquire into this over and over again, [you will find that] "I cannot take hold of it." In that very moment you will see the place where that thought arises, and you will not need to look into it anymore. "I have searched for my mind and I cannot take hold of it." "Now your mind is pacified." This is what I mean.[49]

This is the correct contemplation; what opposes it is a wrongful contemplation. If you do not obtain results, just continue like before, without interruption. Practice cessation and continue with contemplation, practice contemplation and continue with cessation: this is

---

[48] A work by Zhiyi (538–97), the founder of the Tiantai branch of Chinese Buddhism.

[49] These sentences are part of a Chan Buddhist anecdote, recorded in several texts: "Bodhidharma was facing the wall. The Second Patriarch was standing in the snow. He cut off his arm and said, 'My mind has no peace as yet! I beg you, master, pacify my mind!' 'Bring your mind here and I will pacify it for you,' said Bodhidharma. 'I have searched for my mind and I cannot take hold of it,' said the Second Patriarch. 'Now your mind is pacified,' said Bodhidharma."

the method of the conjoined cultivation of concentration and wisdom. This is reversing the Light. "Reversing" is cessation, and "Light" is contemplation. If there is cessation without contemplation, it is called "having reversion without the Light." If there is contemplation without cessation, it is called "having the Light without reversion." Remember this!

APPENDIX

Translator's note: This appendix contains a translation of the most detailed passage concerning the Celestial Heart (*tianxin*) in the *Secret of the Golden Flower*, found in chapter 8.

"Reversing the Light" is only a general term. As the practice progresses, at each stage the radiance becomes more intense and the method of reversion becomes more wondrous. Before, one controlled the inside from the outside; now, one resides in the Center to manage the outside.[50] Before, one supported the ruler; now, one issues orders on behalf of the ruler. The situation is entirely reversed.

When you want to enter the state of quiescence, you should first harmonize and nurture both body and mind, so that they dwell of themselves in rest and harmony. Cast away the ten thousand conditions, so that there is not even a single thread hanging anywhere, and the Celestial Heart is established precisely at the center. Then "lower the curtains" of the eyes,[51] as if a holy edict had summoned a minister: who would dare not comply?[52]

Then use your eyes to illuminate within. Wherever the radiance arrives within the Palace of Kan ☵,[53] the True Yang will come forth in

---

[50] Compare the almost identical sentence in the *Cantong qi* (The Seal of the Unity of the Three), 2:7: "Abide in the Center to control the outside" (see Pregadio, *The Seal of the Unity of the Three*, p. 69).

[51] See p. 234, note 45 above.

[52] "Holy edict" (*shengzhi*) is one of the Chinese terms for an edict issued by the emperor.

[53] The lower Cinnabar Field. In the next paragraph, the text also alludes to the upper Cinnabar Field ("the Yang within Kan rises above"). Note, however,

response. Li ☲ is Yang outside and Yin within; it is the body of Qian ☰. When the Yin line enters it and becomes its ruler, the mind is aroused by following external things; it comes forth in the outward and it roams and wanders. Now, by reversing the Light to illuminate within, [the mind] is not aroused by following external things. The Yin Breath (*qi*) is halted, and the radiance becomes concentrated and illuminates. This is the Pure Yang.

Things of the same kind are necessarily alike; therefore the Yang within Kan rises above. However, this is not the Yang within Kan; it is instead the Yang of Qian responding to the Yang of Qian.[54] The two things meet and coagulate without dispersal. They mesh together and are exceedingly vital, now coming, now going, now floating, now sinking. Within one's own Original Palace, it is as indistinct as the incommensurable Great Emptiness. The body is so light and wondrous that it would like to rise in flight. About this there is a saying: "The clouds fill the thousand mountains."

Then the coming and going leaves no more traces, and the floating and sinking can be no more distinguished. The pulse stills, the breath (*qi*) stops. This is the true conjunction. About this there is a saying: "The moon contains the ten thousand waters."

Wait until the Celestial Heart suddenly moves within the "dim and obscure."[55] That is the return of the Yang; it is the living ZI hour (*huo zishi*).[56]

that in a work like the *Golden Flower*, these and other Neidan technical terms may not be meant in their ordinary senses.

[54] This sentence may be understood as a reference to the Yang within Kan that rises from the lower to the upper Cinnabar Field. See, however, the previous footnote.

[55] *Daode jing*, sec. 21: "Dim and obscure! Within there is an essence."

[56] On the "living ZI hour" see below, p. 249 note 23.

16 Discriminations on Difficult Points in Cultivating Reality

Xiuzhen biannan 修真辨難

Liu Yiming 劉一明 (1734–1821)

Liu Yiming is one of the greatest masters in the history of Neidan. While his views are grounded in some of the most deep-rooted aspects of this tradition, they are also adverse to convention and often do not follow accepted standards. His works represent, however, one of the main instances of an integral exposition of doctrine in the history of Internal Alchemy.

Born in present-day Shanxi province, Liu Yiming was an eleventh-generation master of the Longmen (Dragon Gate) lineage and the founder of one of its northwestern branches. Having recovered from severe illness in his youth, he undertook an extended period of traveling throughout northern China that led him to meet his two main masters. In 1779, he settled on the Qiyun mountains, in present-day Gansu province, and devoted the second half of his life to teaching and writing. His works include commentaries to Neidan texts, the *Daode jing* (Book of the Way and Its Virtue), the *Yijing* (Book of Changes), and Buddhist texts; independent works on Neidan; and a voluminous commentary to the Ming novel, *Xiyou ji* (Journey to the West), explicated in light of Neidan.

The *Xiuzhen biannan*, or *Discriminations on Difficult Points in Cultivating Reality*, is one of the works included in the *Daoshu shi'er zhong* (Twelve Books on the Dao; actually containing about twenty texts). Written in 1798, it is framed as a sequence of questions and answers—about 120 altogether—between Liu Yiming and a disciple. The sequel to this work, entitled *Xiuzhen houbian* (Further Discriminations in Cultivating Reality) has been translated into English under the title *Cultivating the Tao: Taoist and Internal Alchemy* (Golden Elixir Press, 2013).

The original text is not divided into sections. I have added titles to the selected portions.

THE DAO AND YIN AND YANG

He asked: What is the Dao?

I replied: The Dao is the Ancestral Breath prior to Heaven that generates all things. "Watching, you do not see it; listening, you do not hear it; grasping, you do not get it."[1] It envelops and enwraps Heaven and Earth, and gives life and nourishment to the ten thousand things. It is so great that there is nothing outside it, so small that there is nothing inside it. Confucians call it Great Ultimate (*taiji*); Taoists call it Golden Elixir (*jindan*); and Buddhists call it Complete Enlightenment (*yuanjue*). Fundamentally it has no name or title, but if we are forced to give it a name, we call it Dao. If it is determined, one is in error; if it is discussed, one loses it. It has no shape and no image; it is not form and it is not emptiness; it is not Being and it is not Non-Being. If it is attributed the images of form and emptiness, of Being and Non-Being, it is not the Dao.

He asked: If the Dao has no shape and no image, if it is the inchoate One Breath, why does the *Book of Changes* say, "One Yin, one Yang, this is the Dao"?[2]

I replied: The words "one Yin, one Yang, this is the Dao" express the operation (*yong*) of the Dao. The words "it has no shape and it has no image" express the foundation (*ti*) of the Dao. Before the Great Ultimate divides itself [into Yin and Yang], the Dao envelops Yin and Yang. After the Great Ultimate divides itself, it is Yin and Yang that give life to the Dao.

Without Yin and Yang, the Breath of the Dao would not be visible. It is only in the alternation of Yin and Yang that the Breath of the Dao can grow and maintain itself for innumerable kalpas without being damaged.

In the precelestial, there is the Dao; in the postcelestial, there are Yin and Yang. The Dao is the root of Yin and Yang; Yin and Yang are the manifestation of the Dao.

[1] *Daode jing* (Book of the Way and Its Virtue), sec. 14.
[2] *Book of Changes* (*Yijing*), "Appended Sayings" ("Xici"), sec. A.4; see Wilhelm, *The I-ching or Book of Changes*, p. 297.

When we say that the Great Ultimate divides itself and becomes Yin and Yang, and that Yin and Yang join to one another and form the Great Ultimate, we mean that it is One but they are Two, and that they are Two but it is One.

NATURE AND EXISTENCE

He asked: The Internal Medicine fulfills one's Nature (*xing*), the External Medicine fulfills one's Existence (*ming*); thus the cultivation of Nature and of Existence have their respective times. The *Book of Changes* says:

> When he precedes Heaven, Heaven does not go against him; when he follows Heaven, he abides by the time of Heaven.[3]

Therefore inverting the unfolding and following the course [of "creation and transformation"] are unrelated to one another. However, the *Ruyao jing* (Mirror for Compounding the Medicine) says:

> Precelestial Breath,
> postcelestial Breath.
> Those who obtain them
> always seem to be drunk.[4]

What is the reason?

I replied: Our ancestral masters, driven by compassion and sorrow, explained everything clearly. It is you who do not understand.

The Internal Medicine fulfills one's Nature; this is the same as saying, "when he follows Heaven, he abides by the time of Heaven." The External Medicine fulfills one's Existence; this is the same as saying, "when he precedes Heaven, Heaven does not go against him."[5]

---

[3] *Book of Changes*, "Explanation of the Sentences" ("Wenyan") on the hexagram Qian ䷀ (no. 1); see Wilhelm, pp. 382–83.

[4] See above, p. 46.

[5] In the *Book of Changes*, these two sentences describe the person who "accords in virtue with Heaven and Earth." Liu Yiming uses them to describe the two main aspects or stages of the Neidan practice, concerned with

"Heaven does not go against him" means that, using the Way of inverting the course, you take action ahead of events. By doing so, you "seize creation and transformation" and coagulate the Elixir.[6]

"He abides by the time of Heaven" means that, using the Way of following the course, you apply the natural Fire phases; by doing so, you merge the five agents and deliver the Elixir.[7]

The former and the latter are two stages of the practice; therefore we speak of the "conjoined cultivation of Nature and Existence" (*xing-ming shuangxiu*). The Internal and the External [Medicines] are equally cultivated; therefore we speak of the "twofold operation of inverting the course and following the course."

He asked: Nature pertains to Yin, Existence pertains to Yang. Are these the same Yin and Yang that result from the division of the Great Ultimate?

I replied: They are different. Concerning Nature, there are the Nature consisting in one's character and the Nature consisting in what is bestowed by Heaven.[8] Concerning Existence, there are the Existence consisting in one's destiny and the Existence consisting in the Breath of the Dao.

The Nature consisting in one's character and the Existence consisting in one's destiny are the postcelestial Nature and Existence, which are provided with a form. The Nature consisting in what is bestowed by Heaven and the Existence consisting in the Breath of the Dao are the precelestial Nature and Existence, which are formless. To cultivate the postcelestial Nature and Existence, one follows the course of creation and transformation. To cultivate the precelestial

Existence (*ming*) and with Nature (*xing*), respectively. Cultivating Existence requires "inverting the course," and therefore one "precedes Heaven"; cultivating Nature requires "following the course," and therefore one "follows Heaven."

[6] This expression derives from the *Ruyao jing*: "Steal Heaven and Earth, seize creation and transformation." See above, p. 50.

[7] The "natural Fire phases" (*tianran huohou*) are not intentionally timed according to a predetermined sequence, as is usually done in Neidan, but occur spontaneously.

[8] *Qizhi* denotes one's "character" or "personality."

Nature and Existence, one inverts the course of creation and transformation.[9]

Those who practice the great cultivation borrow the postcelestial to return to the precelestial, and cultivate the precelestial to transform the postcelestial. When the precelestial and the postcelestial merge and become one, when Nature and Existence coagulate with one another, this is called "achieving the Elixir."

Nature and Existence are the foundation of Yin and Yang; Yin and Yang are the operation of Nature and Existence. However, there is a distinction between the true and the false, and there is a difference between the precelestial and the postcelestial. Understanding this depends on the subtlety of one's discrimination and the clarity of one's discernment.

TRUE AND FALSE YIN AND YANG

He asked: One's Nature (*xing*) and one's Existence (*ming*) necessarily depend on Yin and Yang in order to coagulate [with one another]. This means that if there is Yin there must be Yang, and if there is Yang there must be Yin. Why is it also said, "When all of Yin is entirely dispelled, the Elixir ripens"?[10] Ultimately, does one use the Yin, or does one not use it?

I replied: What is used is the True Yin and the True Yang; what is not used is the false Yin and the false Yang. The True Yin and the True Yang are the precelestial ones; the false Yin and the false Yang are the postcelestial ones. The precelestial ones are a way of accomplishment; the postcelestial ones are a way of failure.

---

[9] "Existence consisting in the Breath of the Dao" refers to one's formless embodiment within the One Breath (*yiqi*) of the Dao, not manifested in space and time. Later in this chapter, Liu Yiming refers to this embodiment as the "dharma-body." Only secondarily does this body manifest itself as one's physical existence, subjected to birth and death and to a particular "destiny" and life span. See also note 16 below.

[10] *Wuzhen pian* (Awakening to Reality), "Lüshi," poem 13 (see Pregadio, *Awakening to Reality*, p. 60).

THE ONE OPENING OF THE MYSTERIOUS BARRIER

He asked: Not only is it not inside oneself, it is also not outside oneself. Where is actually this thing prior to Heaven?

I replied: It is in the One Opening of the Mysterious Barrier. What we call Mysterious Barrier is the place where the four elements do not stick.[11] It is not Being and is not Non-Being; it is not form and is not emptiness; it is not inside and is not outside. It is also called Gate of the Mysterious-Female, Dwelling of Giving and Taking Life, Opening of Yin and Yang, Barrier of Birth and Death, Cavity of the Inchoate, Altar of the Dragon and the Tiger, Opening of the Turtle and the Snake, Village of the Vague and the Indistinct, Land of the Dim and the Obscure, Door of Exit and Entrance, and Gate of WU and JI. It has many different names, but in general it is called Opening of the Mysterious Barrier.

Within oneself, it is not the heart, the liver, the spleen, the lungs, or the kidneys; it is not the eyes, the ears, the nose, the tongue, or the mind; it is not the 360 bones, and it is not the 84,000 pores. Since ancient times, immortals and realized ones have not been willing to talk about it clearly. Therefore innumerable side gates (*pangmen*)[12] have make reckless conjectures and have developed personal opinions, and have looked for it within the physical features of the body. This is an error, a great error.

Let me tell you one thing. You should know that this Opening is in the land where the six senses do not stick, in the place where the five agents do not reach. "Vague and indistinct!" Within there is an opening. "Dim and obscure!" Within there is a gate.[13] It opens and closes by itself. If you call out, it replies; if you knock, it responds. Luminous and bright! Complete and accomplished! Those who are deluded are one thousand miles away from it; those who are awakened are right in front of it.

---

[11] In Buddhism, the four elements (*sida*) are Earth, Water, Fire, and Wind.

[12] On this term see above, p. 172 n. 30.

[13] These sentences are based on *Daode jing*, sec. 21: "Vague and indistinct! Within there is something. Dim and obscure! Within there is an essence."

Alas! "Understanding this by means of Spirit depends on each person."[14] Unless you inquire into these principles and practice several dozens of years, you will not be able to see it.

THE REVERTED ELIXIR AND THE GREAT ELIXIR

He asked: How should the principles of the Reverted Elixir (*huandan*) and the Great Elixir (*dadan*) be distinguished?[15]

I replied: The Reverted Elixir consists in reverting to the original foundation and in returning from the postcelestial to the precelestial. The Great Elixir consists in cultivating the original foundation and in generating actual images within what is devoid of images.

Indeed, after the Yang culminates and generates the Yin in the human being, day after day the Yin dispels the Yang. The precelestial Breath vanishes, and its amount becomes greatly defective. "Reverting" means to take hold of it by means of a method: you gradually collect and gradually store, and you return to the amount that you originally possessed. It is as if you find something that you had lost, as if what had left comes back. This is the Reverted Elixir.

Yet, even though one has the complete original amount [of precelestial Breath], if it does not undergo refinement by means of Fire, one cannot generate what is provided with form by means of what is devoid of form, and what has substance by means of what is devoid of substance. Therefore after you obtain the Reverted Elixir, you should once again arrange the furnace and newly set up the tripod in order to use Lead to seize Mercury, and Mercury to nourish Lead. Using the natural True Fire, you refine and attain the True Lead and Mercury. They transform themselves into something as indestructible as diamond (*jingang*, *vajra*). Its longevity equals that of Heaven and

---

[14] *Book of Changes*, "Appended Sayings," sec. A.12; see Wilhelm, p. 324.

[15] This question concerns the two main stages of self-cultivation according to Liu Yiming. With the Reverted Elixir, one reverts to the precelestial; with the Great Elixir, one returns to the postcelestial. The first stage is a movement of ascent, achieved by "inverting the course"; the second stage (to be performed after the first one is completed) is a movement of descent, achieved by "following the course."

Earth, and its light contends with those of the Sun and the Moon. Only then can you bring the original foundation to completion.

Otherwise, if you have obtained the Reverted Elixir but do not cultivate the Great Elixir, the original foundation may be there, but it is definitely not solid and stable. There will always be times in which you attain it and then lose it again.

He asked: Are the Reverted Elixir and the Great Elixir the same as the Internal Medicine (*neiyao*) and the External Medicine (*waiyao*)?

I replied: About this there are several discourses. With regard to the Way of the Elixir as a whole, the technique (*shu*) for extending one's Existence (*ming*) is the External Medicine, and the way (*dao*) of fulfilling one's Nature (*xing*) is the Internal Medicine. Without the External Medicine, you cannot shed the illusory body (*huanshen*); without the Internal Medicine, you cannot deliver the dharma-body (*fashen*).[16] By means of the External Medicine you coagulate the embryo; by means of the Internal Medicine you deliver the embryo.

With regard to the Reverted Elixir, Kan ☵ is the External Medicine, and Li ☲ is the Internal Medicine. And with regard to the Great Elixir, True Lead is the External Medicine, and True Mercury is the Internal Medicine.

Each word of the ancients has a purport. You should not be mired in the words and attached to the images.

He asked: True Lead is within Kan ☵, and True Mercury is within Li ☲. When the Reverted Elixir coagulates, Lead and Mercury seize one another. Why are Lead and Mercury once again there in the Great Elixir? Does this mean that there are four Leads and Mercuries?

---

[16] In Buddhism, the dharma-body (*dharmakāya*) is the true and unmanifested body of the Buddha. Liu Yiming and other Neidan masters use this term to mean the equally true and unmanifested body of each person. The *Secret of the Golden Flower* calls this "the body before the birth of Heaven and Earth" (see above. p. 233). Below, Liu Yiming says that this body is equivalent to the "embryo of immortality," delivered at the completion of the Neidan practice.

I replied: In the Reverted Elixir, the Lead within Kan ☵ and the Mercury within Li ☲ are the precelestial Lead and Mercury stored within the postcelestial. Causing this Lead and this Mercury to come forth again is called Reverted Elixir. It also called Golden Elixir, True Seed, and True Lead.

Transmuting your own Yin Mercury with this True Lead is like magnetite attracting iron.[17] This Mercury is the sevenfold Vermilion Powder found within Li ☲.[18] When Mercury finds the Breath of Lead, it instantly dries. Then you use the natural True Fire found within the dead True Mercury, and "nourish [Lead] warmly" for ten months through the operation of extracting and augmenting.[19] Within a short time, the Breath of Lead rises upward and goes away. What is left is only the one Numinous Powder (*lingsha*), Pure Yang without Yin. Then the dharma-body is attained.

He asked: The Golden Elixir is attained when Lead and Mercury coagulate with one another. However, having said that Lead controls Mercury, you also speak of "nourishing [Lead] warmly" for ten months, and of "Lead rising" and "Mercury drying." Is there not a contradiction between the former and the latter?

[17] These words allude to a passage of the *Longhu jing* (Book of the Dragon and the Tiger): "Magnetite attracts iron, covertly going through partitions and obstructions." See *Guwen longhu jing zhushu*, sec. 32.

[18] In his commentary to the *Wuzhen pian* ("Lüshi," poem 4), Liu Yiming explains the term "sevenfold" (*qiban*) as meaning "tears, saliva, semen, juices, breath, blood, and liquids." In Neidan, this is the classical list of Yin essences found within the human body. — When Neidan masters mention the Vermilion Powder (*zhusha*) or the Cinnabar Powder (*dansha*) with regard to the Great Elixir, they do not refer to "cinnabar," although this is the literal meaning of these terms. In Chinese alchemy as a whole, Cinnabar is Yang, but contains the Yin Mercury. In the Neidan use of these terms, "vermilion" (*zhu*) or "cinnabar" (*dan*) means the Yang Cinnabar, and "powder" (*sha*) means the Yin Mercury contained therein. Therefore Vermilion Powder and Cinnabar Powder should be understood as "the True Yin Powder within the Yang Vermilion" or "the True Yin Powder within the Yang Cinnabar."

[19] At this stage of the practice, "extracting and augmenting" (*choutian*) means augmenting Mercury and decreasing Lead.

I replied: From the ancient times to the present day, no one knows how many students have lost their lives because of this celestial mechanism. Among one thousand or ten thousand people, who is able to know it?

Now, the Numinous Powder partakes of the nature of the precelestial utmost Yang. When the Yang culminates and generates the Yin, the precelestial turns into the postcelestial, and within the true there is the false. Unless you obtain the True Lead of the "other house" (*tajia*) to control it, this Numen (i.e., the Numinous Powder) will never be possessed by "me."[20]

Essentially, True Lead stores the precelestial Breath of True Unity. When I transmute my own Numinous Mercury with the Breath of this Lead, Mercury will never leave. However, after this Mercury dies, if I do not entirely extract the Breath of Lead, the Numinous Powder will not coagulate. Why? Because although Lead possesses the precelestial Breath, it comes forth from the postcelestial; as it is Yin outside and Yang inside, it still contains some Yin Breath. Only when this Yin Breath is entirely extracted can it be firm and strong, central and correct. It will manifest itself like a Pearl sized as a grain of millet,[21] radiant and luminous inside and outside, pervading Heaven and permeating the Earth. When it expands, it fills the six poles; when it contracts, it conceals itself within the imperceptible.

The *Wuzhen pian* (Awakening to Reality) says:

> When you use Lead, you should not use ordinary lead—
> but even True Lead is discarded after you have used it.
> These are the wondrous instructions on using Lead:
> use Lead and do not use it—these are truthful words.[22]

Through these words, you can understand the discourses about using Lead.

---

[20] This expression "other house" derives from the *Wuzhen pian*, "Jueju," poem 48; see Cleary, *Understanding Reality*, p. 107. It refers to the postcelestial domain as a whole, which is ruled by the Yin principle and conceals the precelestial True Yang (i.e., True Lead). Liu Yiming discusses these and other related terms in *Cultivating the Tao*, chapter 13.

[21] See above, p. 94 note 21.

[22] *Wuzhen pian*, "Qiyan jueju," poem 9 (see Cleary, *Understanding Reality*, p. 68, where this is poem 10).

THE *ZI* HOUR

He asked: Between the Reverted Elixir and the Great Elixir there are distinctions. Are there also distinctions in the Fire phases (*huohou*)?

I replied: Yes. The Fire phases of the Reverted Elixir are based on the living ZI hour (*huo zishi*). Those of the Great Elixir are based on the true ZI hour (*zheng zishi*). In the living ZI hour, you "distinguish ZI and WU within the time that has no notches."[23] In the true ZI hour, "within a single hour you certainly achieve the Elixir."[24]

As for "ZI and WU within the notches," in each notch there is the mechanism of the birth of Yin and the growth of Yang. When the time of ZI comes, you advance the Yang; when the time of WU comes, you withdraw the Yin. The *Ruyao jing* (Mirror for Compounding the Medicine) says:

> Within one day,
> during the twelve hours,
> wherever the Intention goes,
> all can be done.[25]

This means that the Intention estimates the ebb and flow of Yin and Yang; then "all can be done." This is precisely the living ZI hour for collecting the Medicine within "the time that has no notches."

As for "attaining the Elixir in one hour," in this hour "he joins in his virtue with Heaven and Earth, joins in his light with the Sun and the Moon, joins in his pace with the four seasons, and joins in his

[23] The "living ZI hour" is used in the first stage of the Neidan practice. when one refines the Essence to transmute it into Breath. At this stage, one circulates the Essence within the body along a circular path marked by the celestial stems ZI (the lowest point, near the coccyx) and WU (the highest point, in the upper Cinnabar Field). Although this cycle is framed according to traditional Chinese time computation (where the lowest unit is the "notch" or *ke*, equivalent to about 15 minutes in modern reckoning), Liu Yiming points out that it has nothing to do with ordinary time. The sentence he quotes here is similar to the one attributed to Ma Ziran in the *Jindan wenda* (Questions and Answers on the Golden Elixir); see above, p. 150.

[24] *Wuzhen pian*, "Jueju," poem 18 (see Cleary, *Understanding Reality*, p. 76).

[25] *Ruyao jing*, sec. 15; see above, p. 56.

good and ill fortune with the gods and the spirits."²⁶ This is difficult to obtain and easy to lose: it is connected to life and death and is related to Nature (*xing*) and Existence (*ming*). In this "hour," the accomplished man "seizes the great operation and releases the great mechanism."²⁷ The ciphers of Heaven and Earth are entirely seized, and those of the ten thousand things are also entirely seized. By steering the Dragon you approach the Tiger, and by using the Tiger you harness the Dragon;²⁸ they enter the Yellow Room and coagulate into the utmost Treasure.²⁹ Therefore "coagulating the Elixir in one hour" means the true zi hour of harmonization (*tiaohe*).³⁰

He asked: How can one recognize the coming of the living zi hour and of the true zi hour?

I replied: You do not know how they function. With regard to the living zi hour, the precelestial True Yang is concealed by the postcelestial. It cannot come forth, or rather, it comes forth only from time to time: being muddled by human desires, unavoidably sometimes it is there and sometimes it is lost. Why? Because one discerns the false but does not discern the true. As soon as this precelestial Yang manifests itself, the accomplished person uses a method in order to take hold of it, and gradually collects it and gradually stores it. When one accumulates the Medicine in abundance, one "nourishes it warmly," so that the Breath becomes plentiful and the Spirit becomes whole.

When the true zi hour comes, the Great Medicine comes forth. With an instant of practice, you collect it and ingest it: it conjoins

²⁶ *Book of Changes*, "Explanation of the Sentences" ("Wenyan") on the hexagram Qian ䷀ (no. 1); see Wilhelm, p. 382.
²⁷ Liu Yiming uses these expressions in several works. "Seizing the great operation" derives from the *Ruyao jing* (Mirror for Compounding the Medicine); see above, p. 50. "Releasing the great mechanism" derives from the *Yinfu jing* (Book of the Hidden Agreement); see above, pp. 27 and 29.
²⁸ Phrases similar to these are found in several Neidan texts. As used here, they refer to Yin and Yang being in control of one another, and therefore joining with one another.
²⁹ Yellow Room (*huangfang*) is a synonym of Yellow Court (*huangting*), here a name of the lower Cinnabar Field.
³⁰ For "harmonization" in the Neidan practice see Wang Mu, *Foundations of Internal Alchemy*, pp. 55–63.

with your own True Mercury and it makes the inchoate One Breath whole again. This is joining with the great creation and transformation of things. After the ingestion of the Elixir, "the Inchoate on the seventh day is reborn after death."[31] "Exchanging the trigram lines of the postcelestial, you manifest the roots and the sprouts of the precelestial," and from "doing" you enter "non-doing."[32]

THE YANG SPIRIT AND THE INFANT

He asked: In the practice of "facing a wall for nine years" (*jiunian mianbi*), is one supposed to sit in quiescence for nine years?

I replied: No. What we call "nine years" means "nine reversions." Facing a wall does not consist in sitting in concentration, but only in keeping your attention undivided until it coalesces into Spirit, and in waiting until there is not even the slightest trace of sediments. It is like standing in front of a wall ten thousand fathoms high: nothing at all can be seen, and the ten thousand phenomena (*wanfa*) return to emptiness. This is what it means.

Therefore, unlike the "side gates," what is most important in nourishing the Infant in quiescence and in delivering the Yang Spirit (*yangshen*) is not sitting in quiescence and stopping one's thoughts, or visualizing the [inner] deities while facing a wall. It is taking the nine years as nine cycles.

He asked: Is this infant the same infant that we mean when we speak of "the Infant (*ying'er*) and the Lovely Maid (*chanü*)"?

I replied: They are different. The infant that we mean when we speak of "the Infant and the Lovely Maid" is the Yang within Kan ☵, the

---

[31] The "seventh day" is an image of the rebirth of the Yang principle in Fu ䷗ (shown by the initial solid line at the bottom of this hexagram) after the dominion of the Yin principle (represented by the six broken lines of Kan ䷁). See table 4, p. 260.

[32] "Exchanging the trigram lines of the postcelestial" means restoring Qian ☰ (True Yang) from Li ☲, and Kun ☷ (True Yin) from Kan ☵. Sentences similar to the present ones are found in several texts.

precelestial Breath stored within the postcelestial. The Infant that we mean when we speak of the Embryo of Sainthood is the precelestial Breath that comes from within Empty Non-Being. As it couples with the True Mercury and forms an image, we call it Yang Spirit.

He asked: May I hear about the difference in operation between the Yang Spirit (*yangshen*) and the Yin Spirit (*yinshen*)?

I replied: The Yin Spirit is the postcelestial cognitive spirit; it is what the *Yinfu jing* (Book of the Hidden Agreement) calls "the Spirit that is spirit." The Yang Spirit is the precelestial Original Spirit; it is what the *Yinfu jing* calls "the Spirit that is not spirit."[33]

"The Spirit that is spirit" follows the course of life and death. When one is alive, it maintains itself; when one dies, it leaves. It is the evil root that causes transmigration throughout ten thousand kalpas.

"The Spirit that is not spirit" inverts the course of creation and transformation and is coagulated from Emptiness. Life and death for it are no obstructions: it is "transcendent and alone" (*chaoran ducun*).[34] It is the True Seed that generates the Immortals and accomplishes the Buddhas.

Those who practice the great cultivation cultivate the precelestial and transform the postcelestial. They thoroughly exhaust the root of transmigration throughout countless kalpas, and manifest the Spirit that is as indestructible as diamond (*vajra*). Their longevity equals that of Heaven and Earth, and their light contends with those of the Sun and the Moon.

As for those who practice the middle and the lower vehicles, they do not know the precelestial. In their practices, what they guard in quiescence is only the cognitive spirit, and what they unclose is only the "foolish wisdom."[35] Yet, they believe that they have attained the Dao. How can they know that after the four elements have returned to

---

[33] See above, p. 34. In Liu Yiming's reading of this passage, the "Spirit that is spirit" is the precelestial Spirit that transforms itself into ordinary "spirit" (in particular, the "cognitive spirit" or "thinking spirit"). The "Spirit that is not spirit," vice versa, is the precelestial Spirit in its original state.

[34] This expression is found in several Taoist and Buddhist texts.

[35] *Kuanghui*, a Buddhist term that denotes mere intellectual comprehension.

Emptiness there is nothing for the Yin Numen to rely on? All it can do is look for another dwelling in order to take a new residence. This is what is meant when it is said:

> It is the root of life and death throughout innumerable kalpas, yet the foolish ones call it "the original man."

Tables

Table 1

	WOOD	FIRE	SOIL	METAL	WATER
DIRECTIONS	east	south	center	west	north
SEASONS	spring	summer	(midsummer)	autumn	winter
COLORS	green	red	yellow	white	black
EMBLEMATIC ANIMALS	green dragon	vermilion sparrow	yellow dragon	white tiger	snake and turtle
NUMBERS	3, 8	2, 7	5, 10	4, 9	1, 6
YIN-YANG (1)	minor Yang	great Yang	balance	minor Yin	great Yin
YIN-YANG (2)	True Yin	Yang	balance	True Yang	Yin
STEMS	JIA 甲 YI 乙	BING 丙 DING 丁	WU 戊 JI 己	GENG 庚 XIN 辛	REN 壬 GUI 癸
BRANCHES	YIN 寅 MAO 卯	WU 午 SI 巳	XU 戌, CHOU 丑 WEI 未, CHEN 辰	YOU 酉 SHEN 申	HAI 亥 ZI 子
PLANETS	Jupiter	Mars	Saturn	Venus	Mercury
RELATIONS	father	daughter	forefather	mother	son
VISCERA	liver	heart	spleen	lungs	kidneys
BODY ORGAN	eyes	tongue	mouth	nose	ears

The five agents (*wuxing* 五行) and their associations.

Table 2

AGENT	GENERATION NUMBER	ACCOMPLISHMENT NUMBER
WATER	1	6
FIRE	2	7
WOOD	3	8
METAL	4	9
SOIL	5	10

"Generation numbers" (*shengshu* 生數)
and "accomplishment numbers" (*chengshu* 成數)
of the five agents.

Table 3

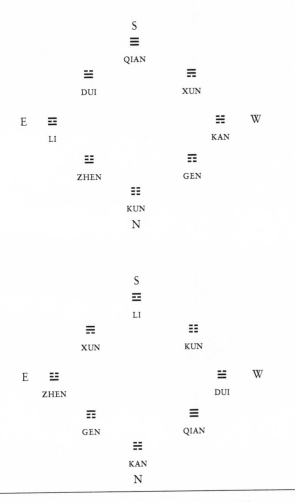

Spatial arrangements of the eight trigrams (*bagua* 八卦) in the
precelestial (*xiantian* 先天, top) and postcelestial (*houtian* 後天,
bottom) configurations.

Table 4

復	臨	泰	大壯	夬	乾	姤	遯	否	觀	剝	坤
FU	LIN	TAI	DAZHUANG	GUAI	QIAN	GOU	DUN	PI	GUAN	BO	KUN
子	丑	寅	卯	辰	巳	午	未	申	酉	戌	亥
zi	chou	yin	mao	chen	si	WU	wei	shen	you	xu	hai
黃鐘	大呂	太蔟	夾鐘	姑洗	仲呂	蕤賓	林鐘	夷則	南呂	無射	應鐘
huangzhong	dalü	taicou	jiazhong	guxi	zhonglü	ruibin	linzhong	yize	nanlü	wuyi	yingzhong
11	12	1	2	3	4	5	6	7	8	9	10
23–1	1–3	3–5	5–7	7–9	9–11	11–13	13–15	15–17	17–19	19–21	21–23

The twelve "sovereign hexagrams" (*bigua* 辟卦)
and their relation to other duodenary series:
earthly branches (*dizhi* 地支), bells and pitch-pipes
(*zhonglü* 鍾律), months of the year,
and "double hours" (*shi* 時). After Kun ䷁, the cycle continues
with Fu ䷗, whose lower line represents the rebirth of the Yang
principle.

Table 5

STEMS			AGENTS	DIRECTIONS	COLORS	VISCERA	NUMBERS
1	JIA	甲	WOOD	east	green	liver	3, 8
2	YI	乙					
3	BING	丙	fiRE	south	red	heart	2, 7
4	DING	丁					
5	WU	戊	SOIL	center	yellow	spleen	5
6	JI	己					
7	GENG	庚	METAL	west	white	lungs	4, 9
8	XIN	辛					
9	REN	壬	WATER	north	black	kidneys	1, 6
10	GUI	癸					

The ten celestial stems (*tiangan* 天干)
and their associations.

Table 6

	BRANCHES		AGENTS	LUNAR MONTHS	HOURS	NUMBERS
1	ZI	子	WATER	11 (solstice)	23–1	1, 6
2	CHOU	丑	SOIL	12	1–3	5, 10
3	YIN	寅	WOOD	1	3–5	3, 8
4	MAO	卯	WOOD	2 (equinox)	5–7	3, 8
5	CHEN	辰	SOIL	3	7–9	5, 10
6	SI	巳	fiRE	4	9–11	2, 7
7	WU	午	fiRE	5 (solstice)	11–13	2, 7
8	WEI	未	SOIL	6	13–15	5, 10
9	SHEN	申	METAL	7	15–17	4, 9
10	YOU	酉	METAL	8 (equinox)	17–19	4, 9
11	XU	戌	SOIL	9	19–21	5, 10
12	HAI	亥	WATER	10	21–23	1, 6

The twelve earthly branches (*dizhi* 地支)
and their associations.

Table 7

1 jiazi 甲子	13 bingzi 丙子	25 wuzi 戊子	37 gengzi 庚子	49 renzi 壬子
2 yichou 乙丑	14 dingchou 丁丑	26 jichou 己丑	38 xinchou 辛丑	50 guichou 癸丑
3 bingyin 丙寅	15 wuyin 戊寅	27 gengyin 庚寅	39 renyin 壬寅	51 jiayin 甲寅
4 dingmao 丁卯	16 jimao 己卯	28 xinmao 辛卯	40 guimao 癸卯	52 yimao 乙卯
5 wuchen 戊辰	17 gengchen 庚辰	29 renchen 壬辰	41 jiachen 甲辰	53 bingchen 丙辰
6 jisi 己巳	18 xinsi 辛巳	30 guisi 癸巳	42 yisi 乙巳	54 dingsi 丁巳
7 gengwu 庚午	19 renwu 壬午	31 jiawu 甲午	43 bingwu 丙午	55 wuwu 戊午
8 xinwei 辛未	20 guiwei 癸未	32 yiwei 乙未	44 dingwei 丁未	56 jiwei 己未
9 renshen 壬申	21 jiashen 甲申	33 bingshen 丙申	45 wushen 戊申	57 gengshen 庚申
10 guiyou 癸酉	22 yiyou 乙酉	34 dingyou 丁酉	46 jiyou 己酉	58 xinyou 辛酉
11 jiaxu 甲戌	23 bingxu 丙戌	35 wuxu 戊戌	47 gengxu 庚戌	59 renxu 壬戌
12 yihai 乙亥	24 dinghai 丁亥	36 jihai 己亥	48 xinhai 辛亥	60 guihai 癸亥

Sexagesimal cycle of the celestial stems (*tiangan* 天干)
and the earthly branches (*dizhi* 地支).

Table 8

EAST				
	1	*jiao*	角	Horn
	2	*kang*	亢	Neck
	3	*di*	氏	Root
	4	*fang*	房	Room
	5	*xin*	心	Heart
	6	*wei*	尾	Tail
	7	*ji*	箕	Winnowing Basket
NORTH				
	8	*dou*	斗	Dipper
	9	*niu (qianniu)*	牛（牽牛）	Ox (or Ox Leader)
	10	*nü (shunnü)*	女（須女）	Maid (or Serving Maid)
	11	*xu*	虛	Emptiness
	12	*wei*	危	Rooftop
	13	*shi (yingshi)*	室（營室）	Encampment
	14	*bi*	壁	Wall
WEST				
	15	*kui*	奎	Stride
	16	*lou*	婁	Bond
	17	*wei*	胃	Stomach
	18	*mao*	昂	Pleiades
	19	*bi*	畢	Net
	20	*zi*	觜	Turtle Beak
	21	*shen*	參	Alignment
SOUTH				
	22	*jing*	井	Well
	23	*gui (yugui)*	鬼（輿鬼）	Spirit (or Spirit Bearer)
	24	*liu*	柳	Willow
	25	*xing (qixing)*	星（七星）	[Seven] Stars
	26	*zhang*	張	Extension
	27	*yi*	翼	Wings
	28	*zhen*	軫	Chariot Platform

The twenty-eight lodges (*xiu* 宿). Translations based on Major, *Heaven and Earth in Early Han Thought*, 127.

Index of Main Terms

Note: Not all occurrences of each term are indexed, but only those that provide the main instances or the clearest explanations of their use. Terms listed in the *Jindan faxiang* (Model Images of the Golden Elixir, translated in chapter 8), as well as terms mentioned in the translator's footnotes, are not indexed.

also clarity and quiescence;
movement and quiescence
Responding Valley (*yinggu*), 119,
140; *see also* middle Cinnabar
Field
"reversing the Light" (*huiguang*),
229–230, 236–237; *see also* "inverting the radiance"
Reverted Elixir (*huandan*), 15–17,
47, 85, 138, 184, 202, 245–247,
249
Reverted Elixir of the Golden
Liquor (*jinye huandan*), 138, 196,
214; *see also* Golden Liquor
River Chariot (*heche*), 9–10, 55, 148
shen, see Spirit
side gates (*pangmen*), 77, 244, 251
sincerity (*cheng*), 24, 27, 32, 38, 88,
227
Soil (one of the five agents), 5–6, 15,
21, 25, 50, 55, 68, 75, 88–89, 148–
149, 207; *see also* True Soil
Spirit (*shen*), 34, 36–37, 90, 94, 111,
141, 147, 168–171, 175, 179, 251–
252; *see also* cognitive spirit;
Cavity of Spirit and Breath; Essence and Spirit; Essence, Breath,
and Spirit; Original Spirit; Spirit
and Breath; Spirit of the Valley;
Yang Spirit; Yin Spirit
Spirit (*shen*) and Breath (*qi*), 30, 53,
58, 88–89, 91, 93, 95–96, 98, 105,
111–112, 154, 159, 167, 169, 172–
173, 188, 220; *see also* Breath;
Spirit
Spirit of the Valley (*gushen*), 28, 47,
82, 117–119; *see also* Spirit
Spirit Water (*shenshui*), 90–91, 97,
192
spleen, 20–21, 111
superior virtue and inferior virtue,
8, 11

Sweet Dew (*ganlu*), 71–72, 93
Three Barriers (*sanguan*), 98, 142,
146
Three Treasures (*sanbao*), 17–18,
170
Tiger, *see* Dragon and Tiger
tongue, 48, 147
True Intention (*zhenyi*), 69, 88; *see
also* Intention
True Lead, 10–11, 15, 20, 72, 74, 76–
77, 88, 98, 192–193, 212, 245–
248; *see also* Lead
True Mercury, 15, 20, 72, 88, 99,
212, 245–246, 251; *see also* Mercury
True Seed (*zhenzhong*), 78, 179–180,
247
True Soil, 52, 56, 79, 88, 97, 104,
107, 207; *see also* Soil
True Yang, 53, 72–73, 76, 79–81,
168, 230, 250; *see also* True Yin
and True Yang
True Yin, 72, 76, 81; *see also* True
Yin and True Yang
True Yin and True Yang, 4, 49, 68–
69, 74–77, 79, 81, 88, 96, 107,
143, 243; *see also* True Yang;
True Yin
true zi hour, 249–250; *see also* living
zi hour; zi hour
Two Eights (*erba*), 72
upper Cinnabar Field, 18, 142, 144;
see also Abyssal Pond; Celestial
Valley; Muddy Pellet
Water (one of the five agents), 9–10,
21, 40, 50, 190; *see also* Water
and Fire; Water of the kidneys;
Water of True Unity
Water and Fire (two of the five
agents), 52–53, 57, 62, 110, 141,
148, 179–181, 189, 219; *see also*
Fire; Water

Glossary of Chinese Characters

an 安 ("to settle"; "rest")

anmo daoyin 按摩導引 ("guiding and pulling")

anyin 按引 ("pressing and pulling")

bagua 八卦 (eight trigrams)

Bai Yuchan 白玉蟾 (1194–1229?)

baixue 白雪 (White Snow)

Baiyun guan 白雲觀 (Abbey of the White Cloud)

Bao zhenren 鮑真人 (Realized Man Bao)

Baopu zi neipian 抱朴子內篇 (Inner Chapters of the Master Who Embraces Spontaneous Nature)

Baopu zi waipian 抱朴子外篇 (Outer Chapters of the Master Who Embraces Spontaneous Nature)

beihai 北海 (Northern Ocean)

beihou sanguan 背後三關 (Three Barriers in the back)

Beizong 北宗 (Northern Lineage)

bi 彼 ("that," "the other")

bian 變 ("change")

bigu 辟穀 ("abstaining from cereals")

BING 丙 (3rd celestial stem)

Biyan lu 碧巖錄 (Blue Cliff Record)

bugang 步罡 ("pacing the celestial net")

caizhan 採戰 ("battle of collecting" [the sexual essences])

Cantong qi 參同契 (The Seal of the Unity of the Three)

Cao Wenyi 曹文逸 (ca. 1125)

Changcun 常存 (Constant Presence)

chanmen 產門 (Gate of Birth)

chanü 姹女 (Lovely Maid)

chaoran ducun 超然獨存 ("transcendent and alone")

chaotuo fenxing 超脫分形 (Transcending Worldliness and Separating from the Form)

CHEN 辰 (5th earthly branch)

Chen Nan 陳楠 (?–1213)

Chen Niwan 陳泥丸 (Chen Nan)

Chen Xubai 陳虛白 (Yuan dynasty)

Chen Zhixu 陳致虛 (1290-ca. 1368)

cheng 誠 (sincerity)

Cheng Xuanying 成玄英 (fl. 631–50)

chonglou 重樓 (Storied Pavilion)

Chongyang lijiao shiwu lun 重陽立教十五論 (Fifteen Essays to Establish the Teaching)

CHOU 丑 (2nd earthly branch)

chouqian 抽鉛 ("extracting Lead")

choutian 抽添 ("extracting and augmenting")

chuilian 垂簾 ("closing the curtains")

Chunyang 純陽 (Lü Dongbin)

chunyang 純陽 (Pure Yang)

Chunyu Fen 淳于棼

ci 此 ("this")

cihuo 雌火 ("feminine Fire")

congming 聰明 ("sharpness of hearing and brightness of sight"; intelligence)

Cui gong ruyao jing zhujie 崔公入藥鏡注解 (Commentary and Explication of the Ruyao jing)

Cui Xifan 崔希範 (ca. 880–940)

Cuixu 翠虛 (Chen Nan)

Cuixu pian 翠虛篇 (The Emerald Emptiness)

cun 存 (to maintain)

cuncheng 存誠 ("maintaining sincerity")

cunxiang 存想 ("visualizing and meditating")

da huandan 大還丹 (Great Reverted Elixir)

dadan 大丹 (Great Elixir)

Dadian Baotong 大顛宝通 (732–824)

dahuan 大還 (Great Reversion)

dan 丹 (Elixir; cinnabar)

danji 丹基 (foundation of the Elixir)

danmu 丹母 (mother of the Elixir)

dansha 丹砂 (cinnabar; "cinnabar powder," "cinnabar sand")

dantian 丹田 (Cinnabar Field)

dantian gong 丹田宮 (Palace of the Cinnabar Field)

Danyang 丹陽 (Ma Yu)

Danyang zhenren yulu 丹陽真人語錄 (Recorded Sayings of the Realized Man Ma Danyang)

danyao 丹藥 (Elixir)

Danyuan 丹元 (Cinnabar Origin)

Dao, *dao* 道 (Way; way)

Daode jing 道德經 (Book of the Way and Its Virtue)

daogui 刀圭 ("knife-point"; "point of the spatula")

daoji 盜機 ("stealing the mechanism")

daoyin 導引 ("guiding and pulling")

Daoshu shi'er zhong 道書十二種 (Twelve Books on the Dao)

Daoyan neiwai bijue quanshu 道言內外祕訣全書 (Complete Writings of Secret Instruction on Inner and External Taoist Teachings)

Daozang 道藏 (Taoist Canon)

Daozang jiyao 道藏輯要 (Essentials of the Taoist Canon)

Daozang xubian 道藏續編 (Sequel to the Taoist Canon)

dapo xukong 打破虛空 ("smashing Emptiness")

daqian shijie 大千世界 ("great chiliocosm")

Daxue 大學 (The Great Learning)

dayong 大用 ("great operation")

dengzhen 登真 ("ascending to the Truth")

dexing shen 德行深 ("deeply virtuous conduct")

dianhua 點化 ("transformation"; realization)

dihu 地戶 (Door of the Earth)

dili 地理 ("patterns of the Earth")

ding 定 (concentration)

ding 頂 ("summit")

ding 鼎 (tripod)

dizhi 地支 (earthly branches)

dongfang 洞房 (Cavern Chamber)

dongfang gong 洞房宮 (Palace of the Cavern Chamber)

Donghua dijun 東華帝君 (Imperial Lord of Eastern Florescence)

dongjing 動靜 (movement and quiescence)

Dongpai 東派 (Eastern Branch)

doubing 斗柄 (Dipper's Handle)

douluo 兜羅 (name of a tree)

du 度 ("crossing over"; ordination)

dui 兌 ("cavity"; "openings"; "mouth")

dumai 督脈 (Control vessel)

Duren shangpin miaojing neiyi 度人上品妙經內義 (Inner Meaning of the Wondrous Book of the Upper Chapters on Salvation)

dushi 度師 (Ordination Master)

erwu 二五 ("two fives")

fan 反 ("to return"; "inverted")

Fang 房 (a constellation)

Fanghu waishi 方壺外史 Secretary of Mount Fanghu)

fangzhong shu 房中術 ("arts of the bedchamber")

fangzhu 方諸 (a mirror used to collect the Yang essences)

fanzhao 反照 ("inverting the radiance")

fashen 法身 (dharma-body)

fashui 法水 (dharma-water)

fawang cheng 法王城 (Citadel of the King of the Dharma)

faxiang ("model images")

feichang 肺腸 ("lungs and intestines")

feng 風 ("wind")

Fengdu 酆都

fengguan 風關 (Barrier of Wind)

Fo yijiao jing 佛遺教經 (Sutra of the Buddha's Bequeathed Teaching)

fu 符 ("to match"; "to be in agreement")

Fu Xi 伏羲

fuhuo 符火 (Matching Fires)

Fusang 扶桑 (a mythical tree)

ganlu 甘露 (Sweet Dew)

GENG 庚 (7th celestial stem)

gongan 公案 ("public cases"; *kōan*)

guan 冠 ("capping" ceremony)

guan 觀 ("contemplation")

guan 關 ("barrier")

guang 光 ("radiance")

guangai 灌溉 ("irrigate")

Guangcheng zi 廣成子

guanjian 關楗 ("barrier and lock")

guanxin 觀心 ("contemplation of the mind")

"Guanyi yin" 觀易吟 (Chant on Contemplating Change)

Guanyin zi 關尹子 (Book of Master Guanyin)

guaqi 卦氣 ("breaths of the hexagrams")

guayang 寡陽 ("solitary Yang")

GUI 癸 (10th celestial stem)

Guizhong zhinan 規中指南 (Compass for Peering into the Center)

gushen 谷神 (Spirit of the Valley)

"Gushen busi lun" 谷神不死論 (Essay on "The Spirit of the Valley does not Die")

Guwen longhu jing zhushu 古文龍虎經注疏 (Commentary and Subcommentary to the Ancient Text of the Book of the Dragon and the Tiger)

guyin 孤陰 ("lone Yin")

HAI 亥 (12th earthly branch)

Haichan 海蟾 (Liu Haichan)

Haiqiong wendao ji 海瓊問道集 (Questions on the Dao by the Master of Haiqiong: An Anthology)

hansan weiyi 函三為一 ("holding the Three into One")

hao 號 (appellation)

Haohua 皓華 (Dazzling Flower)

heche 河車 (River Chariot)

hehe sixiang 合和四象 ("joining the four images in harmony")

heiqian 黑鉛 (black lead)

Heng, Mount 恒山

hou 候 (phases)

houtian 後天 (postcelestial, the postcelestial state)

Hua, Mount 華嶽

huachi 華池 (Flowery Pond)

huaji 化機 ("mechanism of transformation")

huandan 還丹 (Reverted Elixir)
Huandan fuming pian 還丹復命篇 (Returning to Life through the Reverted Elixir)
huanding 換鼎 ("shifting the Tripod")
huangdao 黃道 (Yellow Path)
Huangdi 黃帝 (Yellow Emperor)
Huangdi neijing 黃帝內經 (Inner Book of the Yellow Emperor)
Huangdi neijing lingshu 黃帝內經靈樞 (Inner Book of the Yellow Emperor: The Numinous Pivot)
Huangdi neijing suwen 黃帝內經素問 (Inner Book of the Yellow Emperor: The Plain Questions)
Huangdi suwen 黃帝素問 (Plain Questions of the Yellow Emperor)
huangfang 黃房 (Yellow Room)
huangpo 黃婆 (Yellow Dame)
huangting 黃庭 (Yellow Court)
Huangting jing 黃庭經 (Book of the Yellow Court)
huangwu 黃屋 (Yellow Room)
huangya 黃芽 (Yellow Sprout)
huangyu 黃輿 (Yellow Carriage)
huanshen 幻身 (illusory body)
huashen 化身 (transformation body)
huasheng 化生 ("generate by transformation")
hui 慧 (wisdom)
huiguang 迴光 ("reversing the Light")
huiguang neizhao 迴光內照 ("reversing the light to illuminate within")
huiji 迴幾 ("inverting the mechanism")
hun 婚 (marriage ceremony)
hun 混 ("murky")

Hun 魂 (celestial, Yang "soul")
hunhe 混合 ("inchoate merging")
Hunran zi 渾然子 (Wang Jie)
huo 火 (Fire)
huo zishi 活子時 ("living *zi* hour")
huohou 火候 (Fire phases)
huolong 火龍 (Fire-Dragon)
JI 己 (6th celestial stem)
JIA 甲 (1st celestial stem)
jiaji 夾脊 (Spinal Handle)
jian 鑑 (mirror)
Jiang Yuanting 蔣元庭 (fl. ca. 1800)
jianggong 絳宮 (Crimson Palace)
jiaohe zhi jing 交合之精 ("essence of the intercourse")
jicai 急採 ("quickly collect")
jie 戒 (precepts)
jiehou 節候 ("nodal phases")
jieqi 節氣 ("nodal breaths")
jin 斤 (pound)
jin 金 (metal; gold)
Jin yaoshi 金鑰匙 (The Golden Key)
Jinbi guwen 金碧古文 (Ancient Text on Gold and Jade)
Jinbi jing 金碧經 (Book on Gold and Jade)
jindan 金丹 (Golden Elixir; Metal Elixir)
Jindan da chengji 金丹大成集 (A Great Anthology on the Golden Elixir)
Jindan dayao 金丹大要 (The Great Essentials of the Golden Elixir)
Jindan faxiang 金丹法象 (Model Images of the Golden Elixir)
"Jindan ge" 金丹歌 (Song of the Golden Elixir)
Jindan jiuzheng pian 金丹就正篇 (Rectifying Errors for the Seekers of the Golden Elixir)

Jindan sibai zi 金丹四百字 (Four Hundred Words on the Golden Elixir)

Jindan wenda 金丹問答 (Questions and Answers on the Golden Elixir)

Jindong zhu 金洞主 (Lord of the Golden Cavern)

jing 精 (essence)

jing 鏡 (mirror)

jingang 金剛 (diamond, *vajra*)

Jingang jing 金剛經 (Diamond Sutra)

jingfang 精房 (Room of the Essence)

Jingai 金蓋 (branch of Longmen)

jingong 金公 (Lord of Metals)

jinghua 精華 (essential radiance)

jinhua 金華 (Golden Flower)

Jinhua bijue 金華秘訣 (Secret Instructions on the Golden Flower)

Jinhua zongzhi 金華宗旨 (The Secret of the Golden Flower)

Jinlian zhengzong ji 金蓮正宗記 (Records of the Correct Lineage of the Golden Lotus)

jinshi 金室 (Golden Chamber)

jinwu 金烏 (Golden Crow)

jinxian 金仙 ("Golden Immortal")

jinye huandan 金液還丹 (Reverted Elixir of the Golden Liquor; Golden Liquor reverted to the Cinnabar [Field])

jitu 己土 (one's own "self")

jiuchong 九蟲 (nine worms)

jiudu 九都 (nine capitals)

jiufu 九府 (Nine Palaces)

jiunian mianbi 九年面壁 ("facing a wall for nine years")

jiuqian yishen 九淺一深 ("nine shallow and one deep" penetrations in intercourse)

jiuquan 九泉 (Nine Springs)

jiusi 九思 ("nine concerns")

jiuyou 九幽 (Nine Obscurities)

jixing 己性 ("one's own Nature")

jizhen gong 極真宮 (Palace of Ultimate Truth)

"Jueju" 絕句 (Cut-off lines)

jueli 絕粒 ("cutting off the grains")

kan 看 ("watch")

ke 刻 (notch; instant)

"Koujue" 口訣 ("Oral Instructions")

ku 枯 ("withered")

kuanghui 狂慧 (intellectual comprehension)

Kunlun, Mount 崑崙

Lan Yangsu 藍養素

Laojun 老君 (Lord Lao)

Laozi 老子

leifa 雷法 (Thunder Rites)

Lengyan jing 楞嚴經 (Śūraṅgama sūtra)

li 禮 (rites)

Li Daochun 李道純 (fl. 1288–92)

Li Yuxi 李玉溪

liang 兩 (ounce)

liangneng 良能 (innate capacity)

liangzhi 良知 (innate knowledge)

liaoliao 了了 (complete realization)

Liezi 列子 (Book of Liezi)

Lifeng laoren ji 離峰老人集 (The Old Man of the Solitary Peak: An Anthology)

Lingbao bifa 靈寶畢法 (Complete Methods of the Numinous Treasure)

linggu 靈谷 (Numinous Valley)

lingsha 靈砂 (Numinous Powder)

Lingshu 靈樞 (Numinous Pivot)

Lingshu neijing 靈樞內景 (Inner Book of the Numinous Pivot)

Lingyuan dadao ge 靈源大道歌
(Song of the Great Dao, the Numinous Source)
Liu Chuxuan 劉處玄 (1147–1203)
Liu Haichan 劉海蟾
Liu Yiming 劉一明 (1734–1821)
liuchen 六塵 (six defilements)
liugen 六根 (six senses)
liujia 六甲 (six JIA)
liumai 劉脈 (six pulses)
liuxu 六虛 ("six empty spaces")
liuzhu 流珠 (Flowing Pearl)
liuzhu gong 流珠宮 (Palace of the Flowing Pearl)
lizang 歷臟 ("passing through the viscera")
Longhu jing 龍虎經 (Book of the Dragon and the Tiger)
Longmen 龍門 (Dragon Gate)
Longyan 龍烟 (Dragon Haze)
lu 爐 (furnace)
luchen 陸沈 ("sinking into the ground")
lulu 轆轤 ("pulley")
"Lun chaoyuan" 論朝元 (On Having Audience at the Origin)
"Lun riyue" 論日月 (On the Sun and the Moon)
"Lun sishi" 論四時 (On The Four Seasons)
"Lun wuxing" 論五行 (On the Five Agents)
Lunyu 論語 (Sayings of Confucius)
"Luofu Cuixu yin" 羅浮翠虛吟 (Chant of Emerald Emptiness on Mount Luofu)
Lü Dongbin 呂洞賓
Lu Xixing 陸西星 (1520–1606)
"Lüshi" 律詩 (Regulated verses)
Lüzu zhi 呂祖志 (Monograph on Ancestor Lü)
Ma Yu 馬鈺 (1123–84)

Ma Ziran 馬自然 (11th century)
MAO 卯 (4th earthly branch)
Mao 昴 (a constellation)
mei 梅 (plum)
meiping 媒娉 ("go-between")
Mengzi 孟子 (Book of Mengzi)
mianmian 綿綿 ("unceasing"; "subtle")
mihu 密戶 (Secret Door)
mimi 密密 ("closely")
Min Qian 閔騫 (Confucius' disciple)
Min Yide 閔一得 (1748–1836)
ming 命 (Existence; Life; mandate)
ming 鳴 ("chirping")
mingdi 命蒂 (Stem of Existence)
mingmen 命門 (Gate of Life)
mingtang gong 明堂宮 (Palace of the Hall of Light)
mingxin 明心 (enlightened mind)
muyu 沐浴 (bathing)
na me 那麼 ("so")
nangong 南宮 (Southern Palace)
Nanke 南柯
Nanyue, mount 南嶽
Nanzong 南宗 (Southern Lineage)
naqi 納氣 ("ingesting breath")
nei sanyao 內三要 ("three inner essentials")
Neidan 內丹 (Internal Alchemy; Internal Elixir)
neifu 內符 (internal response)
neiguan 內觀 (inner contemplation)
neishi 內視 (inner observation)
neixing 內省 (inner observation)
neiyao 內藥 (Internal Medicine)
neizhao 內照 ("to illuminate within")
ni 逆 ("inverting the course")
niangniang 娘娘 ("mom")
niejing 躡境 ("climbing up to Reality")

niwan 泥丸 (Muddy Pellet)
niwan gong 泥丸宮 (Palace of the Muddy Pellet)
pangmen 旁門 ("side gates")
Panxi ji 磻溪集 (An Anthology from Panxi)
Peng Haogu 彭好古 (fl. 1586–99)
Peng Si 彭耜 (fl. 1217–51)
Peng Xiao 彭曉 (?–955)
pin 牝 ("female")
pinfu 牝府 (Mansion of the Female)
piyu 譬喻 ("metaphors")
po 破 ("to break")
Po 魄 (earthly, Yin "soul")
qi 氣 (breath; Breath)
Qi bitu 契秘圖 (Secret Charts of the *Cantong qi*)
qian 慳 ("mean")
qiangming 強名 ("forced names"; names used by necessity.)
Qianxu zi 潛虛子 (Lu Xixing)
Qiaoyao ge 敲爻歌 (Songs Metered on the Hexagram Lines)
qiban 七般 ("sevenfold")
"Qifu" 祈父 (Minister of War)
qiji 氣機 ("mechanism of Breath")
qimu 炁母 (Mother of Breath)
qing 情 (emotions, feelings, sentiments, passions; individual qualities)
qingjing 清靜 ("clarity and quiescence")
Qingjing jing 清靜經 (Book of Clarity and Quiescence)
qingke 頃刻 ("a short while")
qingxiu pai 清修派 ("pure cultivation branch")
qingzhuo 清濁 ("clear and turbid"; "pure and impure")
Qinyuan chun 沁園春 (Spring at the Qin Garden)
Qiu Chuji 邱處機 (1148–1227)

qixue 氣穴 (Cavity of Breath)
"Qiyan jueju" 七言絕句 (Heptasyllabic Cut-off Lines)
qizhi 氣質 ("character," "personality")
qizhi zhi xing 氣質之性 ("material nature")
quan 全 ("complete," "intact")
quanmou 權謀 ("strategy")
quanzhen, Quanzhen 全真 (Complete Reality)
"Quanzhen huofa" 全真活法 ("The Way of Life of Complete Reality")
queqiao 鵲橋 (Magpie Bridge)
quzhe 曲折 ("winding courses," "crouchings and bendings")
ren 仁 (humanity)
REN 壬 (9th celestial stem)
renmai 任脈 (Function vessel)
ri 日 (sun)
riguang 日光 ("radiance of the Sun")
ru 如 ("thus")
ruo 若 ("like that")
ruru 如如 ("just so," "thus"; Suchness, *tathatā*)
rushi 入室 ("entering the chamber")
ruyao 入藥 ("to enter the ingredients")
Ruyao jing 入藥鏡 (Mirror for Compounding the Medicine)
sanbao 三寶 (three treasures)
sancai 三才 (Three Powers)
sanfan zhouye 三反晝夜 ("returning three times day and night")
"Sangrou" 桑柔 (The Young Mulberry Tree)
sanguan 三關
sanguang 三光 (Three Luminaries)
sanhua juding 三花聚頂 ("the Three Flowers gather at the summit")

sanjia 三家 (three families)
sanjie 三界 (three worlds)
sanshi 三尸 (three corpses)
seshen 色身 (physical body)
sha 殺 ("taking life")
sha 砂 ("sand," "powder")
shang 上 ("upper"; "to ascend")
Shang 商 (a constellation)
shangde 上德 (superior virtue)
Shangyang zi 上陽子 (Chen Zhixu)
Shao Kangjie 邵康節 (Shao Yong)
Shao Yong 邵雍 (1012–77)
Shen 參 (a constellation)
SHEN 申 (9th earthly branch)
shen 神 (Spirit)
shen 身 (body)
sheng 生 ("giving life")
shengmen 生門 (Gate of Life)
shengren 聖人 (saintly person)
shengshu 生數 (generation numbers)
shengtai 聖胎 (Embryo of Sainthood)
shengzhi 聖旨 ("holy edict")
shenhuo 神火 (Spirit-Fire)
shenming 神明 (Numinous Light)
shenqi xue 神氣穴 (Cavity of Spirit and Breath)
shenshi 神室 (Spirit Chamber)
shenshi 神識 (cognitive spirit; cognitive faculty of Spirit)
shenshui 神水 (Spirit Water)
shentan 深潭 (Deep Pool)
shenwu 神物 (Divine Substance)
shenxi 神息 (breathing of the Spirit)
"Shenxian baoyi" 神仙抱一 (The Divine Immortals Embrace Unity)
shi 師 ("common person"; "soldier")
shi 時 ("double hour"; a time-unit)
Shi Jianwu 施肩吾 (fl. 820–35)

shifu 實腹 ("filling the belly")
Shijing 詩經 (Book of Poems)
shoucheng 守城 ("guarding the citadel")
shu 術 ("technique," "art")
shuihou 水候 (Water phases)
shuihu 水虎 (Water-Tiger)
shun 順 ("following the course")
"Shuo" 說 ("Explanations")
"Shuogua" 說卦 (Explanation of the Trigrams)
SI 巳 (6th earthly branch)
sida 神室 (four elements)
sisheng 四生 ("four kinds of birth")
Sishier zhang jing 四十二章經 (Sutra in Forty-Two Sections)
sixiang 四象 ("four images")
sizheng 四正 (four cardinal points)
Suishu 隨書 (History of the Sui Dynasty)
Sunzi bingfa 孫子兵法 (The Art of War by Master Sun)
tai xuanguan 太玄關 (Great Mysterious Barrier)
Taibai 太白 (Wang Fanggu?)
taihuang gong 太皇宮 (Palace of the Great August One)
taiji 太極 (Great Ultimate)
Taiji tu shuo 太極圖說 (Explication of the Chart of the Great Ultimate)
Taishang 太上 (Most High)
Taixuan jing 太玄經 (Book of the Great Mystery)
Taiyi jinhua zongzhi 太乙金華宗旨 (Ancestral Teachings on the Golden Flower of Great Unity)
Taiyi jun 太一君 (Lord of Great Unity)
taiyuan 太淵 (Great Abyss)
tajia 他家 ("other house")
Tao Sixuan 陶思萱 (?–1692)

ti 體 (foundation)
tiangang 天罡 (Celestial Net)
tiangu 天谷 (Celestial Valley)
tiangui 天癸 (menstruation)
tianhong 添汞 ("augmenting Mercury")
tianmu 天目 (Celestial Eye)
tianran huohou 天然火候 ("natural Fire phases")
Tianshi dao 天師道 (Way of the Celestial Masters)
tianting gong 天庭宮 (Palace of the Celestial Court)
tianwen 天文 ("signs of Heaven")
tianxin 天心 (Heart of Heaven; "celestial mind"; "celestial heart")
tiaohe 調和 (harmonization)
tiaoxie 調燮 (harmonization)
tonglei 同類 ("being of the same kind")
"Tuanzhuan" 彖傳 (Commentary on the Judgments)
tufu 土釜 (Earthenware Crucible)
tugu naxin 吐古納新 ("exhaling the old and inhaling the new [breath]")
wai sanyao 外三要 ("three outer essentials")
Waidan 外丹 (External Alchemy; External Elixir)
waidao 外道 ("external path")
waihuo 外火 (external Fire)
waiyao 外藥 (External Medicine)
wanfa 萬法 ("ten thousand phenomena")
Wang Changyue 王常月 (?–1680)
Wang Chongyang 王重陽 (1113–70)
Wang Daoyuan 王道淵 (Wang Jie)
Wang Fanggu 王方古 (ca. 800)
Wang Jie 王玠 (?-ca. 1380)
Wang Zhe 王嚞 (Wang Chongyang)
Wang Zihua 汪子華 (714–89)

wangjiang 王漿 (royal jelly)
wanyuan 萬緣 ("ten thousand conditions")
Wei 尾 (a constellation)
WEI 未 (8th earthly branch)
Wei Boyang 魏伯陽 (trad. second century CE)
Wei Shilü 魏師呂 (Song or Yuan dynasty)
wei zhi 為之 ("doing")
weilü 尾閭 (Caudal Funnel)
wenda 問答 ("questions and answers")
Weng Baoguang 翁葆光 (fl. 1173)
Wenshi 文始 (Yin Xi)
Wenshi zhenjing 文始真經 (True Book of Master Wenshi)
"Wenyan" 文言 (Explanation of the Sentences)
wenyang 溫養 ("nourishing warmly")
Wenzi 文子 (Book of Wenzi)
WU 午 (7th earthly branch)
WU 戊 (5th celestial stem)
wu 物 (medicine, ingredient)
wuchang 五常 ("five constancies")
wuchang 五長 ("five elders")
Wulou zi 無漏子 (Master Without Contaminations)
Wuming zi 無名子 (Weng Baoguang)
wuqi chaoyuan 五氣朝元 ("the Five Breaths have audience at the origin")
wuwei 無為 ("non-doing")
wuxing quan 五行全 ("the five agents are whole")
wuxing xiangke 五行相剋 ("the five agents conquer each other")
Wuying zi 無隱子 (Master Without Concealment)

Wuzhen pian 悟真篇 (Awakening to Reality)

Wuzhen pian zhushu 悟真篇注疏 (Commentary and Subcommentary to the *Wuzhen pian*)

Wuzhen zhizhi xiangshuo sansheng biyao 悟真直指詳說三乘祕要 (Straightforward Directions and Detailed Explanations on the *Wuzhen pian* and the Secret Essentials of the Three Vehicles)

xia 下 ("lower"; "to descend")

xiade 下德 (inferior virtue)

"Xiang" 象 (Image)

xiangke 相剋 (mutual conquest)

xiangsheng 相生 (mutual generation)

Xiantian daxue shu 先天大學書 (Book on the Great Learning of the Precelestial)

xiantian tu 先天圖 ("precelestial chart")

xiantian 先天 (precelestial, the precelestial state)

xiantian yiqi 先天一氣 (precelestial One Breath)

Xiao Tingzhi 蕭廷芝 (fl. 1260)

Xiao zhiguan shu 小止觀書 (Small Book on Cessation and Contemplation)

xiao zhoutian 小周天 (small celestial circuit)

xiaoxi 消息 (ebb and flow)

"Xici" 繫辭 (Appended Sayings)

"Xijiang yue" 西江月 (West River Moon)

xin 心 (heart; mind)

XIN 辛 (8th celestial stem)

xindi 心地 (mind ground)

xing 形 ([bodily] form)

xing 性 ([inner] Nature)

xinggen 性根 (Root of Nature)

Xingming guizhi 性命圭旨 (Principles of the Conjoined Cultivation of Nature and Existence)

xingming shuangxiu 性命雙修 ("conjoined cultivation of Nature and Existence")

xiongjin 雄金 ("masculine Metal")

xiu 宿 (lodges)

"Xiuxian bianhuo lun" 修仙辨惑論 (Essay on Resolving Doubts in the Cultivation of Immortality)

Xiuzhen biannan 修真辨難 (Discriminations on Difficult Points in Cultivating Reality)

Xiuzhen houbian 修真後辨 (Further Discriminations in Cultivating Reality)

Xiuzhen shishu 修真十書 (Ten Books on the Cultivation of Reality)

Xiyou ji 西遊記 (Journey to the West)

XU 戌 (11th earthly branch)

Xu 虛 (a constellation)

xuan 玄 ("mystery," "mysterious")

xuandan gong 玄丹宮 (Palace of the Mysterious Cinnabar)

xuande 玄德 ("mysterious virtue")

xuangu 玄谷 (Mysterious Valley)

xuanguan 玄關 (Mysterious Barrier)

"Xuanguan xianbi lun" 玄關顯秘論 (Manifesting the Secret of the Mysterious Barrier)

xuanguan yiqiao 玄關一竅 (One Opening of the Mysterious Barrier)

Xuanming 玄冥 (Mysterious Darkness)

xuanpin 玄牝 (Mysterious-Female)

xuanpin zhi men 玄牝之門 (Gate of the Mysterious-Female)

xuanqiao 玄竅 (Mysterious Opening)

xuantai ding 懸胎鼎 (Tripod of the Suspended Womb)

xuanzhu 玄珠 (Mysterious Pearl)

Xue Daoguang 薛道光 (1078?–1191)

xue 血 (blood)

xunzheng 薰蒸 ("fragrant vapor")

Xunzi 荀子 (Book of Xunzi)

xuxin 虛心 ("emptying the heart" or "the mind")

Yan Hui 顏回 (Confucius' disciple)

"Yang" 養 (Nourishment)

Yang Xiong 揚雄 (53 BCE–18 CE)

yanghuo 陽火 (Yang Fire)

yangmen 陽門 (Yang Gate)

yangshen 陽神 (Yang Spirit)

Yangsheng bilu 養生祕錄 (Secret Records on Nourishing Life)

yangsui 陽燧 (a mirror used to collect the Yin essences)

Yangzhou 揚州 (Jiangsu)

yanjin 咽津 ("swallowing saliva")

yanyue lu 偃月爐 (Furnace of the Supine Moon)

yao 藥 (medicine, ingredient)

"Yaotou pi ge" 窑頭坯歌 (Song of the Unbaked Brick in the Kiln)

yaowu 藥物 (medicine, ingredient)

ye 液 (Liquor)

yeniang 爺娘 ("dad and mom")

yezhan 野戰 ("fight in the wild")

"Yi" 抑 (Outward Demeanor)

YI 乙 (2nd celestial stem)

yi 意 (Intention)

yi 易 ("change")

Yi 翼 (a constellation)

Yichuan jirang ji 伊川擊壤集 (Beating on the Ground at Yichuan: An Anthology)

Yijing 易經 (Book of Changes)

yike 一刻 (a time unit; "a short while")

YIN 寅 (3rd earthly branch)

Yin Xi 尹喜

Yin Zhenren 尹真人 (Realized Man Yin)

Yin zhenren Liaoyang dian wenda bian 尹真人廖陽殿問答編 (Questions and Answers of the Realized Man Yin from the Liaoyang Hall)

yin'e 鄞鄂 ("seed")

yinfu 陰符 (Yin response)

Yinfu jing 陰符經 (Book of the Hidden Agreement)

ying'er 嬰兒 (Infant)

Yingchan zi 瑩蟾子 (Li Daochun)

yinggu 應谷 (Responding Valley)

yingyan 應驗 ("sign of response")

yinhai 陰海 (Yin Ocean)

yinshen 陰神 (Yin Spirit)

yinyang pai 陰陽派 ("Yin-Yang branch")

yiqi 一氣 (One Breath)

yixin 一心 (One Heart; One Mind)

yong 用 ("operation"; "function")

YOU 酉 (10th earthly branch)

youshi 幽室 (Obscure Chamber)

youwei 有為 ("doing")

youzuo 有作 ("action")

Yu Yan 俞琰 (1258–1314)

yuan 元 ("origin")

yuan 源 ("source")

yuanchi 淵池 (Abyssal Pond)

Yuandu zi 緣督子 (Zhao Youqin)

yuanjing 元精 (Original Essence)

yuanjue 圓覺 (Complete Enlightenment)

Yuanjue jing 圓覺經 (Sutra of Complete Enlightenment)

Yuanjun 元君 (Original Princess)

yuanqi 元氣 (Original Breath)

yuanshen 元神 (Original Spirit)
yuanzhong 緣中 (center of conditions)
yudi gong 玉帝宮 (Palace of the Jade Emperor)
yue 月 (moon)
yuejing 月精 ("essence of the Moon")
yugan 玉橄 ("jade olive")
yulu 玉爐 (Jade Furnace)
Yunfang 雲房 (Zhongli Quan)
Yunji qiqian 雲笈七籤 (Seven Lots from the Bookbag in the Clouds)
yunü 御女 ("riding women")
yutu 玉兔 (Jade Hare)
Yuwu 玉吾 (Yu Yan)
yuzhen 玉枕 (Jade Pillow)
Zazhu zhixuan pian 雜著指玄篇 (Pointers to the Mystery: A Miscellany)
Zhan Gu 詹谷 (Song or Yuan dynasty)
Zhan Ranhui 湛然慧 (fl. ca. 1920)
Zhang 張 (a constellation)
zhang 章 ("division")
Zhang Boduan 張伯端 (987?–1082)
Zhang Ziyang 張紫陽 (Zhang Boduan)
Zhao Ding'an 趙定庵 (fl. late thirteenth century)
Zhao Youqin 趙友欽 (Yuan dynasty)
zheng zishi 正子時 ("true zi hour")
zhengjue 正覺 ("correct awakening")
zhengqi 正氣 ("correct Breaths")
Zhengyang 正陽 (Zhongli Quan)
zhenren 真人 (realized person)
zhenyi 真一 (True Unity)
zhenyi zhi shui 真一之水 (Water or True Unity)
Zhenyi zi 真一子 (Peng Xiao)

zhenyi 真意 (True Intention)
zhi 止 ("cessation")
zhi 治 ("to control"; "to fix")
zhi 芝 (a "plant of immortality")
zhichao yuandun 直超圓頓 (complete and immediate awakening)
zhiguan 止觀 ("cessation and contemplation")
zhiren 至人 (accomplished person)
zhishu 知術 ("tactics")
Zhixuan pian 指玄篇 (Pointing to the Mystery)
Zhiyi 智顗 (538–97)
zhizhi 知止 ("knowing when to stop")
zhizu 止足 ("knowing what is sufficient")
zhong 中 ("center")
Zhong-Lü 鍾呂 (a branch of Internal Alchemy)
Zhong Lü chuandao ji 鍾呂傳道集 (The Transmission of the Dao from Zhongli Quan to Lü Dongbin: An Anthology)
zhonggong 中宮 (Central Palace)
Zhonghe ji 中和集 (The Harmony of the Center: An Anthology)
zhonghuang 中黃 (Central Yellow)
Zhongli Quan 鍾離權
zhongqiu 中秋 (Mid-Autumn festival)
Zhongyong 中庸 (The Middle Course)
Zhou Dunyi 周敦頤 (1017–73)
zhoutian 周天 (Celestial Circuit)
Zhouyi cantong qi 周易參同契 (Seal of the Unity of the Three, in Accordance with the *Book of Changes*)
Zhouyi cantong qi fenzhang tong zhenyi 周易參同契分章通真義 (The True Meaning of the *Can-*

tong qi, with a Subdivision into Sections)

Zhouyi cantong qi zhujie 周易參同契注解 (Commentary and Explication of the *Cantong qi*)

zhu 朱 ("vermilion")

zhu 銖 ("scruples")

Zhu Xi 朱熹 (1130–1200)

Zhu Ziyang 朱紫陽 (Zhu Xi)

Zhuangzi 莊子 (4th century BCE)

Zhuangzi 莊子 (Book of Zhuangzi)

zhuji lianji 筑基煉己 ("laying the foundations for refining oneself")

zhuliu 朱硫 (Red Sulphur)

zhusha 朱砂 (Vermilion Sand; Vermilion Powder)

Zhuzi yulei 朱子語類 (Classified Sayings of Zhu Xi)

ZI 子 ("son"; 1st earthly branch)

zi 字 ("graph")

zifan 自反 ("to examine oneself")

Zifu 紫府 (Purple Prefecture)

Zihua zi 子華子 (Book of Zihua zi)

Ziqing 紫清 (Bai Yuchan)

ziran 自然 ("being as it is")

Ziyang 紫陽 (Zhang Boduan)

zongzhi 宗旨 ("ancestral teaching")

zuqi 祖氣 (Ancestral Breath)

Works Cited

CHINESE SOURCES

The bibliography of Chinese sources only includes works cited with references to chapters, sections, or pages. Works cited in the list of main sources of this anthology (pp. xi-xiii) are not duplicated here. *Abbreviations*: DZ = *Zhengtong daozang* 正統道藏 (Taoist Canon); T. = *Taishō shinshū daizōkyō* 大正新脩大藏經 (Buddhist Canon).

Baopu zi neipian 抱朴子內篇 (Inner Chapters of the Master Who Embraces Spontaneous Nature). Ge Hong 葛洪 (283–343). Ed. by Wang Ming 王明, *Baopu zi neipian jiaoshi* 抱朴子內篇校釋 (second revised edition, Beijing: Zhonghua shuju, 1985).

Baopu zi waipian 抱朴子外篇 (Outer Chapters of the Master Who Embraces Spontaneous Nature). Ge Hong 葛洪 (283–343). Ed. by Yang Mingzhao 楊明照, *Baopu zi waipian jiaojian* 抱朴子外篇校箋 (Beijing: Zhonghua shuju, 1991).

Cantong qi 參同契 (The Seal of the Unity of the Three). Attr. Wei Boyang 魏伯陽 (trad. second century CE). Text in Fabrizio Pregadio, *The Seal of the Unity of the Three: A Study and Translation of the Cantong qi, the Source of the Taoist Way of the Golden Elixir* (Mountain View, Golden Elixir Press, 2011).

Chongyang quanzhen ji 重陽全真集 (Complete Reality: A Collection by Wang Chongyang). Wang Chongyang 王重陽 (1113–70). DZ 1153.

Cuixu pian 翠虛篇 (The Emerald Emptiness). Chen Nan 陳楠 (?–1213). DZ 1090.

Daode jing 道德經 (Book of the Way and Its Virtue). Mid-fourth century BCE (?). Sibu beiyao 四部備要 ed.

Daxue 大學 (The Great Learning). Ca. fourth century BCE. In *Liji* 禮記 (Book of Rites), sec. 42. Shisan jing zhushu 十三經注疏 ed., 1815.

Duren shangpin miaojing neiyi 度人上品妙經內義 (Inner Meaning of the Wondrous Book of the Upper Chapters on Salvation). Complete title: *Yuanshi wuliang duren shangpin miaojing neiyi* 元始無量度人上品妙經內義. Commentary by Xiao Yingsou 蕭應叟, 1226. DZ 90.

Fo yijiao jing 佛遺教經 (Sutra of the Buddha's Bequeathed Teaching). Alternative title: *Fochui banniepan lüeshuo jiaojie jing* 佛垂般涅槃略説教誡經. Ca. 400 CE. T.389.

Guizhong zhinan 規中指南 (Compass for Peering into the Center). Complete title: *Chen Xubai guizhong zhinan* 陳虛白規中指南. Chen Xubai 陳虛白 (Yuan dynasty). DZ 243.

Guwen longhu jing zhushu 古文龍虎經注疏 (Commentary and Subcommentary to the Ancient Text of the Book of the Dragon and the Tiger). Commentary by Wang Dao 王道 (fl. 1185). DZ 996.

Haiqiong wendao ji 海瓊問道集 (Questions on the Dao by the Master of Haiqiong: An Anthology). Bai Yuchan 白玉蟾 (1194–1229?). DZ 1308.

Huangdi neijing suwen 黃帝內經素問 (Inner Book of the Yellow Emperor: The Plain Questions). Originally ca. third-second century BCE. Sibu congkan 四部叢刊 ed.

Huangting jing 黃庭經 (Book of the Yellow Court). Complete title: *Huangting neijing jing* 黃庭內景經. Late fourth century. Text in Kristofer Schipper, *Concordance du Houang-t'ing king: Nei-king et Wai-king* (Paris: École Française d'Extrême-Orient, 1975).

Jin yaoshi 金鑰匙 (The Golden Key). Peng Xiao 彭曉 (?–955). In *Yunji qiqian* 雲笈七籤, ch. 70.

Jindan da chengji 金丹大成集 (A Great Anthology on the Golden Elixir). Xiao Tingzhi 蕭廷芝 (fl. 1260). In *Xiuzhen shishu* 修真十書, ch. 9–13.

Jindan dayao 金丹大要 (The Great Essentials of the Golden Elixir). Chen Zhixu 陳致虛 (1290-ca. 1368). DZ 1067.

Jindan sibai zi 金丹四百字 (Four Hundred Words on the Golden Elixir). Attr. Zhang Boduan 張伯端 (987?–1082). In *Xiuzhen shishu* 修真十書, ch. 5.

Jinlian zhengzong ji 金蓮正宗記 (Records of the Correct Lineage of the Golden Lotus). Qin Zhi'an 秦志安, 1241. DZ 173.

Liezi 列子 (Book of Liezi). Originally ca. fourth century BCE, received text ca. fourth century CE. Ed. by Yang Bojun 楊伯峻, *Liezi jishi* 列子集釋 (Beijing: Zhonghua shuju, 1979).

Lifeng laoren ji 離峰老人集 (The Old Man of the Solitary Peak: An Anthology). Yu Daoxian 于道顯 (1168–1232). DZ 1264.

Lingbao bifa 靈寶畢法 (Complete Methods of the Numinous Treasure). Attr. Zhongli Quan 鐘離權 and Lü Dongbin 呂洞賓. DZ 1191.

Lunyu 論語 (Sayings of Confucius). Fifth to third centuries BCE. Text in *Lunyu zhuzi suoyin* 論語逐字索引 (Hong Kong: Shangwu yinshuguan 1995).

Lüzu zhi 呂祖志 (Monograph on Ancestor Lü [Dongbin]). Late sixteenth century. DZ 1484.

Mengzi 孟子 (Book of Mengzi). Fourth century BCE. Text in *Mengzi zhuzi suoyin* 孟子逐字索引 (Hong Kong: Shangwu yinshuguan, 1995).

Panxi ji 磻溪集 (An Anthology from Panxi). Qiu Chuji 邱處機 (1148–1227). DZ 1159.

Suishu 隨書 (History of the Sui Dynasty). Wei Zheng 魏徵 (580–643) et al. Zhonghua shuju ed. (Beijing, 1973).

Sunzi bingfa 孫子兵法 (The Art of War by Master Sun). Attr. Sun Wu 孫武 (trad. sixth century BCE). Text in *Bingshu sizhong zhuzi suoyin* 兵書四種逐字索引 (Hong Kong: Shangwu yinshuguan 1992).

Taixuan jing 太玄經 (Book of the Great Mystery). Yang Xiong 揚雄 (53 BCE–18 CE). Text in *Fayan zhuzi suoyin, Taixuan jing zhuzi suoyin* 法言逐字索引、太玄經逐字索引 (Hong Kong: Shangwu yinshuguan, 1995).

Wuzhen pian zhushu 悟真篇注疏 (Commentary and Subcommentary to the *Wuzhen pian*). Weng Baoguang 翁葆光 (fl. 1173) and Chen Daling 陳達靈 (fl. 1174); compiled by Dai Qizong 戴起宗 (fl. 1335–37). DZ 141.

Xiuzhen shishu 修真十書 (Ten Books on the Cultivation of Reality). Late thirteenth or early fourteenth century. DZ 263.

Xunzi 荀子 (Book of Xunzi). Third century BCE. Text in *Xunzi zhuzi suoyin* 荀子逐字索引 (Hong Kong: Shangwu yinshuguan 1996).

Yangsheng bilu 養生祕錄 (Secret Records on Nourishing Life). Xiao Tingzhi 蕭廷芝 (fl. 1260–64). DZ 579.

Yichuan jirang ji 伊川擊壤集 (Beating on the Ground at Yichuan: An Anthology). Shao Yong 邵雍 (1012–77). DZ 1042.

Yijing 易經 (Book of Changes). Original portions ca. ninth century BCE, commentaries and appendixes ca. 350 to 250 BCE. Text in *Zhouyi yinde* 周易引得 (Peking: Harvard-Yenching Institute, 1935).

Yin zhenren Liaoyang dian wenda bian 尹真人廖陽殿問答編 (Questions and Answers of the Realized Man Yin from the Liaoyang Hall). Ca. 1800. Daozang xubian 道藏續編 ed.

Yunji qiqian 雲笈七籤 (Seven Lots from the Bookbag in the Clouds). Zhang Junfang 張君房, ca. 1025. DZ 1032.

Zhongyong 中庸 (The Middle Course). Ca. fourth century BCE. In *Liji* 禮記 (Book of Rites), sec. 31. *Shisan jing zhushu* 十三經注疏 ed., 1815.

Zhouyi cantong qi fenzhang tong zhenyi 周易三同契分章通真義 (The True Meaning of the *Cantong qi*, with a Subdivision into Sections). Peng Xiao 彭曉 (?–955). DZ 1002.

Zhuzi yulei 朱子語類 (Classified Sayings of Zhu Xi). Li Jingde 黎靖德, 1270. Zhonghua shuju ed. (Beijing, 1986).

Zhuangzi 莊子 (Book of Zhuangzi). Original portions fourth century BCE, completed in the second century BCE. Ed. by Guo Qingfan 郭慶藩, *Zhuangzi jishi* 莊子集釋 (Beijing: Zhonghua shuju, 1961).

WESTERN-LANGUAGE STUDIES AND TRANSLATIONS

Baldrian-Hussein, Farzeen. *Procédés Secrets du Joyau Magique: Traité d'Alchimie Taoïste du XIe siècle*. Paris: Les Deux Océans, 1984.

Cleary, Thomas. *The Secret of the Golden Flower: The Classic Chinese Book of Life*. San Francisco: Harper, 1991.

Cleary, Thomas. *Understanding Reality: A Taoist Alchemical Classic*. Honolulu: University of Hawaii Press, 1987.

Graham, A.C. *The Book of Lieh-tzu*. London: John Murray, 1960.

Legge, James. *The Chinese Classics*. Vol. 1: *Confucian Analects, The Great Learning, and The Doctrine of the Mean*. Second revised edition. Oxford: Clarendon Press, 1893.

Legge, James. *The Chinese Classics*. Vol. 2: *The Works of Mencius*. Second revised edition. Oxford: Clarendon Press, 1895.

Liu Yiming [1734–1821]. *Cultivating the Tao: Taoist and Internal Alchemy*. Mountain View, CA: Golden Elixir Press, 2013.

Major, John S. *Heaven and Earth in Early Han Thought: Chapters Three, Four and Five of the Huainanzi*. Albany: State University of New York Press, 1993.

Pregadio, Fabrizio. *Awakening to Reality: The "Regulated Verses" of the Wuzhen pian, a Taoist Classic of Internal Alchemy*. Mountain View, CA: Golden Elixir Press, 2009.

Pregadio, Fabrizio. *The Seal of the Unity of the Three: A Study and Translation of the Cantong qi, the Source of the Taoist Way of the Golden Elixir*. Mountain View, CA: Golden Elixir Press, 2011.

Wang Jie [?-ca. 1380]. *Commentary on the Mirror for Compounding the Medicine*. Mountain View, CA: Golden Elixir Press, 2013)

Wang Mu. *Foundations of Internal Alchemy: The Taoist Practice of Neidan*. Mountain View, CA: Golden Elixir Press, 2011.

Watson, Burton. *The Complete Works of Chuang Tzu*. New York: Columbia University Press, 1968.

Wilhelm, Richard. *The I-ching or Book of Changes*. New York: Bollingen, 1950.

Wilhelm, Richard. *The Secret of the Golden Flower: A Chinese Book of Life*. Translated into English by Cary F. Baynes. London: Routledge and Kegan Paul, 1962; New York: Harcourt, Brace and World, 1962; several later reprints.

Golden Elixir Press
www.goldenelixir.com

From the Catalogue

The Seal of the Unity of the Three: A Study and Translation of the Cantong qi, the Source of the Taoist Way of the Golden Elixir, by Fabrizio Pregadio.

Under an allusive poetical language teeming with images and symbols, the *Cantong qi* sets forth the teaching that gave origin to Internal Alchemy.

Cultivating the Tao: Taoism and Internal Alchemy, by Liu Yiming (1734–1821).

Written by one of the greatest masters of this tradition, *Cultivating the Tao* offers a comprehensive overview of the main principles of Internal Alchemy in 26 short chapters.

Foundations of Internal Alchemy: The Taoist Practice of Neidan, by Wang Mu.

A clear description of the practice of Internal Alchemy, based on the system of the *Wuzhen pian* (Awakening to Reality) with about two hundred quotations from original Taoist texts.

Awakening to Reality: The "Regulated Verses" of the Wuzhen pian, a Taoist Classic of Internal Alchemy, by Zhang Boduan (987?–1082).

The *Wuzhen pian* (Awakening to Reality) is one of best-known Taoist alchemical texts. Written in the 11th century, it describes in a poetical form the main facets of Internal Alchemy.

Commentary on the Mirror for Compounding the Medicine: A Fourteenth-Century Work on Taoist Internal Alchemy, by Wang Jie (?-ca. 1380).

Dating from the 10th century, the *Ruyao jing* (Mirror for Compounding the Medicine) describes the principles of Internal Alchemy in 20 poems. This book contains a complete translation of the text and of the commentary by Wang Jie, affiliated with the Quanzhen (Complete Reality) tradition.

The World Upside Down: Essays on Taoist Internal Alchemy, by Isabelle Robinet.

Four essays on Neidan translated for the first time into English. Their subjects are: (1) The alchemical principle of "inversion"; (2) The devices used by the alchemists to "manifest the authentic and absolute Tao"; (3) The role of numbers in Taoism and Internal Alchemy; (4) The meanings of the terms External Elixir and Internal Elixir.

Made in the USA
Middletown, DE
30 November 2022

16549559R00182